Mark Roome
1990

TM

BOOKS BY THOMAS MERTON
AVAILABLE IN PAPERBACK EDITIONS
FROM HARCOURT BRACE JOVANOVICH, PUBLISHERS

The Ascent to Truth

Disputed Questions

The Last of the Fathers

Love and Living

No Man Is an Island

The Seven Storey Mountain

The Sign of Jonas

The Waters of Siloe

Thomas Merton

DISPUTED QUESTIONS

A Harvest/HBJ Book
Harcourt Brace Jovanovich, Publishers
San Diego   New York   London

Copyright © 1960, 1959, 1953 by
The Abbey of Our Lady of Gethsemani

All rights reserved. No part of this publication may be reproduced or transmitted
in any form or by any means, electronic or mechanical, including photocopy,
recording, or any information storage and retrieval system, without permission in
writing from the publisher.

Requests for permission to make copies of any part of the work should be mailed
to: Permissions, Harcourt Brace Jovanovich, Publishers, Orlando, FL 32887.

Library of Congress Cataloging in Publication Data
Merton, Thomas, 1915–1968.
   Disputed questions.
   "A Harvest/HBJ book."
   Reprint. Originally published: New York : Farrar,
Straus, and Cudahy, c1960.
    1. Catholic Church—Addresses, essays, lectures.
I. Title.
BX891.M45   1985   230'.2   84-27905
ISBN 0-15-626105-7

Printed in the United States of America

First Harvest/HBJ edition 1985

  B C D E F G H I J

Ex parte ordinis
NIHIL OBSTAT:
   Fr. M. Gabriel O'Connell, O.C.S.O.
   Fr. M. Shane Regan, O.C.S.O.
   Fr. M. Paul Bourne, O.C.S.O.
   Fr. M. Thomas Aquinas Porter, O.C.S.O.
IMPRIMI POTEST:
   Fr. M. Gabriel Sortais, O.C.S.O.
April 30, 1960

NIHIL OBSTAT:
   Daniel V. Flynn, JCD, Censor Librorum
IMPRIMATUR:
   Francis Cardinal Spellman
   Archbishop of New York
June 8, 1960

The nihil obstat and imprimatur are official declarations that a book is free of doctrinal or moral error. No implication is contained therein that those who have granted the nihil obstat and imprimatur agree with the contents, opinions or statements expressed.

PREFACE

A title like *Disputed Questions* may, from the author's point of view, have at least one definite advantage: it can preserve the reader from the delusion that the book is "inspirational." That is certainly not the case. The book is meant to stimulate thought and to awaken some degree of spiritual awareness. But it is not supposed to make anyone break out with a sudden attack of spiritual happiness, still less with pious enthusiasm and the conviction that all's right with the world as long as we make up our minds to concentrate on the bright side of things. For this, as I understand it, is what an "inspirational" book is supposed to do. If that is true, then I should like to lay claim to the honor of never having written one.

On the other hand, the title should not confuse those who are familiar with the traditions of scholastic philosophy. These essays are by no means *questiones disputatae*, in the medieval sense. The subjects are all more or less controversial, but that does not mean that I am engaging in controversy with anyone in particular. I am simply thinking out loud about certain events and ideas which seem to me to be significant, in one way or another, for the spiritual and intellectual life of modern man. Anyone who reads the table of contents might be inclined to disagree with that statement, and thus to make it the first and most hotly disputed question of them all. Pasternak? All right, the Pasternak affair is a contemporary issue of some significance. Modern religious art? Well, perhaps in some quarters this topic is important. Christianity and Totalitarianism? There we certainly have a burning spiritual and social question since, in the choice which is offered us today between two brands of totalitarian society, certain Christian elements seem to be leaning heavily toward one. And this fact is by no means encouraging. But, one might ask, what on earth do Mount Athos, the reformer of the Camaldolese hermits, the early Carmelite Friars, and most of all Saint John Climacus, have to do with the contemporary world? I freely admit that their social significance is not immediately apparent, and even, in the last analysis, that it may turn out to be apparent to me only. Let us settle for the fact that the subjects may have some interest in themselves and may, perhaps, obliquely reflect some light upon contemporary spiritual life which can be seen if one looks closely. But perhaps even without that close and patient scrutiny, which no author has a right to demand of his readers in a hectic day like this, it will be possible to enjoy the book and get some new light on the spiritual life in general, if not on modern life in particular.

If I say that I think these essays all have some reference to our present situation, however remote they may seem from it at first, it is because I think there is one theme, one question above all, which runs through the whole book. It is a philosophical question: the relation of the *person* to the *social organization*. Sometimes this question takes the shape of a more ancient one: solitude vs. community, or the hermit vs. the cenobite. At other times, as in the Pasternak essays, it takes an acutely concrete and actual form, in discussing the struggle of one outstanding and gifted person isolated in the presence of a huge antagonistic totalitarian machine which turns against him the full force of its disapproval and stops short only of his physical destruction.

The problem of the person and the social organization is certainly one of the most important, if not the most important problem of our century. Every ethical problem of our day—especially the problem of war—is to be traced back to this root question. We meet it everywhere, but since we tend to be more and more "organization men" (in the west) or "new-mass-men" (in the east) we are getting so conditioned that we fail to see that it is a problem.

I know from my own experience that in the last twenty years the world has moved a very long way towards conformism and passivity. So long a way that the distance is, to me, both frightening and disconcerting. I have been all the more sensitive to it because I have spent this time in the isolation of a contemplative monastery, and have only recently come back into contact (through certain discrete readings and conversations) with the America which I used to know as a rather articulate, critical and vociferously independent place. It is certainly not so any more. Not that the people do not complain and criticize, but their complaints and criticisms, indeed their most serious concerns, seem to be involved in trivialities and illusions—against a horrifying background of impending cosmic disaster. It seems to me that for all our pride in our freedom and individuality we have completely renounced thinking for ourselves. What passes for "thinking" is mass-produced, passively accepted, or not even accepted. We simply submit to the process of being informed, without anything actually registering on our mind at all. We are content to turn on a switch and be comforted by the vapid, but self-assured slogans of the speaker who, we fondly hope, is thinking for the whole nation.

I believe one of the reasons for the excitement over Pasternak was the fact that the "free world" sought to justify itself and sustain its ideal image of itself by appealing to the example of this one man who really had something personal to say and said it in spite of all opposition. As if Pasternak's courage could have served to palliate the whole world's apathy and stupor!

When I say I am concerned with the *person*, I do not mean that I am interested primarily in the *individual*. There is a great difference. Individualism is nothing but the social atomism that has led to our present inertia, passivism and spiritual decay. Yet it is individualism which has really been the apparent ideal of our western society for the past two or three hundred years. This individualism, primarily an economic concept with a pseudospiritual and moral façade, is in fact mere irresponsibility. It is, and has always been not an affirmation of genuine human values but a flight from the obligations from which these values are inseparable. And first of all a flight from the obligation to *love*. Hence the long essay on love is one in which the personalist foundation of the other studies is laid down. The individual, in fact, is nothing but a negation: he is "not someone else." He is not everybody, he is not the other individual. He is a unit divided off from the other units. His freedom may not seem like an illusion, when he is surrounded by the social mirage of comfort and ample opportunity. But as soon as the structure of his society begins to collapse, the individual collapses with it and he who seemed to be a person soon becomes nothing but a number. Yet he is still an "individual." Hence it is clear that mass society is constructed out of disconnected individuals—out of empty and alienated human beings who have lost their center and extinguished their own inner light in order to depend in abject passivity upon the mass in which they cohere without affectivity or intelligent purpose.

The vocation of the *person* is to construct his own solitude as a *conditio sine qua non* for a valid encounter with other persons, for intelligent cooperation and for communion in love. From this cooperation and communion—which is anything but the ludicrous pantomime called "togetherness"— there grows the structure of a living, fruitful and genuinely human society.

The great error and weakness of our time is the delusion of "humanism" in a culture where man has first been completely alienated from himself by economic individualism, and then precipitated into the morass of mass-technological society which is there to receive us in an avalanche of faceless "numbers." Under such conditions, "humanism" is nothing but a dangerous fantasy.

The various studies in this book in which hermits appear are meant to examine, in a dispassionate way, the full dimension of human and religious solitude. This does not mean that the solution of the problems of our time is for everyone to become a hermit. Far from it! But it does mean that we cannot save ourselves if we gain control of the world and of the moon besides, and suffer the loss of our own souls. In order to find our own souls we have to enter into our own solitude and learn to live with ourselves. This is the beginning of true humanism, because we cannot know man until we find him in ourselves. And when we find him in this way we find that he is the image of God. This discovery makes it impossible for us to evade the obligation of loving everyone else who bears in himself the same image. (For the benefit of those who think the term "image of God" is a piece of gratuitous verbalism, let it be said that the Fathers of the Church identify the diving image in man with his freedom and capacity to love, like God who "is love.")

The perspectives of the present volume are, then, the perspectives of true Christian humanism and personalism. I need not add that without such perspectives the contemplative life would be, to me, completely unthinkable. I cannot be content with the idea that a contemplative monk is one who takes flight from the wicked world and turns his back on it completely in order to lose himself in antiquarian ritualism, or worse still, to delve introspectively into his own psyche. I admit that this illusion also exists and is dangerous—and that the monks themselves are largely responsible for creating it. The "flight from the world" in the true sense of this hoary expression is simply a movement of liberation, the acquiring of a new and higher perspective, at the price of detachment—a perspective from which the mystifying, absurd chaos of human desires and illusions gives place not to an *a priori* dogmatic symbol, but to a concrete intuition of providence and mercy at work even in the natural constitution of man himself, created in the image of God and destined, by the divine mercy, for participation in God's life and light—His freedom and His love. The vocation of man is to live freely and spiritually as a son of God in and through Christ, and, moved by the Spirit of Christ, to work for the establishment of that "Kingdom of God" which is the unity of all men in peace, creativity and love.

I do not believe that this Kingdom and its peace can be established by the power of money. I do not believe it can be established by the noise of slogans, or by dynamos, or by marching armies whether militant or pacific. I do not believe that this Kingdom can ever be the work either of individualists or of mass-men. It can only be the work of persons who have reached not only natural maturity but the full supernatural stature of Christ.

FATHER M. LOUIS, O.C.S.O.

Abbey of Gethsemani, June 1960

PART ONE

THE PASTERNAK AFFAIR

1 . *In memoriam*

On the night of Monday, May 30, 1960, the Pasternak Affair was finally closed. The lonely Russian poet's mysterious life of seventy years came to a peaceful end in the *dacha* at the writer's colony which he had made famous—Peredelkino, twenty miles outside of Moscow.

A year and a half had passed since the brief orgy of political animosity and righteous indignation which had celebrated the award of the Nobel Prize for Literature in the fall of 1958. The prize had been offered to Pasternak, not for his novel *Dr. Zhivago* alone but for his whole life work in poetry, for his other prose works and presumably also for his translations. Under Soviet pressure Pasternak refused the prize. He also refused a proffered opportunity to "escape" from Soviet Russia, pointing out that he did not want to "get away" from his native country because he did not feel that he could be happy anywhere else.

There was a great deal of excitement everywhere. The press made much of the Pasternak case, with the usual gesticulations on both sides of the iron curtain. While the smoke was still thick, and the excitement over the explosion still general, all one could do was to hope and pray that Pasternak would survive. There seems to have been every expectation, both in the west and in Russia, that Pasternak was about to become a "non-person." The Russian writers fell all over one another in their eagerness to become as disassociated from him as they possibly could. Western writers, in appeals that were probably more effective than anyone expected them to be, asked that Pasternak's case be examined with the cool objectivity of non-partisan fairness. Although the poet was menaced in every way, especially when his case was front-page news, after the excitement died down he was left alone. The visits of foreign newsmen, the "pilgrimages" of western men of letters to Peredelkino, were suffered to continue. Pasternak's immense correspondence was apparently not much interfered with, and things went on "as usual" except that the poet could not write poetry or work on the historical play or on the new novel which he had planned. He was kept too busy with visitors and the writing of letters. The last phase of his extraordinary life was the most active of all. The whole world (including many of the younger writers in the Soviet Union) had turned to him as to a prophetic figure, a man whose ascendency was primarily spiritual. The impact of this great and sympathetic figure has been almost religious, if we take that term in a broad and more or less unqualified sense.

It is true that there are striking and genuinely Christian elements in the outlook of Pasternak, in the philosophy that underlies his writing. But of course to claim him as an apologist for Christianity would be an exaggeration. His "religious" character is something more general, more mysterious, more existential. He has made his mark in the world not so much by what he said as by what he was: the sign of a genuinely spiritual man. Although his work is certainly very great, we must first of all take account of what is usually called his personal "witness." He embodied in himself so many of the things modern man pathetically claims he still believes in, or wants to believe in. He became a kind of "sign" of that honesty, integrity, sincerity which we tend to associate with the free and creative personality. He was also an embodiment of that personal warmth and generosity which we seek more and more vainly among the alienated mass-men of our too organized world. In one word, Pasternak emerged as a genuine human being stranded in a mad world. He immediately became a symbol, and all those who felt it was important not to be mad attached themselves in some way to him. Those who had given up, or sold out, or in one way or another ceased to believe in this kind of human quality turned away from him, and found appropriate slogans or catchwords to dismiss him from their thoughts.

This does not mean, of course, that everyone who was "for" Pasternak was a real human being and all the rest were squares. On the contrary, one of the most salient characteristics of the Pasternak Affair in its most heated moments was the way Pasternak got himself surrounded by squares coming at him from all directions with contradictory opinions. Naturally, those who "believed" in Pasternak were not thereby justified, sanctified, or reborn. But the fact remains that he stirred up the unsatisfied spiritual appetites of men for ideals a little more personal, a little less abstract, than modern society seems to offer them.

But what, after all, has been the precise importance of Pasternak? Is this the last, vivid flareup of the light of liberal and

Christian humanism? Does he belong purely to the past? Or is he in some way the link between Russia's Christian past and a possibly Christian future? Perhaps one dare not ask such questions, and the following two studies are not by any means attempts to do so.

The first essay is the more literary of the two. The second examines, in detail, the development of the "Pasternak Affair" and tries to assess its significance for the spiritual and intellectual life of our time. In neither do I try to appropriate Pasternak for any special cultural or religious movement, to line him up with any religious position that may be familiar in the west, or to claim that he stands four-square for culture and democracy as against barbarism and dictatorship.

I might as well admit that, looking at the divisions of the modern world, I find it hard to avoid seeing somewhat the same hypocrisies, the same betrayals of man, the same denials of God, the same evils in different degrees and under different forms on either side. Indeed, I find all these things in myself. Therefore I cannot find it in myself to put on a mentality that spells war. These studies of Pasternak are by no means to be interpreted as my contribution to the cold war, because I don't want any part of the war, whether it is cold or hot. I seek only to do what Pasternak himself did: to speak my mind out of love for man, the image of God—not to speak a set piece dictated by my social situation.

I am happy to record the fact that Pasternak himself read the first of these two studies, and accepted it with kind approval.* The second was not sent to him, being to a great extent "political." Because of my own warm personal admiration for this great poet, and because of the debt of gratitude I owe him for many things, this book is dedicated to his memory. I am persuaded that Russia will one day be as proud

* See page 291 (Appendix) for text of his last letter to the author.

of Pasternak as she is of all her other great writers, and that *Dr. Zhivago* will be studied in Russian schools among the great classics of the language. I can think of no better and more succinct comment upon the life and death of Pasternak than these words of his own which express his belief in immortality and which I have quoted again in the second study. Because of the coming of Christ, says Zhivago, speaking the mind of Pasternak himself: "Man does not die in a ditch like a dog—but at home in history, while the work toward the conquest of death is in full swing; *he dies sharing in this work*."

ii . *The people with watch chains*

> My sister-called-life, like a tidal wave breaking
> Swamps the bright world in a wall of spring rain:
> But people with watch-chains grumble and frown
> With poisoned politeness, like snakes in the corn.
> From *My Sister Life*.

It is perhaps not quite fair to start a discussion of Pasternak with lines from an early poem. He repudiated his earlier style, together with much that was written by the futurists and symbolists who were his friends forty years ago. (He did not, of course, repudiate his friends. For someone like Pasternak, friends cannot become "non-persons.") He may or may not have pardoned us for enjoying the freshness of this early verse, but in any case it is clear that Life who was his "sister" in 1917 became his bride and his very self in *Doctor Zhivago* ("Doctor Life"). Life is at once the hero and the heroine (Lara) of this strange, seemingly pessimistic but victorious tragedy: not, however, Life in the abstract, certainly not the illusory, frozen-faced *imago* of Life upon which Communism constructs its spiritless fantasies of the future. Life for Pasternak is the painful, ambivalent, yet inexhaustibly fecund reality that is the very soul of Russia. A reality which, with all its paradoxes, has certainly manifested itself in the Russian revolution and all that followed, but which overflows all the possible limits of recorded history. Hundreds of pages of turbulent and exquisite prose give us some insight into the vastness of that reality as it was experienced, quite providentially, by one of the few sensitive and original spirits that survived the storm. And since Life cannot be confined within the boundaries of one nation, what Pasternak has to say about it overflows symbolism, into every corner of the world. It is the mystery of history as passion and resurrection that we glimpse obscurely in the story of the obscure Doctor who gives his name to the novel. This frustrated, confused and yet somehow triumphant protagonist is not only Pasternak himself and even Russia, but mankind,—not "twentieth-century man" but man who is perhaps too existential and mysterious for any label to convey his meaning and his identity. We, of course, are that man.

That is the mark of a really great book: it is in some way about everybody and everybody is involved in it. Nothing could be done to stop the drab epic of Zhivago, like the downpour in the 1917 poem, from bursting on the heads of all and swamping them whether they liked it or not. For that is exactly what Life cannot refrain from doing.

The appearance of *Doctor Zhivago*, and all the confused and largely absurd reactions which followed upon it, form a very meaningful incident at the close of an apparently meaningless decade. Certainly the surprise publication and instant success of the novel everywhere (including Russia, where it has been avidly read in manuscript by all the young

intellectuals who could get hold of it) has more to say in
retrospect than all the noise and empty oratory of the Soviet
fortieth anniversary. This significance will of course be
missed by all those who insist on taking a purely partisan
and *simpliste* view of events, and who therefore interpret the
book as all black or all white, all good or all bad, all left or
all right. The dimensions of Pasternak's world view are more
existential and spiritual and are decidedly beyond left and
right.

In bursting upon the heads of all, Zhivago inevitably deluged first of all those simple and pontifical souls whose
Gospel is passive conformity with the politicians and big-
shots, with the high priests of journalism and the doctors of
propaganda: upon those who though they no longer deco-
rate their paunches with cheap watch chains, still thrive on
conformity with the status quo, on either side of the iron
curtain.

Zhivago is one of those immensely "popular" books that
has not really been popular. It has been bought by more
people than were able to read it with full understanding.
No doubt many of those who have had Pasternak's heavy
volume in their hands have approved of it only vaguely and
for the wrong reasons. And others who have read it have
put it down with the unquiet feeling that it was somehow
not sufficiently business-like. For such as these, "life" has
ceased to mean what it means to Pasternak. For the people
with watch chains, a life that gets along independently of
the plans of politicians and economists is nothing but a reactionary illusion. This has been brought home to Pasternak
in no uncertain terms by his devoted confrères in the Soviet Writers' Union. But the same judgment has finally
worked its way out in the West also, where Isaac Deutscher,
the biographer of Stalin, has accused *Zhivago* of being an-

other Oblomov and scolded him for considering the revolution "an atrocity." Let us face it, the people with watch chains can easily reconcile themselves with any atrocity that serves their own opportunism, whether it be in the form of a revolution or of an atomic bomb. Life (claimed as a sister by escapists and cosmopolitan mad-dogs) had better learn to get along in these new circumstances. The atrocities are here to stay.

All great writing is in some sense revolutionary. Life itself is revolutionary, because it constantly strives to surpass itself. And if history is to be something more than the record of society's bogging down in meaningless formalities to justify the crimes of men, then a book that is at the same time great in its own right, and moreover lands with a tremendous impact on the world of its time, deserves an important place in history. The reason why *Doctor Zhivago* is significant is precisely that it stands so far above politics. This, among other things, places it in an entirely different category from Dudintsev's *Not by Bread Alone*. Attempts to involve Pasternak in the cold war have been remarkable above all by their futility. The cloud of misunderstandings and accusations that surrounded the affair did not engulf Pasternak: the confusion served principally to emphasize the distance which separated him from his accusers and his admirers alike.

Both as a writer and as a man, Pasternak stands out as a sign of contradiction in our age of materialism, collectivism and power politics. His spiritual genius is essentially and powerfully solitary. Yet his significance does not lie precisely in this. Rather it lies in the fact that his very solitude made him capable of extraordinarily intimate and understanding contacts with men all over the face of the earth.

The thing that attracted people to Pasternak was not a social or political theory, it was not a formula for the unification of mankind, not a collectivist panacea for all the evils in the world: it was the man himself, the truth that was in him, his simplicity, his direct contact with life, and the fact that he was full of the only revolutionary force that is capable of producing anything new: he is full of love.

Pasternak is then not just a man who refuses to conform (that is to say, a rebel). The fact is, he is not a rebel, for a rebel is one who wants to substitute his own authority for the authority of somebody else. Pasternak is one who *cannot* conform to an artificial and stereotyped pattern because, by the grace of God, he is too much alive to be capable of such treason to himself and to life. He is not a rebel but a revolutionary, in the same way that Gandhi was a revolutionary. And in fact those who have said: "Passive resistance is all right against the English but it would never work against Russia" must stop and consider that in Pasternak it did, to some extent, work even in Russia. Pasternak is certainly a man to be compared with Gandhi. Though different in so many accidental ways, his protest is ultimately the same: the protest of life itself, of humanity itself, of love, speaking not with theories and programs but simply affirming itself and asking to be judged on its own merits.

Like Gandhi, Pasternak stands out as a gigantic paradox in a world of servile and mercenary conformities. His presence in such a world has had an inescapable effect: it has struck fear into the hearts of everyone else, whether in Russia or in America. The reaction to Pasternak, the alternate waves of love, fear, hate and adulation that have rushed toward him from every part of the world, were all set in motion by the *guilt* of a society that has consciously and knowingly betrayed life, and sold itself out to falsity, formalism and spiritual degradation. In some (for instance, the pundits of Soviet literature) this guilt has produced hatred and rage against Pasternak. The fear he aroused was intolerable. His colleagues in the Soviet Writers' Union began to yell for his blood, and yelled all the more loudly in proportion as they were themselves servile and second rate. There were a few notable exceptions, rare writers of integrity and even talent, like Ilya Ehrenburg.

The politicians of the Kremlin, on the other hand, not being writers, not thoroughly understanding what it was all about anyway, were less moved to guilt, felt less fear, and were slow to do much about the case at first.

In the West the reaction was different. We felt the same guilt, the same fear, but in a different mode and degree. On the whole our reaction was to run to Pasternak with fervent accolades: to admire in him the courage and integrity we lack in ourselves. Perhaps we can taste a little vicarious revolutionary joy without doing anything to change our own lives. To justify our own condition of servility and spiritual prostitution we think it sufficient to admire another man's integrity.

I think that later pages of this study will show that Pasternak's witness is essentially Christian. That is the trouble: the problematical quality of Pasternak's "Christianity" lies in the fact that it is reduced to the barest and most elementary essentials: intense awareness of all cosmic and human reality as "life in Christ," and the consequent plunge into love as the only dynamic and creative force which really honors this "Life" by creating itself anew in Life's—Christ's—image.

As soon as *Doctor Zhivago* appeared everybody began comparing Pasternak with Tolstoy and Dostoievsky. The comparisons were obvious, sometimes trite, but basically legitimate. However, they run the risk of creating misconceptions. Pasternak does not merely work on an enormous canvas, like the classical novelists of the nineteenth century. Sholokov also has done that, and Pasternak is immensely more important than Sholokov, competent as the latter may be. But to be a twentieth-century Tolstoy is in fact to disqualify oneself for comparison with one who was an original and unique genius of his own age. The thing that makes Pasternak a new Tolstoy is precisely the fact that he is *not* Tolstoy, he is Pasternak. He is, that is to say, a writer of great power, a man of new and original vision, whose work takes in an enormous area, creates a whole new world. But it is not the world of *War and Peace* and it is not constructed in the same way. In fact, Pasternak has as much in common with Joyce and Proust as he has with Tolstoy. He is a poet and a musician which Tolstoy was not, and the structure of *Zhivago* is symphonic, thematic, almost liturgical. Both writers are "spiritual" in a very deep way, but the spirituality of Tolstoy is always more ethical and pedestrian.

Like Dostoievsky, Pasternak sees life as a mystic, but without the hieratic kenoticism of the *Brothers Karamazov*. The mysticism of Pasternak is more latent, more cosmic, more pagan, if you like. It is more primitive, less sophisticated, free and untouched by any hieratic forms. There is therefore a "newness" and freshness in his spirituality that contrasts strikingly with the worn and mature sanctity of Staretz Zossima purified of self-consciousness by the weariness of much suffering. Pasternak's simple and moving poem on "Holy Week" illustrates this point. It is the death and resurrection of Christ seen in and through nature. Only discreetly and for a brief moment do ritual forms present themselves, as when we see a procession emerge from a country church. The birch tree "stands aside" to let the worshippers come forth but the procession soon returns into the church.

> And March scoops up the snow on the porch
> And scatters it like alms among the halt and lame—
> As though a man had carried out the Ark
> And opened it and distributed all it held.

All the reality of Holy Week is there, but in a very simple, elementary shape—a shape given to it by Pasternak's humility and contact with the "sacred" earth.

The very scarce and slight expressions of explicit spirituality in *Doctor Zhivago* are uttered by people who might have qualified for a place in the *Brothers Karamazov* (Uncle Nikolai and the seamstress of Yuriatin), but they have about them the ingenuousness of a spirituality that has never yet become quite conscious of itself and has therefore never needed to be purified.

If Pasternak's view of the universe is liturgical, it is the cosmic liturgy of Genesis, not the churchly and hierarchal liturgy of the Apocalypse, of pseudo-Dionysius and of the Orthodox Church. And yet Pasternak loves that liturgy, and belongs to that Church. It even occurs to him to quote from the liturgy frequently and in strange places: for instance, these words which he declared indicate a basic liturgical inspiration in the poets Blok and Mayakovsky:

"Let all human flesh be silent and let it remain in terror, and in trembling, and let no living being think within itself. For behold, there cometh the King of Kings and the Lord of Lords to offer Himself in immolation and to become the food of the faithful."

Notice, though, in what a subdued and apologetic manner Pasternak himself makes use of this powerful text. In the

last stanza of the poem on "Holy Week," we read his lines
on the Easter Vigil:

> And when midnight comes
> All creatures and all flesh will fall silent
> On hearing Spring put forth its rumor
> That just as soon as there is better weather
> Death itself can be overcome
> Through the power of the Resurrection.

To say then that *Zhivago* has a liturgical character is not
to accuse it of hieratic ceremoniousness. On the contrary, it
is to praise the spontaneity with which cries of joy and reverence spring up on every page to hymn the sanctity of Life
and of that Love which is the image of the Creator.

And so, though Pasternak is deeply and purely Christian,
his simplicity, untainted by ritualistic routine, unstrained by
formal or hieratic rigidities of any sort, has a kind of *pre-
Christian* character. In him we find the ingenuous Christianity of an *anima naturaliter Christiana* that has discovered
Christianity all by itself. It is a Christianity that is not perfectly at home with dogmatic formulas, but gropes after
revealed truth in its own clumsy way. And so in his Christianity and in all his spirituality Pasternak is exceedingly primitive. This is one of his most wonderful qualities and we owe
it no doubt to the persecution of Christianity by the State
in Russia. Where the Church was free we got the complex,
tormented Christianity of Dostoievsky. Where the Church is
confined and limited we get the rudimentary, "primitive"
Christianity of Pasternak.

What *Zhivago* opposes to Communism is therefore not a
defense of Western democracy, not a political platform for

some kind of liberalism, and still less a tract in favor of formal religion. *Zhivago* confronts Communism with life itself and leaves us in the presence of inevitable conclusions. Communism has proposed to control life with a rigid system and with the tyranny of artificial forms. Those who have believed in this delusion and yielded themselves up to it as to a "superior force" have paid the penalty by ceasing to be complete human beings, by ceasing to live in the full sense of the word, by ceasing to be men. Even the idealistic and devoted Strelnikov becomes the victim of his own ideals, and Lara can say of him:

> It was as if something abstract had crept into his face and made it colorless. As if a living human face had become the embodiment of a principle, the image of an idea. . . . I realized that this had happened to him because he had handed himself over to a superior force that is deadening and pitiless and will not spare him in the end. It seemed to me that he was a marked man and that this was the seal of his doom.

The fact that this judgment is so closely akin to Freudianism and is yet explicitly Christian gives one much food for reflection. The Christian note is sounded in a strong and definite way at the very beginning of the book, as one of the themes which will recur most strongly in all its various parts. The "beast in man" is not to be tamed by threats, but must be brought into harmony with life and made to serve creativeness and love by the influence of inner and spiritual music.

> What has for centuries raised man above the beast is not the cudgel but an inward music; the irresistible power of unarmed truth, the powerful attraction of its example. It has always been assumed that the most important things in the Gospels are the ethical maxims and commandments. But for me the

most important thing is that Christ speaks in parables taken from life, that He explains the truth in terms of everyday reality. The idea that underlies this is that communion between mortals is immortal, and that the whole of life is symbolic because it is meaningful.

The words about the "irresistible power of unarmed truth" are pure Gandhi. The rest, about the inextricable union of symbolism and communion, in life itself, is what gives Pasternak's vision of the world its liturgical and sacramental character (always remembering that his "liturgy" is entirely nonhieratic and that in him sacrament implies not so much established ritual form as living mystery).

Everyone has been struck, not to mention embarrassed, by the overpowering symbolic richness of *Doctor Zhivago*. In fact, Pasternak, whether he knows it or not, is plunged fully into midstream of the lost tradition of "natural contemplation" which flowed among the Greek Fathers after it had been set in motion by Origen. Of course the tradition has not been altogether lost, and Pasternak has come upon it in the Orthodox Church. The fact is clear in any case: he reads the Scriptures with the avidity and the spiritual imagination of Origen and he looks on the world with the illuminated eyes of the Cappadocian Fathers—but without their dogmatic and ascetic preoccupations.

However, it is not with scriptural images that Pasternak is primarily concerned. The Fathers of the Church declared that the Scriptures are a recreated world, a Paradise restored to man after Adam had disturbed the cosmic liturgy by his fall. Pasternak is not the prophet of this regained Paradise, as were Origen and Gregory and Nyssa. Rather he is a prophet of the original, cosmic revelation: one who sees symbols and figures of the inward, spiritual world, working themselves out in the mystery of the universe around him and above all in the history of men. Not so much in the formal, and illusory, history of states and empires that is written down in books, but in the living, transcendental and mysterious history of individual human beings and in the indescribable interweaving of their destinies.

It is as artist, symbolist and prophet that *Zhivago* stands most radically in opposition to Soviet society. He himself is a man of Eden, of Paradise. He is Adam, and therefore also, in some sense, Christ. Lara is Eve, and Sophia (the Cosmic Bride of God) and Russia. One should examine, for instance, the description of the Eden-like garden at Duplyanka in the very beginning of the book. The fragrant fields, the heat, the flowerbeds, the lonely coppice where Yurii speaks with his angel or his mother whose presence (again a sophianic presence) seems to surround him here. Here too Lara, as a girl, is shown to us in the beginning of the book (in one of those innumerable coincidences which Pasternak himself regards as of supreme significance in his novel):

> Lara walked along the tracks following a path worn by pilgrims and then turned into the fields. Here she stopped and, closing her eyes, took a deep breath of the flower-scented air of the broad expanse around her. It was dearer to her than her kin, better than a lover, wiser than a book. For a moment she rediscovered the purpose of her life. She was here on earth to grasp the meaning of its wild enchantment, to call each thing by its right name, or, if this were not in her power, to give birth out of love for life to successors who would do it in her place.

The allusion to that primeval, Edenic existence in which Adam gave the animals their names, is transparently obvious. And Eve is the "Mother of all the living."

Yurii and Lara will be united in another Eden, at Vary-kino, but a strange Eden of snow and silence, lost in a vast landscape wasted by armies. There Yurii will give himself, in the night, to his most fruitful work of poetic creation.

In contrast to the Eden image which symbolizes the sophianic world of Yurii and Lara, of Adam, of Christ, stands the House of the Sculptures in Yuriatin. One of the most significant chapters of the book is called "Opposite the House of the Sculptures." It is the one where the seamstress develops the typological figures of the Old Testament, speaking by lamplight in the same enchanted atmosphere of warmth that pervaded the fields of Duplyanka. The opposition is obvious.

(Lara) Antopova lived at the corner of Merchant Street opposite the dark, blue-grey house with sculptures. . . . It did indeed live up to its name and there was something strange and disturbing about it. Its entire top floor was surrounded by female mythological figures half as big again as human beings. Between two gusts of the dust storm it seemed to him as if all the women in the house had come out on the balcony and were looking down at him over the balustrade. . . .

At the corner there was a dark grey house with sculptures. The huge square stones of the lower part of its façade were covered with freshly posted sheets of government newspapers and proclamations. Small groups of people stood on the sidewalk, reading in silence. . . .

With uncanny insight, the poet has portrayed the bourgeois world of the nineteenth century, a grey façade covered with "sculptures"—enormous and meaningless figures of nothingness, figures for the sake of figures. Yet a dust storm gives them an illusory life. Decorations with no inner reference: advertisements of a culture that has lost its head and has run soberly raving through its own backyards and factories with a handful of rubles. All that remained was for the house itself behind the façade to be gutted and emptied of its semi-human content: then everything was set for the Posters and Proclamations of the Red state. If the editors of *Novy Mir* read *Doctor Zhivago* with understanding they would have found in this passage a much more profound condemnation of Communism than in the description of the Partisan battle which they picked out for special reproof.

On the one hand we have the revolution: "what they mean by ideas is nothing but words, claptrap in praise of the revolution and the regime. . . ." Against this pseudo-scientific array of propaganda clichés, stands the doctor and poet, the diagnostician. One of his greatest sins (the term is chosen advisedly) is his belief in intuition. By his intuition, he is able to get "an immediate grasp of a situation as a whole" which the Marxists vainly hope to achieve by pseudo-science. But what does he seek most of all? What is his real work? As poet, his function is not merely to express his own state of mind, and not merely to exercise his own artistic power. Pasternak's concept of the poet's vocation is at once dynamic and contemplative: two terms which can only be synthesized in the heat of a prophetic ardor.

Language is not merely the material or the instrument which the poet uses. This is the sin of the Soviet ideologist for whom language is simply a mine of terms and formulas which can be pragmatically exploited. When in the moment of inspiration the poet's creative intelligence is married with the inborn wisdom of human language (the Word of God and Human Nature—Divinity and Sophia) then in the very flow of new and individual intuitions, the poet utters the voice of that wonderful and mysterious world of God-man-hood—it is the transfigured, spiritualized and divinized cosmos that speaks through him, and through him utters its praise of the Creator.

> Language, the home and receptacle of beauty and meaning, itself begins to think and speak for man and turns wholly into music, not in terms of sonority but in terms of the impetuousness and power of its inward flow. Then, like the current of a mighty river polishing stones and turning wheels by its very movement, the flow of speech creates in passing, by virtue of its own laws, meter and rhythm and countless other relationships, which are even more important, but which are as yet unexplored, insufficiently recognized, and unnamed. At such moments, Yurii Adreievitch felt that the main part of the work was being done not by him but by a superior power that was above him and directed him, namely the movement of universal thought and poetry in its present historical stage and in the one to come. And he felt himself to be only the occasion, the fulcrum, needed to make this movement possible.

This is the very key to Pasternak's "religious philosophy." He is a complete existentialist (in the most favorable and religious sense of the word). One might ask, in the light of this passage, if his Christian images were nothing more than secondary symbols, subordinated to this great, dynamic worldview. The answer is no. What we have here is a Christian existentialism like that of Berdyaev, and of course far less articulate and less developed than that of Berdyaev. The Christian cosmology of Dante, for example, was static and centripetal. But Christianity is not bound up with Ptolemaic astronomy. Pasternak is absorbed in his vision of a fluid, ever moving, ever developing cosmos. It is a vision appropriate to a contemporary of Einstein and Bergson: but let us not forget that it is also akin to the vision of St. Gregory of Nyssa.

It is not necessary at this point to investigate further the depth and genuineness of the Christian elements in Pasternak. They are clearly present, but their presence should not delude us into any oversimplifications in his regard. There are many differences between his Christianity and the Protestant, or even the Catholic Christianity of the West. To what extent are these differences fundamental? We may perhaps return to this question elsewhere. Sufficient to remember that if in the first pages of the book Christ becomes a kind of ideological or symbolic center for the whole structure, this does not alter the fact that Uncle Nikolai propounds his belief in the following terms, which cannot help but perplex the average believer:

> One must be true to Christ. . . . What you don't understand is that it is possible to be an atheist, it is possible not to know whether God exists or why, and yet believe that man does not live in a state of nature but in history, and that history as we know it now began with Christ, and that Christ's Gospel is its foundation.

Without commenting on this passage, let us simply remark that it is typical of the "religious statements" made here and there in the book which very frequently are much tamer and more simple than they appear to be at first sight. Here the difficulty arises largely from a misuse of the word "atheist." What Pasternak really means, in our terminology, is "agnostic," as is clear from his own explanation. Note that Pasternak does not necessarily make himself personally answerable for the theology of Uncle Nikolai, and that he records with full approval the remarkable discourse of Sima on the miracles of the Old Testament as "types" of the greatest miracle, the Incarnation. It is clear that Christ, for Pasternak, is a transcendent and Personal Being in the sense generally understood by such orthodox theologians as Soloviev or the Russian existentialist Berdyaev. The Christ of Pasternak is the Christ of Soloviev's "God-manhood." His view of the cosmos is, like Berdyaev's, "sophianic" and his "sister Life" has, in fact, all the characteristics of the Sancta Sophia who appeared to Soloviev in Egypt. His protestations that for him "believing in God" or in "the Resurrection" is not quite the same thing as it might be to the popular anthropomorphic mind is, after all, quite legitimate self-defense for one who has no pretension of talking like a professional theologian. So much for his terms. But as for his intentions and his spirit, of these there can be no doubt: they are genuinely religious, authentically Christian and all the more so for their spontaneous unconventionality.

But the important thing to realize is that here, as with all deeply spiritual thinkers, to concentrate on a strict analysis of concepts and formulas is to lose contact with the man's basic intuitions. The great error, the error into which the Communists themselves plunge headlong at the first opportunity, is to try to peg genius down and make it fit into some ready-made classification. Pasternak is not a man for whom there is a plain and definite category. And we must not try to tag him with easy names: Christian, Communist; anti-Christian, anti-Communist; liberal, reactionary; personalist, romanticist, etc.

As Lara says, in one of her most "sophianic" moods: "It's only in mediocre books that people are divided into two camps and have nothing to do with each other. In real life, everything gets mixed up! Don't you think you'd have to be a hopeless nonentity to play only one role all your life, to have only one place in society, always to stand for the same thing?" Both the admirers and the enemies of Pasternak have tried to do him this great dishonor: to write him into one of their own "mediocre books," and to make of him a stereotype to fit and to excuse their own lamentable prejudices. Thus do the "people with watch chains" complain—and not too politely—"like snakes in the corn."

It is true that some names fit Pasternak better than others, and that he is certainly very much of a Christian and not very much of a Communist. Nevertheless his Christianity is first of all quite personal, then quite Russian. His politics are personal first of all and then again Russian, though it might be a lot safer to say that he is anti-political rather than political. But it would be utterly false to say (as his accusers said) that he had rejected the Russian revolution as a whole.

Where precisely does he stand? The answer is that like life itself he stands nowhere, but *moves*. He moves in a definite direction, however, and this is what must be taken into account if he is to be properly understood. From the very first we must realize that this direction does not lie, simply, west of Russia. Pasternak's tendencies are neither geographical nor political. His movement is into the new dimension of the future which we cannot yet estimate because it is not yet with us. He looks beyond the rigid, frozen monolith of Soviet society; he looks beyond the more confused, shifting and colliding forms that make up the world of the West. What does he see? Freedom. Not the freedom of Soviet man after the mythical "withering away of the state." Not the chaotic irresponsibility that leaves Western man the captive of economic, social and psychological forces. Not even that vision which has been irreverently described as "pie in the sky," but really the freedom of the sons of God, on earth, in which "individual life becomes the life story of God and its contents fill the vast expanses of the universe."

III . *Spiritual Implication*

Boris Pasternak established himself in 1958 as one of the very few unquestionably great writers of our century. For forty years this deeply sensitive and original poet had remained hidden and practically unknown in a Russia that seemed entirely alien to his genius. It would be an understatement to say that Soviet official criticism relegated him to oblivion, scorning him as a bourgeois individualist and an internal émigré. But the events of October and November, 1958, were to bring out the fact that Pasternak had remained one of the most admired and loved Russian poets, even in Russia itself. It is true, both in Russia and outside it he was a poet's poet. But that was precisely his importance. He was a rare, almost miraculous being, who had survived the Stalin purges not only with his life but with his full spiritual independence: a kind of symbol of freedom and creativity in the midst of an alienated society—an alienated world.

The fact that the prize award followed closely on the publication and the world-wide success of *Dr. Zhivago* made it easy for politicians to say that the whole thing was a plot, a new gambit in the Cold War. This popular oversimplification obscured the literary importance of the novel which represented the final maturing of a great talent that had been waiting in silence for many years, unable to express itself. A long discipline of sorrowful gestation had given the book a kind of unruly, explosive sincerity that demanded to be heard. And it was heard, in spite of the fact that critics took occasion to complain of many things in it. Was the story too involved? Were the characters really characters? Did the book really have a structure? Was it absurd to compare

such a writer to Tolstoy? And above all, why so many curious and arbitrary coincidences? When all these things were
said, it was still evident that the people who said them were
wasting their time in doing so. It was somehow clear to anyone who had really penetrated the meaning of *Dr. Zhivago*
that all these questions were really irrelevant. The book was
much too big and too vital a creation for such criticisms to
have much meaning. It swept them all away by its own overwhelming strength and conviction. The story was involved
because life is involved: and what mattered was that the
book was alive. You could not only forgive the complexity
of the plot, but you were drawn to lose yourself in it, and to
retrace with untiring interest the crossing paths of the different characters. *Dr. Zhivago* is one of those books which
are greater than the rules by which critics seek to condemn
them: and we must remember that it is precisely with such
books as this that literature advances.

In the end, when everyone had had his say, and the first
pronouncements on the book could be evaluated and
summed up, it was clear that the deeper and more original
critical minds were sold on it. They were obviously preparing to undertake a deeper and more detailed study of the
work. This was the case with Edmund Wilson, for example,
who came out with one of the most serious and favorable
studies of the novel (*The New Yorker*, November 15, 1958)
and who later plunged more deeply into what he believed to
be the book's symbolism (*The Nation*, April 25, 1959.) It is
interesting that Wilson's enthusiasm led him into a kind of
Joycean labyrinth of allegory which he imagined he had discovered in the book, and this evoked an immediate protest
on the part of the author. Pasternak emphatically denied any
intention of creating the allegorical structure Wilson had
"discovered." But the effect of this protest was to increase

one's respect for *Dr. Zhivago*. It is not by any means another *Ulysses* or *Finnegans Wake*. The genius of Pasternak is quite other than the genius of Joyce, and to imagine him plotting out and landscaping his symbolism is to miss what he is really doing.

In any case, it is quite clear that the publication of *Zhivago* was one of the most significant literary events of the century. This is confirmed by the fact that every scrap of poetry or prose Pasternak ever published is being dug up, translated and printed in every language and that his great novel is already beginning to be the object of exhaustive study. We shall now undoubtedly have a lush crop of doctoral dissertations on every aspect of Pasternak's life and work, and this is certainly no cause for rejoicing. The perfectionistic critics, the group who have been turning over and over the least relics of Melville and Henry James will probably leave Pasternak alone, which is fortunate for everyone concerned. But a great many sensitive and alert writers are going to dive into Pasternak and come up with wonderful things for the rest of us, because Pasternak is a great sea full of sunken treasures and in him we have, for once, riches that are not fully expended in a column and a half of the Sunday Book Section.

It is not out of place to start by this affirmation that the award of the 1958 Nobel Prize for Literature was a *literary* event. Last year it was treated almost exclusively, both in Russia and out of it, as political event. It was to be expected that Soviet officialdom would react a little hysterically to the prize award. Since Marxists think entirely in political categories, their hysteria was necessarily political. The publication of the book was a vile and sweeping attack on the Revolution. The prize award was a direct blow at the Soviet Union. The whole thing was a reactionary plot cooked up on Wall Street. Pasternak was an unregenerate relic of the bourgeois past who had somehow been suffered to survive and to pollute the pure air of a new Soviet world. The capitalist wolves had taken advantage of this occasion to howl for Soviet blood. One mixed metaphor after another denounced the shameless author.

No one was, or should have been surprised at this mechanical routine. It was inevitable, and so familiar as to have been supremely boring to everyone except the author and to those who appreciated his talent and personality enough to fear for his life. Nor was it entirely surprising that our side picked up the ball and got into the same game without a moment's delay. To the Western journalists, Pasternak at once became a martyr, a symbol of democracy fighting for recognition under Red tyranny, another proof of the arbitrary perversity of Soviet dictatorship. And of course all this was partly true. But it was slanted and given a political emphasis that was not really there, because *Dr. Zhivago* is in no sense a defense of Western democracy or of the political and economic systems that prevail here. The liberty that Pasternak defends is a liberty of the spirit which is almost as dead in the West as it is behind the Iron Curtain. Perhaps, in a certain way, it is *more* dead in those situations where men fondly believe that the spirit can continue to live in an atmosphere of crass materialism. Let us remember that the vilest character in *Dr. Zhivago* is not one of the Communist automatons but the shrewd, lecherous businessman, Komarovsky.

The fact that Christ is mentioned with sympathetic approval in all parts of the book and that there are quotations from the Bible and from the liturgy was perhaps overstressed by those who were too eager to find in *Dr. Zhivago* an apologia for a vague and superficial Christianity. Here too,

Pasternak does not lend himself so easily to exploitation in favor of a cause. This is not a book that can be used to prove something or to sell something, even if that something happens to be the Christian faith. The dogmatic ambiguity of Pasternak's religious statements takes good care of that. Pasternak himself denies that there is an explicitly religious "message" in his book. But this does not mean that the book is not deeply religious and even definitely Christian. The sincerity of the author's own religious feeling is overpoweringly evident, even though it is not always easy to see how that feeling is to be translated into clear theological propositions. But can we not believe that this too is not only understandable, but much to be desired? Who would think of asking a citizen of the Soviet Union today to burst out periodically with a little homily, couched in the exact technical language of a manual of Catholic moral or dogma? Is it not perhaps all too evident that to demand such a thing would be to put ourselves unconsciously on the same footing as the Soviet Writers' Union who insisted that Pasternak must have secret connections in the West, and must be engaged in an ideological plot?

To me, on the contrary, one of the most persuasive and moving aspects of Pasternak's religious mood is its slightly off-beat spontaneity. It is precisely because he says practically nothing that he has not discovered on his own, that he convinces me of the authenticity of his religious experience. When one is immersed in a wide and free-flowing stream of articulate tradition, he can easily say more than he knows and more than he means, and get away with it. One can be content to tell his brethren in Christ what they devoutly desire and expect, no more and no less. But *Dr. Zhivago*, and the deeply religious poems printed in its final section, is the work of a man who, in a society belligerently hostile to

religion, has discovered for himself the marvels of the Byzantine liturgy, the great mystery of the Church, and the revelation of God in His word, the Sacred Scriptures. The newspapermen who interviewed Pasternak in his *dacha* were all
struck by the big Russian Bible that lay on his desk and gave
evidence of constant use.

Pasternak's Christianity is, then, something very simple,
very rudimentary, deeply sincere, utterly personal and yet for
all its questionable expressions, obviously impregnated with
the true spirit of the Gospels and the liturgy. Pasternak has
no Christian message. He is not enough of a Christian "officially" to pretend to such a thing. And this is the secret to
the peculiar religious strength that is in his book. This
strength may not be at all evident to most of us who are
formally and "officially" members of the visible Church. But
it is certainly calculated to make a very profound impression
on those who think themselves unable to believe because
they are frightened at the forbiddingly "official" aspects our
faith sometimes assumes. *Dr. Zhivago* is, then, a deeply
spiritual event, a kind of miracle, a humble but inescapable
portent.

It is my purpose to bring out and to emphasize the essentially spiritual character of the Pasternak affair. That is precisely its greatest importance for it is one of the few head-
line-making incidents of our day that has a clearly spiritual
bearing. The literary significance of *Dr. Zhivago* and of Pasternak's verse would never have accounted for the effect
they have had on our world. On the other hand, the real
political content of Pasternak's work is negligible, and the
brief political upheaval that accompanied his prominence in
the news was quite accidental, except in so far as it was a
tacit recognition of Pasternak as a *spiritual* influence in the
world. Those who have been struck by the religious content

of his work have been responding, consciously or otherwise, not so much to a formal Christian witness as to a deep and uncompromising *spirituality*.

Pasternak stands first of all for the great spiritual values that are under attack in our materialistic world. He stands for the freedom and nobility of the individual person, for man the image of God, for man in whom God dwells. For Pasternak, the person is and must always remain prior to the collectivity. He stands for courageous, independent loyalty to his own conscience, and for the refusal to compromise with slogans and rationalizations imposed by compulsion. Pasternak is fighting for man's true freedom, his true creativity, against the false and empty humanism of the Marxists —for whom man does not yet truly exist. Over against the technological jargon and the empty scientism of modern man, Pasternak sets creative symbolism, the power of imagination and of intuition, the glory of liturgy and the fire of contemplation. But he does so in new words, in a new way. He speaks for all that is sanest and most permanently vital in religious and cultural tradition, but with the voice of a man of our own time.

This is precisely what makes him dangerous to the Marxists, and this is why the more intelligent and damning pro-Soviet critics (for instance Isaac Deutscher) have done all they could to prove that *Dr. Zhivago* is nothing but a final, despairing outburst of romantic individualism—a voice from the dead past.

On the contrary, however, the fervor with which writers and thinkers everywhere, both in the West and in Russia, have praised the work and the person of Pasternak, quickly made him the center of a kind of spontaneous spiritual movement. This has not received much publicity in the press, but it still goes on. Pasternak became the friend of scores of men still capable of sharing his hopes and fighting for the same ideal. The beauty of this "movement" is that it has been perfectly spontaneous and has had nothing to do with any form of organized endeavor: it has simply been a matter of admiration and friendship for Pasternak. In a word, it is not a "movement" at all. There were none of the "secret connections" the Soviet Police are always hopefully looking for. There was no planned attempt to make a systematic fuss about anything. The protests of Western writers like Camus, T. S. Eliot, Bertrand Russell, and so on, were perfectly spontaneous. And at the same time, it is not generally known that in Moscow several of the leading members of the Writers' Union conspicuously refused to take part in the moral lynching of Pasternak. The most important of these was Ilya Ehrenburg.

The peculiar strength of Pasternak lies then not only in his own literary genius and in his superb moral courage, but in the depth and genuineness of his spirituality. He is a witness to the spirituality of man, the image of God. He is a defender of everything that can be called a spiritual value, but especially in the aesthetic and religious spheres. He is a thinker, an artist, a contemplative. If at times he seems to underestimate the organized ethical aspect of man's spiritual life it is for two reasons: first because he is portraying a world that has become an ethical chaos, and secondly because in that chaos ethics have been perverted into a nonsensically puritanical system of arbitrary prohibitions and commands. There are moments when *Dr. Zhivago* seems so much a creature of impulse as to have lost his ethical orientation. But this is deliberate: and we shall see that it is part of a protest against the synthetically false "moralism" that is inseparable from the totalitarian mentality today.

In order to understand the events of 1958, it is necessary to review briefly Pasternak's own career and the part played by him in the literary history of twentieth-century Russia. In particular we must examine his real attitude toward the Russian revolution which has been by no means simple. For Pasternak was one of those poets who, in 1917, received the Revolution with hopeful, though perhaps not unmixed, enthusiasm and who, though he never succeeded in confining his genius within the paralyzing limitations of the Communist literary formulary, at times attempted to write in praise of the Revolution. There are in fact many passages in *Dr. Zhivago* itself which favor the Revolution in its early stages. In a word, Pasternak was one of that legion of writers, artists and intellectuals who, though they began by a more or less fervent acceptance of the Revolution, were forced sooner or later to reject it as a criminal perversion of man's ideals—when they did not pay with life itself for their fidelity to it. The special importance of Pasternak lies in the symbolic greatness of the protest of one who, having survived the worst of the purges conducted under Stalin, emerged after Stalin's death to say exactly what he thought of Stalinism and to say it not in France, or in England, or in America, but in the heart of Soviet Russia.

Everyone is familiar by now with the salient facts of Pasternak's life. He was born in 1890, in Moscow, the son of a painter, Leonid Pasternak, who was the friend and illustrator of Tolstoy. His mother was a concert pianist. In his early years, young Pasternak conceived a great admiration for two friends of his father—the poet Rilke and the musician Scriabin, and at first the boy planned to become a musician. He wrote: "I love music more than anything else, and I loved Scriabin more than anyone else in the world of music. I began to lisp in music not long before my first acquaintance with him. . . ." In other words, he had already begun to compose, and he soon played some of his compositions for Scriabin who "immediately began to assure me that it was clumsy to speak of talent for music when something incomparably bigger was on hand and it was open to me to say my word in music" (*Safe Conduct*, p. 23).

In 1912 Pasternak studied Kantian philosophy under Cohen at the University of Marburg in Germany, and returning to Russia became involved in the futurist movement, publishing poems in the review *Tsentrifuga*. He had already long since been under the spell of the symbolist, Alexander Blok, and Blok plays an important, though hardly noticeable part, in the symbolic structure of *Dr. Zhivago*. The crucial symbol of the candle in the window, which flashes out to illuminate a kind of knot in the crossing paths of the book's main characters, sets Zhivago to thinking about Blok. The connection of ideas is important, because the candle in the window is a kind of eye of God, or of the Logos (call it if you like *Tao*), but since it is the light in the window of the sophianic figure, Lara, and since Blok in those days (1905) was absorbed in the cult of Sophia he had inherited from Soloviev, the candle in the window suggests, among other things, the Personal and Feminine Wisdom Principle whose vision has inspired the most original Oriental Christian theologians of our day.

Among the futurists, the one who seems to have made the greatest impression on Pasternak is Mayakovsky. In the early autobiographical sketch, *Safe Conduct*, Pasternak speaks of admiring Mayakovsky with all the burning fervor which he had devoted to Scriabin. Later, however, in his more recent memoir, *I Remember*, he has corrected the impressions created by his earlier sketch. "There was never any intimacy between us. His opinion of me has been exaggerated." The two had "quarreled" and Pasternak says that he found May-akovsky's propagandist activities for the Communists "incomprehensible." Mayakovsky devoted a turbulent and powerful talent to the Bolshevist cause and turned out innumerable *agitkas* (political playlets) and a long propaganda poem in honor of Lenin. But Pasternak himself wrote a fine poem about the bleak days of the Revolution, in which he traces a vigorous and sympathetic portrait of Lenin.

> I remember his voice which pierced
> The nape of my neck with flames
> Like the rustle of globe-lightning.
> Everyone stood. Everyone was vainly
> Ransacking that distant table with his eyes:
> And then he emerged on the tribune,
> Emerged even before he entered the room,
> And came sliding, leaving no wake
> Through the barriers of helping hands and obstacles,
> Like the leaping ball of a storm
> Flying into a room without smoke.

(From *The High Malady*, trans. by Robert Payne)

This, however, is no propaganda poem. Nowhere in it does Pasternak betray the truth in order to conform to some preconceived idea about the Revolution. His vision is direct and sincere: he says what he sees. He describes not what he thinks he feels or "ought to feel," but what he actually feels.

These facts are important since Pasternak, who has been accused, by the Communists, of having always been in inveterate reactionary, obviously felt sympathy and admiration for Lenin and for the October Revolution. As for the 1905 Revolution, his position is unequivocal. Lara, for instance, walks down the street listening to the guns in the distance and saying to herself, "How splendid. Blessed are the down trodden. Blessed are the deceived. God speed you, bullets, You and I are of one mind" (p. 53). Her exultation is symbolic. The revolution means that she is temporarily delivered from her captivity to Komarovsky, the smart lawyer, the opportunist and man of business who, all in all, is the most sinister figure in the whole book and who typifies the wealthy ruling class. It is significant of course that after the Revolution Komarovsky remains a powerful, influential figure: he is the type that revolutions do not get rid of but only strengthen.

All that Pasternak has to say both for and against the Bolshevik Revolution—and there is very much of it—is summed up in a paragraph spoken by Sima, in Yuriatin (a very minor character who nevertheless expresses the clear ideological substance of the whole book). She says:

> With respect to the care of the workers, the protection of the mother, the struggle against the power of money, our revolutionary era is a wonderful, unforgettable era of new, permanent achievements. But as regards the interpretation of life and the philosophy of happiness that is being propagated, it is simply impossible to believe that it is meant to be taken seriously, it's such a comic survival of the past. If all this rhetoric about leaders and peoples had the power to reverse history it would set us back thousands of years to the Biblical times of shepherd tribes and patriarchs. But fortunately this is impossible (*Dr. Zhivago*, p. 413).

Pasternak's writing in the twenties is by no means purely an evasion of contemporary reality. It is true that in the collection of stories by him printed in 1925 there is only one, "Aerial Ways," which has anything to do with the revo-

lution and this is by no means a glorification of the new order. That is in fact the thing that Pasternak has never really
been able to do. He has not been able to believe in Communism as any kind of an "order." He has not been able to
accept the myth of its dialectical advance toward an ever
saner and better world. Even in his most sanguine moments
he always viewed the revolution as a chaotic surging of blind
forces out of which, he hoped, something new and real
might perhaps evolve. *Dr. Zhivago* by and large represents
his judgment that the whole thing was a mountain that gave
birth to a mouse. No new truth has been born, only a
greater and more sinister falsity. It is this that the Communists cannot forgive him. They do not seem to realize that
this very fact confirms his judgment. If Communism had
really achieved what it claims to have achieved, surely by
now it could tolerate the expression of such opinions as are
to be found in *Dr. Zhivago*.

In 1926 Pasternak published a poem on the 1905 Revolution and in 1927 he followed with another revolutionary
poem, "Lieutenant Schmidt." The former of these received
a lengthy and favorable exegesis from Prince Dimitry
Mirsky who had at that time returned to Russia and was
temporarily in favor as a Marxist critic—prior to his exile and
death in one of the far north camps of Siberia.

Pasternak's writings about the revolution never quite succeeded with the Party because he was always interested too
much in man and not enough in policies and the party line.
It cannot really be said that he ever seriously attempted to
write about the Revolution from a Communist viewpoint
and it is certainly false to think that he ever sacrificed any of
his integrity in order to "be a success." The fact remains that
he has been consistently criticized for "individualism,"
"Departure from reality" and "formalist refinement." In

other words he remained an artist and refused to prostitute his writing to politics.

No original work from Pasternak's pen was to appear from 1930 until 1943 when "Aboard the Early Trains", appeared and was condemned by Zhdanov as "alien to socialism." During the rest of these years he worked at translations.

That Pasternak fell silent was not a matter of isolated significance. Blok had died in 1921, disillusioned by the Revolution. The Party's literary authorities were discussing whether or not "The Twelve" was really a Communist poem. Gumilyov had been executed in 1922. Esenin had written his last poem in his own blood and killed himself in 1925. Mayakovsky, at the height of fame and success as a "proletarian poet," committed suicide at the precise moment when, in the words of a historian, he was considered "the embodiment of socialist optimism." The last remaining representatives of the poetic ferment of the war years and the early twenties disappeared into the background, and remained silent, if they were not liquidated in the thirties. Pasternak was one of the few to survive. He was able to find support and expression for his genius by publishing remarkable translations of Shakespeare, Rilke, Verlaine, Goethe and other poets of the West.

One of the most mysterious aspects of the Pasternak story is his survival during the great purges of the 1930's. The current guesses as to how he escaped death are barely satisfactory. Some allege that since Pasternak was supposed to have been Mayakovsky's "best friend," and Mayakovsky was now canonized, Stalin allowed Pasternak to live. But anyone who knows anything of Stalin and the purges knows perfectly well that the fact of being the "best friend" of someone who had died might just as well have meant a one-way ticket to the far-north camps. Others believe that because Pasternak had translated the Georgian poets so brilliantly, Stalin could not kill him. But Stalin found it no hardship to kill the Georgian poets themselves—like Pasternak's friend Tabidze. Whey then should he spare a translator?

By all the laws of political logic, or lack of logic, Pasternak should have died in the thirties and in fact he nearly did so, for the strain of living through those times undermined his health. Not only was he obviously suspect as a nonpolitical, antipolitical and therefore automatically reactionary poet, but also he distinguished himself by openly defying official literary dogmas in meetings and conferences. Not only that, but he refused to sign several official "petitions" for the death of "traitors," and his friends barely saved him by covering up his defection. The general opinion is that Pasternak could not possibly have survived the purges unless Stalin himself had given explicit orders that he was to be spared. Why?

There has been much speculation, and an article by Mr. Mikhail Koryakov, published in Russian in the *Novy Zhurnal* (in America) and quoted by Edmund Wilson (*The Nation, loc. cit.*) seriously lines up some of the quasi-legendary possibilities. What they add up to is that because of some cryptic statement made by Pasternak in refererence to the mysterious death of Stalin's wife, Allelueva, Stalin conceived a superstitious fear of the poet. The Georgian dictator is said to have imagined that Pasternak was endowed with prophetic gifts, was a kind of dervish, and had some kind of unearthly insight into the cause of Allelueva's death. Since Stalin himself has been credited with the murder of his wife, this does not make the mystery of Pasternak's survival any less mysterious.

The intolerably dreary history of art and literature under

Stalin might have seemed hopeful to those who firmly believed that the Leader could really make Russia over and create a new, mass-produced Soviet man in his own image and likeness. But the death of Stalin and the "thaw" that followed showed on all sides that the need for originality, creative freedom, and spontaneity had not died. Even men like Ehrenburg and Simonov, successful Communist writers who could be relied upon to do exactly what the Party leaders wanted, discreetly began to suggest the possibility of a rebirth of initiative and even a certain frankness on the part of the writer. As if socialist realism might soon be replaced with something remotely related to real life!

The history of the "thaw" is well known. A few months proved that the slightest relaxation in favor of individual liberty and self-determination, in any field whatever, would bring about the collapse of everything that had been built up by Stalin. The events in Poland and Hungary in the fall of 1956 make this abundantly clear. In both these countries, outspoken writers had led the resistance against Moscow. There was no choice but a hasty and devout return to the principles used so effectively by Stalin. While notable ex-members of the Praesidium began to wend their way to places like Outer Mongolia, the millionaire novelist and editor, Simonov, became overnight a leading literary figure of Uzbekistan.

Yet no show of official severity has yet been able to discourage the determined resistance of a younger generation of writers. This resistance is in no sense overtly political; it takes the form of a dogged, largely passive protest against the dreariness and falsity of Communist life. It is a silent, indirect refusal to seek any further meaning in copybook formulas and in norms handed down from above by politicians. A young poet of today, Evgeny Evtushenko, has been publicly scolded by Khrushchev in person. Evtushenko, as a kind of prophet of the New Generation, defies the limitations imposed on his spiritual and artistic freedom. He describes a friend returning from a forced labor camp bursting with interest in everything new, listening to the radio and seeking out all kinds of information: "everything in him breathes character." Evtushenko himself cries out in protest at not being able to fraternize and speak with the people of Buenos Aires, New York, London or Paris. He wants art, but not socialist realism. He wants to defy the directives of a dying generation and "speak new words." He actively resents the attempts of the Party to regiment his talent, and replies to official criticism with startling lines:

> Many do not like me
> Blaming me for many things
> And cast thunder and lightning at me.
> Sullen and tense they pour scorn on me
> And I feel their glares on my back.
> But I like all this
> I am proud that they cannot handle me,
> Can do nothing about me.[1]

One cannot help but admire the courage of this young poet—it is a fact of deep significance. It shows that the boots of the MVD have never succeeded in stamping out the fires of independent thought in Russia: and that these fires can, at any time, blaze out more brightly than ever.

We are reminded of the revolutionists of a century ago. But there is one significant difference: the resistance of Russian youth so far has been largely nonpolitical. It is not revo-

[1] See "The Young Generation of Soviet Writers," by A. Gaev, in *Bulletin of the Institute for Study of the U.S.S.R.*, Munich, Sept. 1958, pp. 38 ff.

lutionary in the nineteenth-century sense. It is moral and personal. Even when there is protest against the pharisaism and obscurantism of Soviet propaganda and censorship, it is not the protest of men who want to overthrow the regime. It is singularly free from attempts to exercise political pressure. It is this special innocence from political bias that strikes us most forcibly, for this is a resistance of people who have become *utterly fed up with everything that savors of politics.* This is the most significant thing about the protest, and it is the key to the Pasternak affair.

To try to place in a well-defined political category the moral rebellion of Russian youth against Communism is not only to misunderstand that rebellion: it is the very way by which the Communist themselves would try to frustrate it. Communism is not at home with nonpolitical categories, and it cannot deal with a phenomenon which is not in some way political. It is characteristic of the singular logic of Stalinist-Marxism, that when it incorrectly diagnoses some phenomenon as "political," it corrects the error by forcing the thing to *become* political. Hence the incessant cries of treachery and attack on all sides. Everything that happens that is unforeseen by Russia, or somehow does not fit in with Soviet plans, is an act of capitalist aggression on the Soviet Union. If a late frost ruins the fruit trees of the Ukraine, this is a political event, fomented by Wall Street. When Pasternak writes a great novel, which for political reasons cannot be printed in the USSR; and when this novel is hailed as a masterpiece outside the USSR—even though the novel is obviously not a political tract against the Soviet system, its success becomes an act of political betrayal on the part of the author. Reasons: for propaganda purposes, the USSR has to appear to be the home of all true literature and the only sound judge of what is and what is not a masterpiece. To produce a book that is hailed as a masterpiece after it has been rejected by the Soviet publishers is therefore an act of treachery, for which Pasternak was publicly and officially called "a pig who dirties the place where he sleeps and eats." No one thinks of admitting that it was a sign of weakness and impotency on the part of the Soviet publishers not to be able to print this great work themselves!

Dr. Zhivago was written in the early fifties and finished shortly after Stalin's death in 1953. In 1954, the Second Congress of Soviet writers, with its rehabilitation of condemned writers living and dead, seemed to offer hope for the future. *Dr. Zhivago* was offered for publication to *Novy Mir*. In 1954 some of the poems from *Dr. Zhivago* appeared in a literary magazine and the prospects for the publication of the entire book really seemed to be good. Ilya Ehrenburg had read it, apparently with enthusiasm, as had many other writers. Meanwhile the manuscript had been given personally by Pasternak to the publisher Feltrinelli, of Milan.

In 1956, *Dr. Zhivago* was rejected by *Novy Mir* with a long explanation which we shall discuss in a moment. But Feltrinelli refused to give up the manuscript and manifested his intention to go ahead and publish it. From that time on, guarded attacks on Pasternak were frequent in the Soviet literary magazines. He was reminded that though he might have talent he "had strayed from the true path" and one critic, Pertsov, accused him of a happy acceptance of "chaos" and of being in his element in confusion. Nevertheless in June, 1958, a sympathetic discussion of *Dr. Zhivago* was held over Radio Warsaw. Meanwhile of course the book had appeared in Italy, France and Germany and had taken Europe by storm. The English edition came out in late summer of 1958 and the Nobel Prize was awarded to Pasternak on October 23.

This was hailed by an immediate uproar in the Russian press. The decision was regarded as an act of open hostility, a new maneuver in the Cold War. The award was "steeped in lies and hypocrisy" and *Dr. Zhivago* was a "squalid" work in which Pasternak manifested his "open hatred of the Russian people. He does not have one kind word to say about our workers." *Pravda* discussed the whole thing under the delightfully confusing headline: "A Reactionary hue and cry about a Literary Weed."

On October 27 Pasternak was solemnly expelled from the Soviet Writers' Union. This automatically made it impossible for him to be published or to make any kind of a living by his pen. On October 30 Pasternak, seeing the political storm that had been raised about the award, communicated to Stockholm his regretful decision not to accept the prize. Nothing had been said officially one way or another by the Kremlin. Of all the attacks on Pasternak, the most concentrated and bitter were those which came from his colleagues in the Union of Soviet Writers. The day after his refusal of the Prize, 800 members of the Union which had already expelled him now passed a resolution demanding that he be deprived of Soviet citizenship.

At the same time, the issue continued to be discussed with a certain amount of frankness in Moscow. Pasternak was visited by newspapermen and friends. Poems and parts of *Zhivago* continued to circulate from hand to hand in typewritten or mimeographed editions.

The reports in the Western press tended, by and large, to miss the nuances and gradations of the Pasternak affair in Russia. Everything was presented as either black or white.

The Russians were *all* against Pasternak. The Kremlin was completely opposed to him, and would have done away with him if the protest of the West had not been so strong. In the West, on the contrary, everything was white, everyone was *for* Pasternak.

It is true that the protest of Western thinkers and intellectuals was decisive in arresting the all-out campaign against Pasternak in Russia, and in helping to keep him free. Nevertheless, his friends inside Russia were by no means idle. Efforts to organize a positive movement in his behalf were not very successful. But several of the most influential members of the Writers' Union refused to participate in the meetings where Pasternak was condemned. Ilya Ehrenburg sent word that he was "absent from Moscow" when everyone knew he was in his Gorky Street apartment. Leonid Leonov remained conspicuously aloof. Another writer tried actively to bring about Pasternak's rehabilitation and used his influence with Khrushchev for this end. A well-informed Western observer in Moscow reported that the Kremlin in general was disturbed by the fact that the Moscow intelligentsia remained at least passively pro-Pasternak, and that the campaign was met with deep anxiety and even mute protest on the part of the young writers who admired him. Mute protest is not much, of course. But in Russia, any protest at all is significant.

It is said that Pasternak received a fair number of letters from people in the USSR who deplored the attacks on him. Later, many of the Soviet writers who had participated in the voting at the Writers' Union privately expressed their regrets to him. All this is true. But at the same time it must not be forgotten that a real wave of indignation and hostility toward Pasternak swept the Soviet Union, incited by the speeches and articles against him, and one night a resentful crowd put on a demonstration outside his *dacha* and even threatened to burn it down.

The political noise that has surrounded *Dr. Zhivago* both in the East and in the West does nothing whatever to make the book or its author better or worse. As far as politics are concerned, Pasternak takes the position of a "nonpartici-pant," or *obyvatel,* and as *Life* comments, "Pasternak's detachment sounds a little like the faraway voice of a monk in a beleaguered Dark Age monastery, a mood with which Americans cannot easily sympathize." For my own part, being not only an American, but also a monk, I do not find sympathy so terribly hard. On the contrary, it would seem that Pasternak's ability to rise above political dichotomies may very well be his greatest strength. This transcendence is the power and the essence of *Dr. Zhivago.* One of the more important judgments made by this book is a condemnation of the chaotic meaninglessness of all twentieth-century political life, and the assertion that politics has practically ceased to be a really vital and significant force in man's society. This judgment is pronounced upon the political confusion of the nineteen-twenties in Soviet Russia, but it also falls by implication, and with proper modifications, on the West as well as on the East. What Pasternak says about Russia goes, in a different way, for the Western Europe of Hitler and Mussolini, and for the whole world of the last war—not to mention the America of the '50's.

The protest of *Dr. Zhivago* is spiritual, not political, not sociological, not pragmatic. It is religious, aesthetic and mystical. We cannot fully understand the author's view of the modern world if we insist on interpreting him by standards which have nothing to do with his work and his thought. We cannot fit into simple political categories one for whom the whole political chaos of our world is a kind of enormous spiritual cancer, running wild with a strange, admirable and disastrous life of its own and feeding on the spiritual substance of man. The deep interest of *Dr. Zhivago* is precisely its diagnosis of man's spiritual situation as a struggle for freedom *in spite of* and *against* the virulence of this enormous political disease. For, to be more accurate, since man's spiritual substance is his freedom itself, it is precisely this freedom which is devoured by politics and transmuted into a huge growth of uncontrollable precocity. Hope of attaining true freedom by purely political means has become an insane delusion.

The great success of *Dr. Zhivago* is by no means attributable to the mere fact that it happens to contain sentences which level devastating blows against the Communist mentality. Anyone with any perception can see that these blows fall, with equal power, on every form of materialistic society. They fall upon most of the gross, pervasive and accepted structures of thought and life which go to make up our changing world. The book is successful not because these blows are dealt, but because, as they land, we gradually begin to realize that Pasternak seems to know what is wrong. He seems to know what has happened to our spiritual freedom. He seems to realize why it is that most of the world's talk about freedom, peace, happiness, hope for the future is just talk and nothing more. He knows all too well that such talk is only a palliative for despair. But at the same time he has a true and solid hope to offer.

The author who most reminds me of Pasternak in this respect is Ignazio Silone. His heroes too, perhaps on a smaller scale and in a more restricted area, travel the same road as *Dr. Zhivago*, but with a more explicitly political orientation. Silone's men, with all the pathetic yet admirable smallness of genuinely human heroes, are true to man, true to his real history, true to man's vocation to "be Christ."

Zhivago of course is not a saint or a perfect hero. He is weak-willed, and his life is a confused and unsatisfactory mess. He himself knows that he has not been able to make a success of it. But the point is, he sees that in the circumstances in which he lives it is not possible to make a real success out of life—that the only honest thing is to face meaninglessness and failure with humility, and make out of it the best one can. Under such conditions his tragic life is lived "successfully" under the sign of wisdom.

It seems that the main difference between Pasternak and Western authors who have sensed the same futility, is that he is not defeated by it as they are. Nowhere in Pasternak does one get the impression that his heroes are up a blind alley, beating their heads against a wall. In the West one sees very little else. For a great majority of Western writers, though in varying degrees, man finds himself as he does in Sartre, with "No Exit"—*Huis Clos*—that is to say, in hell. The Communists would explain this as a feature of capitalist decay. Yet their own society is up the same blind alley, pretending that the wall at the end is not there, and that the business of beating your head against it is proof of optimism and progress. Pasternak sees the blind alley and sees the wall, but knows that the way out is not through the wall, and not back out by the way we came in. The exit is into an entirely new dimension—finding ourselves in others, discovering the inward sources of freedom and love which God has put in our nature, discovering Christ in the midst of us, as "one we know not."

This exit is not a mere theoretical possibility. Nor is it even a mere escape. It is a real and creative solution to man's problems: a solution that can bring meaning out of confusion and good out of evil. It is something that has been sought after with hope and conviction by the greatest Russian minds of the past century: Dostoievsky, Tolstoy, Soloviev, and by Russians of our own time like Nicholas Berdyaev.

The solution is *love* as the highest expression of man's spirituality and freedom. Love and Life (reduced to one and the same thing) form the great theme of *Dr. Zhivago*. In proportion as one is alive he has a greater capacity and a greater obligation to love. Every degree of true and false love makes its appearance in the book—from the self-assured and bestial selfishness of Komarovsky, the businessman, to the different shades of compulsive and authoritarian falsity in the various revolutionaries. There are all aspects of parental and conjugal love (Zhivago really loves his wife Tonia, for example). Lara though seduced by Komarovsky in her girlhood remains the embodiment of a love that is simple, unadulterated spontaneity, a love that does not know how to be untrue to itself or to life. Her love is perfectly aware of the difference between sin and goodness, but her repentance (the Magdalen theme) has a creative power to transcend limitations and to emerge into a new world. Lara is thus the embodiment of the goodness and love of God immanent in His creation, immanent in man and in Russia, and there left at the mercy of every evil. Far from being a trite and prissy concept, this is both deep and original. One can see in Pasternak a strong influence from Soloviev's *Meaning of Love* and his theory of man's vocation to regenerate the world by the spiritualization of human love raised to the sophianic level of perfect conscious participation in the mystery of the divine wisdom of which the earthly sacrament is love.

At the same time we must remember that Zhivago's victory is tragic Lara vanishes "without a trace" to die, probably, in a concentration camp. Nothing has been "transformed." It is the victory that shines forth in apparent defeat—the victory of death and resurrection. We notice too, that resurrection remains curiously implicit in the strange, impoverished death of the unsuccessful doctor who falls to the pavement with a heart attack while getting out of a Moscow streetcar. There is a strange parallel between the double death rite of Marina and Lara for Zhivago and the terribly impressive scene of lamentation at the end of *Safe Conduct* in which Mayakovsky's sister raves with Oriental passion over the body of the suicide. There is a gleam of hope in the Epilogue where Tania, the child of Zhivago and Lara, the "child of the terrible years" is seen, for a moment, in her own simplicity. The things she has had to go through have not ruined her. And we realize that the strange mystical figure of Evgraf, the "guardian angel," "will take care of her." She is the Russia of the future.

One of the singularly striking things about *Dr. Zhivago* is its quality of tragedy without frustration. Here everything is clean and free from ambivalence. Love is love and hate is hate. Zhivago says and does what he means, and when he is uncertain he is not dishonest about it. It is this spiritual cleanliness, this direct vision and fidelity to life here and now which Pasternak opposes to the grandiose and systematic ravings of politicians who turn all life into casuistry and bind man hand and foot in the meticulous service of unrealities.

It is time to quote. These are the thoughts of Zhivago, half starved and faint from hardships and exposure, as he reads a political proclamation pasted on a wall:

Had (these words) been composed last year, the year before? Only once in his life had this uncompromising language and single-mindedness filled him with enthusiasm. Was it possible that he must pay for that rash enthusiasm all his life by never hearing year after year, anything but these unchanging, shrill, crazy exclamations and demands which became progressively more impractical, meaningless and unfulfillable as time went by? . . . What an enviable blindness, to be able to talk of bread when it has long since vanished from the face of the earth! Of propertied classes and speculators when they have long since been abolished by earlier decrees! Of peasants and villages that no longer exist! Don't they remember their own plans and measures, which long since turned life upside down? What kind of people are they, to go on raving with this never cooling feverish ardor, year in, year out, on non-existent, long-vanished subjects, and to know nothing, to see nothing around them. (*Dr. Zhivago,* p. 381)

Pasternak was morally compelled to refuse the Nobel Prize in order to remain in Russia. Writers in England, France and the United States protested against Russia's flat rejection of her only great writer since the Revolution. *Pravda* devoted eighteen columns to an unprecedented publication of the "original letter" which had been sent to Pasternak by the magazine *Novy Mir* refusing to serialize the novel in Russian. The letter was signed, curiously enough, by a poet, A. T. Tvardovsky, who, since writing it, had himself fallen under an official ban. The document is notable for its surprising lack of abusiveness and its relatively sympathetic effort to reason with the author. Pasternak was evidently respected in this case by a devoted colleague. The chief objection is not made against the passages in which Marxism is explicitly condemned, for these are relatively few and could have been expunged. The whole fault of the book, from the Soviet point of view, is something "which neither the editors nor the author can alter by cuts or revision . . . the spirit of the novel, its general tenor, *the author's view of life.*"

This view of life, as we have indicated above, is that the individual is more important than the collectivity. His spirit, his freedom, his ability to love, raise him above the state. The state exists for man, not man for the state. No man has the right to hand himself over to any superior force other than God Himself. Man has no right to alienate his own liberty to become a cog in a machine. Man is of no use to man if he ceases to be a person and lets himself be reduced to the status of a "thing." A collectivity that reduces the members to the level of alienated objects is dooming both itself and its members to a sterile and futile existence to which no amount of speeches and parades can ever give a meaning. The great tragedy of the revolution, for Pasternak, was the fact that the best men in Russia submitted to mass insanity and yielded up their own judgment to the authority of Juggernaut.

It was then that untruth came down on our land of Russia. The main misfortune, the root of all evil to come, was the loss of confidence in the value of one's own opinion. People imagined that it was out of date to follow their own moral sense, that they must all sing in chorus, and live by other people's notions, notions that were being crammed down everybody's throat. . . . The social evil became an epidemic. It was catching, and it affected everything, nothing was left untouched by it. Our home too became infected. . . . Instead of being natural and spontaneous as we had always been, we began to be idiotically pompous with each other. Something showy, arti-

ficial, forced, crept into our conversation—you felt you had
to be clever in a certain way about certain world-important
themes. . . . (*Dr. Zhivago*, p. 404)

Like Dostoievsky, Pasternak holds that man's future depends on his ability to work his way out from under a continuous succession of authoritarian rulers who promise him
happiness at the cost of his freedom. Like Dostoievsky, also,
Pasternak insists that the fruit of Christ's Incarnation, Death
and Resurrection, is that true freedom has at least become
possible: but that man, ignoring the real meaning of the
New Testament, prefers to evade the responsibility of his
vocation and continues to live "under the law." This is not
a new complaint: it goes back to St. Paul.

Ironically enough, one of the most brilliant analyses of
man's alienation came from the pen of Marx. Modern Russia, while paying lip-service to Marx's theory on this point,
has forgotten his full meaning. Yet in so doing, the Soviets
have brought out the inner contradiction of Marx's thought:
for the complete spiritual alienation of man which Marx
ascribed in part to religion has been brought about by militant atheism, as well as by the economic system which claims
to be built on an orthodox Marxian foundation. It is of
course not fair to blame Stalin's police state directly on
Marx, though Marx cannot be absolved from indirect responsibility.

At any event, Pasternak's "view of life" is what has
brought upon him the outraged and unanimous condemnation of Soviet officialdom. While the letter from *Novy Mir*
reproves Pasternak as immoral, the Soviet critics after the
Nobel Prize award did not hesitate to find in *Dr. Zhivago*
and in its author every possible kind of moral depravity.

Pasternak, the lowest of the low, could not even be compared to a pig. He could no longer claim a right to breathe the pure air of Soviet Russia.

It would be a great mistake to think that for the Communists such accusations are taken as mere words without specific reference, to be used with cynical opportunism. The curious fact is that Communism today has forged its own rigid and authoritarian code of morals, which can be called "an ethic" only by doing violence to the meaning of words, but which nevertheless claims with puritanical self-assurance to show men how to "live."

The ideal Communist is a combination of a beaver and a wolf. He unites machine-like industry with utter insensitiveness to deep human values whenever they come into conflict with political duty. He either knows at all times the course of history and "the one correct thing" to do at the moment, or, if he does not know it, he obeys someone else who claims to know it. In either case, he "acts" with all the complacent self-assurance of a well-adjusted machine, and grinds to pieces anything that comes in his way, whether it be his own idea of truth, his most cherished hopes for this world or the next, or the person of a wife, friend, or parent.

All through *Dr. Zhivago* we find an extraordinary and subtle range of such characters portrayed: some of them pure Communist types, others much more complicated and hard to label. The hero himself, Yurii Zhivago, *is in all respects the exact opposite to the New Soviet Man*. This, of course, is what constitutes, in Soviet eyes, the depth of moral degradation. To have human feelings, to follow the lead of spontaneous inner inspiration, to be moved by love and pity, to let oneself be swayed by appreciation of what is *human* in man—all this is nothing but bourgeois depravity and shameless individualism.

It almost seems that Pasternak has gone out of his way to make Zhivago act on impulse in a way that would seem utterly foolish to Communists. It always remains clear that this yielding to impulse is not presented (as it sometimes is in Western novels) as the ideal of freedom. No, freedom is something higher and more spiritual than that. But Pasternak makes the point that if one does at times follow a crazy urge and do something completely pointless, it is not an act to be ashamed of. Must one always be reasonable? Must one always have a ponderous ethical justification for every action he performs? Must one fear spontaneity and never do anything that is not decreed by some program, some form or other of duty? On the contrary, it is compulsiveness that warps life and makes it pointless. The apparent pointlessness of man's impulses may perhaps show the way to what he is really seeking.

This, for a Marxist, is deadly heresy: everyone knows that for a Marxist everything has to fit in with his fantasies of omniscience. Everything has to have a point, everything has to be guided toward some specific purpose. To this, Zhivago replies:

> You find in practice that what they mean by ideas is nothing but words—claptrap in praise of the revolution and the regime. . . . One of my sins is a belief in intuition. And yet see how ridiculous. They all shout that I am a marvelous diagnostician, and as a matter of fact it's true that I don't often make mistakes in diagnosing a disease. Well, what is this immediate grasp of the situation as a whole supposed to be if not this intuition they find so detestable? (p. 407)

It is therefore understandable that *Novy Mir* should have singled out with horror the passage where Yurii Zhivago finds himself accidentally in the middle of a battle between

Red Partisans and White Russian volunteers (pp. 332-6). There can be no question that such a passage would make any good Communist squirm in his chair with acute moral discomfort. It would repel and horrify him in much the same way as a chapter of Sartre or Moravia might horrify a nun. It is the kind of thing he would take not only as alien and unpleasant, but as a threat to the whole foundation of his moral security and peace of mind. I do not doubt that Pasternak wrote this section deliberately with his tongue in his cheek. The Reds have responded admirably. The *Novy Mir* letter as reprinted in *Pravda* contains the whole passage quoted *in extenso*, in order to let each loyal Communist taste the full deliciousness of scandalized horror.

What happens? Zhivago, as a doctor, is not supposed to fight. But he is caught in this battle which like all battles is a silly and tragic mess. Zhivago impulsively takes the gun of a fallen comrade, but deliberately aims at a dead tree trunk, and only hits one of the enemy by accident. After the skirmish, he finds that his fallen Red comrade and the White soldier he has wounded each wear a locket containing the text of Psalm 90, which was devoutly believed to be a protection against death. The Red soldier, with a corrupt text of the Psalm, is dead. The White, with a correct text, is alive. Taking pity on him, Zhivago clothes him in the uniform of the fallen Red Partisan and looks after him among the Communist fighters, until he escapes, threatening that he will continue to fight the Reds.

This scene, which is essentially comical, contains just about every mortal sin in the Communist code. I leave the reader to discover them for himself.

The situation being what it was, the Soviet Leaders were faced with the problem of blackening Pasternak in the eyes of East and West at the same time. He had to be regarded not only as a dangerous criminal by Russia, but as a hypocrite and coward by the West. Realistic politicians knew well enough that denunciations would not be enough to ruin Pasternak in the eyes of the young writers who undoubtedly looked up to him as a model and a hero. Soviet attacks on Pasternak could only add to his prestige in the West. For this reason, far from categorically forbidding him to accept the prize, they left the door wide open and urged him to leave Russia as long as he did not try to return. It would have been admirable, from their viewpoint, to have "proof" that Pasternak was a traitor to his country. At the same time their benevolence would remain to "prove" that "Pasternak has been left perfectly free to accept the Nobel Prize." Pasternak refused to abandon Russia, not out of political astuteness but merely because he loved his own country and did not feel that he would be able to write anywhere else.

Once again, he was acting with perfect consistency as one who is the exact opposite of a Communist. His staying in Russia was another victory for his personal integrity as an artist and as a human being. But perhaps there was some advantage to be gained here by the Reds. Perhaps Pasternak could be pressed a little further, and so diminish in the eyes of the West. Pasternak came out in *Pravda* with a letter of "apology," declared that he had made a "mistake" in accepting the Nobel Prize, and that his subsequent refusal of it had been "entirely voluntary." He stated that he had not been threatened and that his life had not been imperiled. This letter, which saddened and shocked readers in the West, but which could have been regarded as inevitable, was probably extracted from him in order to save face for the Soviet Government and pay the price of his moral victory.

If one reads the letter carefully, he can detect the difference between passages written by Pasternak and those inserted by others to "make his meaning clear." The passages obviously written by Pasternak are clear and consistent with his position. He asks to be dissociated from the "political campaign around my novel" which he regrets and did not intend. "I never had the intention of causing harm to my state and my people." That is only a reaffirmation of the obvious fact that the book is not a political tract. In regard to the "political errors" of which he "might be accused," he declares that they are not to be found in the novel. This passage is interesting and entirely true. Here is what Pasternak writes: "*It would appear* that I am *allegedly maintaining* the following erroneous principles. *I am supposed to have alleged* that any revolution is an historically illegal phenomenon, that the October Revolution was such, and that it brought unhappiness to Russia and the downfall of the Russian intelligentsia." It is quite obvious that Pasternak nowhere holds that all revolution is "historically illegal" —nor does anybody else. Nor does he maintain that the October Revolution was "illegal." The texts we have quoted certainly show that Russia after the revolution is not portrayed in *Dr. Zhivago* as a bed of roses and that Pasternak plainly ascribes many bad effects to Communism. At the same time we have seen clearly that he accepted the necessity of the Revolution, first of all in 1905, then in 1917. No one in his right senses could imagine that Pasternak was trying in *Dr. Zhivago* to lead Russia back to capitalism or to the old regime. But it is equally clear that he has maintained a perfect independence and objectivity with regard to the revolution, and after living through Stalin's five-year plans and the purges, he has concluded (with the vast majority of intellectuals everywhere in the world) that the Bolshevik

Revolution was a failure and that Marxism had nothing to offer man but a Gospel of delusions. His apology as it stands does nothing to alter the substance of this belief. All that he regrets, about *Zhivago*, is the manner in which it was published and the way it was exploited by anti-Communist journalism. These two things were obviously not the fault of the author.

Pasternak's letter ends with a pious sigh which is utterly alien to his thought and his style and was almost certainly inserted by somebody else: "I firmly believe that I shall find the strength to redeem my good name and restore the confidence of my comrades."

The mystery of this letter has not fully been cleared up, but after its publication and the publication of other similar statements Pasternak cautioned a friend against believing any statement that was supposed to have emanated from him.

Meanwhile, November and December 1958 were months of bitterness and conflict. We have already considered the open explosions of hostility which occurred at the time of the Prize award, when the Soviet authorities were trying to get Pasternak out of Russia. These explosions soon ceased, and the case vanished from the pages of *Pravda*. It ceased to be front-page news in the West and soon disappeared altogether but for a few sporadic flare-ups.

Meanwhile, Pasternak was exhausted and ill. In order to forget his troubles, he kept himself busy on a translation of a Polish play, a job that had been deliberately steered his way by sympathetic friends in the Polish Writers' Union. Letters continued to arrive from the West. Friends and even reporters continued to visit the *dacha*—where the presence of newspapermen did nothing to improve the peace of the household. Mrs. Pasternak strenuously objected to them, and uttered vigorous protests, all of which were dutifully reported in the Western newspapers.

December came, and with it the distribution of the Nobel Prizes. Western journalists gloated over the possibility that it might turn into a good show—with an empty chair in evidence for Pasternak. No such thing was done, fortunately. It would have been very entertaining for minds that rejoice in devious forms of moral aggression, but it would not have made life any more comfortable for Pasternak.

At the end of the year a story broke in the Western press, stating that a Spanish exile in London, José Vilallonga, had arranged to tour free Europe and America with Pasternak, giving lectures. It was alleged that Pasternak's life had been insured for three million dollars. The Russians seem to have taken this story seriously and *Pravda* reported a telegram in which Pasternak was supposed to have rejected the offer. In reality, as Pasternak himself made clear, he had never been in contact with Vilallonga and everything about the story was "pure invention" including the supposed telegram.

Early in the new year, Pasternak was again featured in a disturbing story. A reporter of the London *Daily Mail* printed a poem in which Pasternak complained bitterly at being rejected by his own countrymen. Pasternak did not deny having written the poem but protested against its publication as a breach of confidence. Once again it was felt that his life might be in danger. When in February, Pasternak suddenly disappeared from his *dacha*, many came to the conclusion that he had been imprisoned and that the game was now up. The explanation given by the Soviet Press was that he had gone away for a "vacation" and in order "to avoid the newspapermen who were coming from London to Moscow with Prime Minister Macmillan." As it turned out, this explanation may have been substantially true.

Actually, Pasternak had left Peredelkino of his own free will and had gone to spend a few weeks at Tiflis, Georgia, as the guest of Mrs. Tabidze, the widow of the Georgian poet shot by Stalin's police. He returned home in good health, and gradually, as the affair ceased to appear in the press and began to be forgotten in the West, prospects began to look good for the harassed writer. In May, for example, a shake-up in the Soviet Writers' Union led to the replacement of Pasternak's enemy Surkov, as head of the Union, by Fedin who is friendly to Pasternak.

This was not a mere coincidence. The removal of Surkov was certainly a consequence of the Pasternak Affair, and those who interpreted this change in the Writer's Union as evidence that Pasternak's friends had won over the favor of Khrushchev are perhaps not too far wrong. Whatever may be the real facts, which remain to be discovered and made public, we can agree with the writer of the *New York Times* who said: "It was apparent that there were profound second thoughts about the persecution of Mr. Pasternak. All of the leading literary and party figures who participated in the verbal lynching were downgraded or demoted." And this is highly significant. It shows at least that the qualities of freedom and integrity for which Pasternak stood in the eyes of west and east alike were able in some measure to get themselves recognized in Soviet Russia.

This is no small achievement. It is quite clear that Pasternak emerged from the whole affair as the moral and spiritual conqueror of Stalinism, and that he conquered, not for himself alone but even for those of his compatriots who were able to share to some degree in his outlook. And if he did this, it was not only because of his natural and human qualities but, I might venture to say, because of the depth and clarity of his Christian faith. Not that Pasternak is an explicit witness for the Christian message, in the face of Communism: his faith was never directly involved in the debate at all. And yet his resistance was spiritual and his spirit was essentially Christian not only because of his belief in "Christ as the center of history" but because of his existential dedication to the supreme inner value of personalism, which is one of the characteristic Christian contributions to western humanistic thought.

Let us now draw a few conclusions.

Pasternak's book was offered for publication in Russia after the death of Stalin, during the "thaw" when, at the Twentieth Party Congress, Khrushchev openly admitted the "crimes and errors" of Stalin, implicitly showing that Russia needed to move back from extreme dictatorial authoritarianism to a freer and more flexible way of life. Pasternak obviously thought that his book could claim to represent the thought and aspirations of the intelligentsia, including many Communists, at that time. No doubt there would have to be changes, but the *substance* of his book was, it seemed, just what Russia was waiting for. As far as the young intellectuals are concerned, this may have been true.

Unfortunately, as regards the Party, he was premature! The fact that *Dr. Zhivago* could never be made acceptable by editing showed that Soviet Russia could never accept so fundamental an idea of freedom. The end of the thaw soon made this very plain.

A providential accident led to the publication of the novel outside the USSR by an Italian publisher who refused obedience to Moscow when the edition was condemned. When Pasternak was awarded the Nobel Prize, it showed that the whole world was glad that at last a great book had come out of Russia. The acclaim of critics and readers was certainly not primarily a political matter. Unquestionably,

Western readers have not studied Pasternak's estimate of Communism without satisfaction. And of course the newspapers have turned the book into a political weapon, which was not the intention of the author. But the Nobel Prize was awarded on nonpolitical grounds to a book great in its own right.

The fact remains that if Soviet Russia had been strong enough to absorb the powerful contents of this book in the first place, and had been able to publish it, even in a somewhat edited version, the prestige achieved by this act would have been tremendous. One Nobel Prize winner in literature is of more value to Russia than a thousand winners in physics, no matter how set the Soviet government is on science. It is one thing to produce atomic counters or to win the pentathlon, and another to be recognized as a leader in the field of literature. If Russia wins the Nobel award in science it is because she has good scientists. If her athletes excel, it is because they are good. But her scientists and athletes are good because dialectical materialism cannot directly interfere in their speciality. (The attempt to do so in biology has been given up.) What remains but the conclusion that if Russian writers were not forced to sabotage their talent and their integrity and grind out political clichés, they too might win Nobel Prizes? Here is one who has done it: but without benefit of a blessing from the Kremlin. The implications are so plain that even the Kremlin can see them, and, like the Hungarian Revolution, the spectacle has proved disconcerting.

So much for Russia. But what does Pasternak have to say to the Western intellectual? The first thing, of course, is said by the triumphant artistic achievement of his novel and the poetry which accompanies it. *Dr. Zhivago* itself is greater than any "message" that might be distilled out of it. It is a superb novel which recovers the full creative fecundity that seems to have vanished from our cramped and worried literature; a book with a sense of orientation and meaning in strong contrast with our Western frustration and despair.

Pasternak has become a best seller and a widely read author in the West, but he will always be a writer's writer. His greatest impact has been on the *writers* of the West. He has received letters from all kinds of people, but especially from other writers, in many different countries, not the least being Camus and Mauriac. Pasternak answered all these letters with profound warmth of understanding, and those who were privileged to be in contact with him felt that he had given them much more than they expected—an inspiration and sense of direction which they had ceased to hope for from any other writer!

We have learned from Pasternak that we must never yield to the great temptation offered by Communism to the writer. I do not mean the temptation to be a member of a privileged and respected class, but the far more insidious one of becoming a "writer for the future." Surely there is something apocalyptic about the sinister complacency with which Communism, which has hitherto proved effective only in killing writers or ruining them, proposes itself as Master of the future of literature. "Write for us, you will be remembered forever in the Kingdom of the Messias who has now come! Refuse our offer, and you will be buried with the world that we are about to bury."

It is against such insinuations of the Beast that Pasternak replies with his doctrine of life and resurrection. This is a doctrine with a strongly Christian basis, using exclusively Christian symbolism. Needless to say, not all of Pasternak's expressions can be fully reconciled with those to be found in a manual of dogma. The Christ of Pasternak is the Christ

Who has liberated man from death and Who lives in man, waiting for man's liberty to give Him a chance to transform the world by love. Love is the work not of states, not of organizations, not of institutions, but of persons. Hence:

> Gregariousness is always the refuge of mediocrities. . . . Only individuals seek the truth, and they shun those whose whole concern is not the truth. How many things in this world deserve our loyalty? Very few indeed. I think one should be loyal to immortality, which is another word for life, a stronger word for it. One must be true to immortality—true to Christ (p. 9).

Pasternak looks at our world, dismembered by its obsessions and its factions, each one claiming to be on the side of the angels and calling everyone else a devil. Egged on by journalists, politicians and propagandists, we cling with mad hope to fanatical creeds whose only function is to foment violence, hatred, and division. Will we never begin to understand that the "differences" between these factions are often so superficial as to be illusory and that all of them are equally stupid? Will we never grow up, and get down to the business of living productively on this earth, in unity and peace?

History is not a matter of inexorable scientific laws, it is a new creation, a work of God in and through man: but this theandric work is unthinkable not only without man's desire but also without his *initiative*. Christ has planted in the world the seeds of something altogether new, but they do not grow by themselves. Hence history has never yet really had a chance to become a Christian creation. For the world to be changed, man himself must begin to change it, he must take the initiative, he must step forth and make a new kind of history. The change begins within himself.

You can't advance in this direction without a certain faith. You can't make such discoveries without a spiritual equipment. And the basic elements of this equipment are in the Gospels. What are they? To begin with a certain love of one's neighbor, which is the supreme form of vital energy. Once it fills the heart of man it has to overflow and expend itself. And then the two basic ideals of modern man—without them he is unthinkable—the idea of free personality and the idea of life as sacrifice. . . . There is no history in this sense among the ancients. They had blood and beastliness and cruelty and pockmarked Caligulas who had no idea how inferior the system of slavery is. They had the boastful dead eternity of bronze monuments and marble columns. It was not until after the coming of Christ that time and man could breathe freely. Man does not die in a ditch like a dog—but at home in history, while the work toward the conquest of death is in full swing; he dies sharing in this work (p. 10).

Here is the deep meaning of Pasternak's critique of Communism. It is blindness and sin to seek immortality in the bronze and stone which are already stamped with lifelessness and twice dead when they are frozen into an art without inspiration. "Why seek ye the living among the dead?" Communism, like all characteristically modern political movements, far from opening the door to the future is only a regression into the past, the ancient past, the time of slavery before Christ. Following these movements, mankind falls backward into an abyss of ancient, magical laws; man comes under the authority of numbers and astrological systems and loses all hope of freedom. But with the coming of Christ

The reign of numbers was at an end. The duty, imposed by armed force to live unanimously as a people, a whole nation, was abolished. Leaders and nations were relegated to the past.

They were replaced by the doctrine of individuality and free-dom. *Individual human life became the life story of God and its contents filled the vast expanses of the universe.*

These words occur on page 413, far into the book, in an apparently colorless, "unexciting" chapter which is in reality very important to Pasternak's great work—one of the nerve centers where all his meaning is fully experienced.

If we stop to think about what it says, we will realize that if Pasternak is ever fully studied, he is just as likely to be re-garded as a dangerous writer in the West as he is in the East. He is saying that political and social structures as we under-stand them are things of the past, and that the crisis through which we are now passing is nothing but the full and ines-capable manifestation of their falsity. For twenty centuries we have called ourselves Christians, without even beginning to understand one tenth of the Gospel. We have been tak-ing Caesar for God and God for Caesar. Now that "charity is growing cold" and we stand facing the smoky dawn of an apocalyptic era, Pasternak reminds us that there is only one source of truth, but that it is not sufficient to know the source is there—we must go and drink from it, as he has done.

Do we have the courage to do so? For obviously, if we consider what Pasternak is saying, doing and undergoing, to read the Gospel with eyes wide open may be a perilous thing!

MOUNT ATHOS

For over a thousand years Mount Athos has been one of the greatest monastic centers in all Christendom. Perhaps those who have heard of this ancient republic have cherished a vague idea that Athos was simply a "monastery." Actually, the 35-mile-long peninsula near Thessalonica, in northern Greece, is a whole nation of monks and monasteries. The capital of this small country, which for a long time enjoyed a completely independent political existence, is a town called Karyes in the center of the peninsula; it is the seat of Synaxis or Synod, the representative body of monks elected by the various monasteries at the beginning of each year. Karyes is a town of monks with a monastic school, a small hotel, and various shops and stores run by monks and laymen, plus a small force of Greek policemen who are obliged to remain celibate as long as they serve on Athos. The peninsula is absolutely forbidden to all women, for, as legend says, the Blessed Virgin excluded all other women from Athos when she claimed it as "her garden," after she was driven ashore by a storm, near the site of the present monastery of Iviron.

Whether or not the Blessed Virgin ever came there, Athos has been for a thousand years a "desert" cut off from the world and a jealously guarded stronghold of asceticism and contemplation. The mountain itself stands at the south end of the peninsula, and rises to a height of 5,000 feet. The rest of the territory is rugged, stony, wooded and truly wild. Wolves and wild boars still roam there. The mountain is criss-crossed by mule tracks. Automobiles, trucks, and tractors do not exist on Athos; there are no motor roads. Some of the monasteries have telephone connections with each other. Only one has electric lights, and in consequence is devised by the others. Some of the communities make their living by selling timber. Others survive by the production of wine or olive oil. All are poor and even the best of them does not measure up to minimum standards of comfort for Western Europeans, let alone for Americans. Recent books written about Athos tend to be at once exciting and deceptive. Often they are illustrated by magnificent photographs which one can contemplate with insatiable wonder. But the text is generally trivial by comparison. We find the sardonic remarks of hardened tourists who are ready for anything, and who will not hesitate to ride miles on mule back, drink ouzo and eat octopus fried in olive oil (provided that they can regard all this with the amused detachment of westerners dropping, as it were, from another planet). In such books one rarely receives any insight into the profound religious mystery of Athos. Even one of the most sympathetic and understanding accounts, that written by a Scot, the late Sidney Loch, who lived for years just outside the borders of Athos and knew its monks and hermits very well, nevertheless lacks a deep religious perspective. Nowhere has any modern western writer given us a witness to the spirit of Athos comparable to the profoundly moving pages of Henry Miller about Epidaurus, Mycenae and especially Phaestos (in Crete). It is perhaps true that Athos is out of touch with our times, far more so than any monastery in the Western world. But precisely because of this it has much to teach us, since our salvation consists not in keeping up with the times but in transcending them or, as St. Paul would say, in redeeming them.

Athos is the last important Christian survival of the typical ancient monastic colonies which flourished in the fourth and fifth centuries when monasticism began in the Church. In those days men did not enter this or that religious order (there were no "orders")—they fled to a "desert" or to a mountain area in the wilderness where monks gathered in twos or threes, or in small colonies of ten, twenty, or fifty, or even in large groups of several hundred. Others lived alone as hermits and recluses. There the monastic way was followed not according to a fixed legislative code, but according to traditional customs which could be adjusted very flexibly to the needs of each one in his spiritual journey to God. So too at Athos, even today. The different monasteries, *skites* and cells are not representatives of various "orders" in the Orthodox Church. There are still no formal orders, in our sense, in the Greek Church, only various kinds of monks.

At Athos the two main groups are cenobitic and idiorrhythmic monks. The cenobites live a systematic community life resembling that of Cistercians or Benedictines in the Western Church. Yet they do not, as one might suppose, "follow the Rule of St. Basil" or any other rule. The Rule of St. Basil is in any case rather a "spiritual directory" than a formal rule like that of St. Benedict. The Athonites are bound to keep the *typicon* (monastic customs) of their individual monasteries, and the cenobite's life is still in many ways much stricter than the strictest observance in the Western Church. The monks sometimes chant in choir sixteen or eighteen hours at a stretch for the offices of the greater feasts, and their fasts are more numerous and more arduous than ours. The general condition of poverty in the cenobitic monasteries is all the more notable now that these once prosperous houses have been gradually ruined. The monks work hard to earn a meager living. Wars, revolutions and iron curtains have cut off their supply of vocations as well as their revenues. And if life in the monasteries themselves is austere, it is all the more so out in the cells and hermitages where men live on the rugged mountainside in conditions on a level with those of the poorest of the poor in the Balkan countries.

The idiorrhythmic monks are peculiar to the Oriental Church, if we except those modern religious congregations in the West whose members are allowed to retain title to their property and to keep their individual earnings. The idiorrhythmic monks, whether in monasteries or out of them, retain proprietorship of what property they have, and live on the income from their labor. The monastery furnishes them with shelter and work, in a rudimentary organization which is controlled not by an abbot but by an elected committee. The monks chant the office together in choir, but work and live on their own, in or out of the monastery, cooking their own meals which can include meat on certain days. The monastic shops in Karyes are run by idiorrhythmic monks. It is a loose kind of life, not necessarily decadent, though it dates from a period of relaxation in the history of Athos, in the days when it was ruled by the Turks.

Monasteries can choose to be either idiorrhythmic or cenobitic and some have passed back and forth from one to the
other several times in the course of centuries.

There are twenty large autonomous monasteries on Athos.
The oldest of these is Lavra, founded by St. Athanasius of
Athos in 963. Though there were hermits and small groups
of monks on the Mountain before this time, and though St.
Anthanasius himself first came to Athos in 958, the thou-
sandth anniversary of Athonite monasticism will probably
be celebrated in 1963. The monastery of Simopetra, standing on a high cliff overhanging the sea, is probably familiar
to many who have seen photographs of Mount Athos; the
flimsy balconies on which the monks may sit suspended
hundreds of feet above the sea leave one with an indelible
impression of the Holy Mountain. Another ancient monastery is Iviron, founded in 980 by three knights from Georgia. The community was originally Georgian, and chanted
the liturgy in its own tongue, though for centuries now
Iviron has been under the control of Greeks. Later I will
mention the once flourishing Russian monastery on Athos,
St. Panteleimon.

The score of smaller groups, *skites*, *kalybes*, *kellia* and
hermitages, all depend on one or other of the main monasteries, which alone can be represented by delegates (one
each) in the synod at Karyes.

The general level of life for the idiorrhythmic monks is
a little more comfortable and a great deal more independent
than it is for the cenobites. The largest and most prosperous
Greek monasteries are idiorrhythmic. Cenobitism flourished
most of all among the Russians, who are now rapidly de-
clining in numbers and significance. The idiorrhythmic
monastery of Vatopedi, one of the largest and least primi-

tive, is the only one that has electric light and a few water closets which may or may not work. It is also the only Athonite community that has adopted the Gregorian calendar, so that Vatopedi celebrates the feasts of the liturgical year with the Western Church, thirteen days ahead of the other monasteries on Athos.

Only at Vatopedi does twelve o'clock mean noon. Other monasteries, following the Turkish practice, put twelve at sunset. Iviron, different from all the rest, puts twelve at sunrise, as it used to be done in Persia. The atmosphere of independence on Athos is therefore something quite unusual in this world of ours where no one dreams of disregarding the clocks of his time-belt, no matter how nonconformist he may be in other respects.

The so-called *skites* are dependent monasteries, not necessarily smaller than the twenty autonomous communities that have a voice in the synod. On the contrary, Stavronikita, which today numbers only 22 monks, is an autonomous house, while the Russian *skite* of St. Andrew once outnumbered it by several hundred but never managed to become autonomous.

Besides the *skites*, the Holy Mountain is dotted with *kalybes* (cottages) where two or three monks live and work together, and then there are caves and cells for hermits, some of whom still live in the same seclusion and austerity as the primitive monks of the desert. The great variety of vocations on Athos, the respect for individual differences of vocation, the liberty allowed to the grace of the Holy Spirit: all this remains a significant characteristic of this monastic nation, and a sign of its vitality.

Not everyone can become a hermit: this depends on the permission of monastic superiors who jealously guard the privilege and grant it only to those who have proved their spiritual strength and purity of heart and are ready to be "kissed by God."

At the same time we must not take too romantic a view of the solitaries on Athos. They lead a life that is, from our Western viewpoint, utterly squalid, filthy and miserable. Yet they seem to get along well enough at it, and they really are, for the most part, deeply spiritual men. (In fact it is quite possible that they are more spiritual than the monks of our more hygienic and up-to-date monasteries with their spotless dairy cows and well-washed pigs.) The hermits on Athos are, generally, men of peasant extraction who are physically prepared to live a life exposed to heat, cold, vermin and near-starvation.

The population of Athos has had its ups and downs since the tenth century. Perhaps the highest number was reached in the sixteenth century when it is estimated that from 15,-000 to 20,000 monks and hermits lived on the Holy Mountain. This was when the monastic republic enjoyed its greatest material prosperity, in spite of the fact that Turkish government imposed a levy on the monks, in return for leaving them in peace. There was a sharp decline after the Greek revolution in 1821. Many monks joined the rebel army and fought for Greece, leaving the monasteries half empty.

The nineteenth century saw the great tide of Russian vocations to Athos, astutely promoted by the Tsars who took over a ruined, abandoned Greek monastery (St. Panteleimon) and built it up into a powerful community of 1,500 Russian cenobites. The Russiko, as this cenobium is called, became a kind of political nightmare for all the rest of Athos. The Greeks fought with all their power to prevent the populous and wealthy Russian *skites,* like that of St. Andrew, from becoming independent monasteries and thus gaining a seat in the synod. They already suspected that half the monks of the Russiko were Tsarist soldiers in disguise, and were afraid that the Russians might gain control of the governing body of the peninsula.

In 1912, the population of Athos was about 7,000, of whom over half were Russians. By 1930 this number had been cut almost in half, and of course the biggest decline of all was among the Russians, who had received no voca- tions since the Bolshevist revolution. One by one the de- pendent cells and *kalybes* closed down and the aging Rus- sian monks fell back upon the larger monasteries which, even with these reinforcements, remained half empty and began to go to ruin.

Vocations from other Iron Curtain countries have also rapidly declined. The Serbian idiorrhythmic monastery of Chilandari has dwindled from eighty monks in 1930 to 43 in 1950. The same rate of decline is found in Zographou (Bulgarian) and the Rumanian *skite* of Prodromos. But the Greek monasteries themselves are in no better condition. The population of the Holy Mountain was 4,600 in 1930 and must be little more than half that number today.

Lavra, one of the most flourishing Greek idiorrhythmic houses, and said to be the best on Athos, had six hundred monks in 1930 and only two hundred in 1953—a drastic loss in 23 years. The outlook for the future of Athos is not reassuring and, in parentheses, the Russian ambassador in Athens has taken a discreet, disquieting interest in the Rus- siko. (The remaining monks are all loyal to the memory of the Tsars whose portraits are everywhere at St. Pantelei- mon.) It is known that monasticism is tolerated today within the USSR for reasons of political expediency. Per-

haps the Kremlin might suddenly one day find it dialecti-
cally correct to take over the Russiko for its own monastic
purposes—and revive the nightmare that kept the Greeks
of Athos uneasy all through the nineteenth century.

The typical Athos monastery is a fortified village of ram-
bling, balconied buildings centered around the main church
or *katholikon*. There are always other churches and chapels
—seventeen, for example, at Vatopedi. In these churches
and chapels are innumerable ikons, some of which represent
the best of Byzantine painting and many of which figure in
miraculous legends.

The sacred art of Mount Athos is hieratic but austerely
resplendent in the darkness and silence of churches where
there is no room for curiosity and aestheticism, only for worship. We of the west have become so unaccustomed to seeing sacred painting in its proper situation—the sanctuary of
the Living God, and are so familiar with the bare lighted
wall of the museum, that we might at first fail to appreciate
the mystical technique of the great painters of Athos. Here
the saints, the angels, the Mother of God and Christ the
Pantokrator shine at us dimly from the shadowy walls lit by
candles and votive lamps. Their beauty is part of the mystery
of the liturgy and speaks to us in harmony with the ancient
Greek hymns. In such frescoes we look in vain for realism
or anecdote. We find instead the powerful language of prayer
and of spiritual vision. It is true that on Athos as well as
everywhere else, sacred art has declined into vulgarity and
pastiche. As far as I know there has not yet been any significant attempt at a revival of the ancient spirit and the pure
tradition of Greek sacred painting.

Sculpture is an altogether negligible element in Eastern
Church art. We find nothing at Athos to correspond to the

tympan of Vezelay or of Autun, nor to the saints around the
doors of Rheims and Chartres. Fortunately we find nothing
either to correspond to the sculpture of Saint Sulpice.

Most of the monasteries, particularly those near the sea-
shore, have arsenals as well as crenelated walls, a reminder of
the days when they had to be ready to defend themselves at
any time against pirates or Latin raiders from the West.
Though in the earliest days of Athos, before the schism of
1054, there was a monastery of Italian Benedictines on
Athos, the Western Church has not been popular there since
the Crusades. Too often parties of Crusaders or other groups
of Western knights raided and sacked the monasteries of
Athos, and the memory of these events has not died.

Theological suspicion of the west has also been kept alive
on the Holy Mountain by memory of the Palamite controversy in the fourteenth century. Athos in the Middle Ages
was the center of a powerful mystical revival—the so-called
hesychast movement. The hesychasts were contemplatives,
solitaries for the most part, who followed a tradition supposed to have originated on Mount Sinai and which later
flourished in Russia. The term hesychasm has had a very
bad press in the west where it has been grossly misunderstood. St. Gregory Palamas, a monk of Athos who later became Archbishop of Salonika, was the chief defender of
hesychasm, in the fourteenth century, against a Greek from
Italy called Barlaam of Calabria. Barlaam has sometimes
been represented as a westernizing pseudo-Thomist. In actual fact, he was a humanist who, in the name of classical
ideals, turned the weapon of his skeptical nominalism
against the mystical theology of Palamas. Barlaam, in practice, considered all mystical experience more or less illusory.
At best, it was only a product of refined aesthetic fervor en-

kindled by symbols. St. Gregory Palamas, on the other hand, defended the thesis that the "divine light"—the same light that was seen by the three Apostles who saw the vision of the Transfigured Savior on Mount Thabor—could be experienced directly in this present life. He held that this light was not a mere symbol of the divinity, but an experience of the "divine energies"—though not of the divine essence. Barlaam was formally defeated in the lists of theological controversy and the Oriental Church upheld the teachings of Palamas. At this, Barlaam withdrew to the west and went over to Rome (or rather to Avignon)—not so much because of devotion to Church unity, as because he found the climate of nominalism in the west at that time more congenial to his own mentality.

Hesychasm, which has always been regarded with extreme caution, if not outright suspicion, by Western writers, has perhaps been treated too shabbily by them. It is clearly something more than a technique of autohypnosis by which one pretends to "procure" or "induce" a state of mystical illumination. Hesychasm has some technical points in common with hatha-yoga, but it is an authentically Christian and deeply simple way of prayer.

Gregory Palamas taught that the "uncreated energies" of God could communicate themselves directly to men even in the present life (he rejected the idea of created grace). All these points are questionable and might seem, to Western theologians, to be unacceptable. But perhaps we should not reject them without first having made sure we know what they really mean. In practice, the hesychast "way of contemplation" is simply a method of recollection which relies on slow, rhythmical breathing and silent repetition of an aspiratory prayer like "Lord Jesus Christ have mercy on me a sinner."

It would be a great mistake to idealize the monasticism of Mount Athos. But it would be a far greater one to underestimate it. Here, as everywhere, human frailty and the miseries of man as a political animal have made themselves evident from age to age. And yet Athos remains, for all its deficiencies, one of the most authentic and integral examples of Christian monasticism. After a thousand years it is still quite close to the original pattern of monastic life that was first developed in the deserts of Egypt and Syria. It is above all the fullness and variety of Athos that impress us. Like everything else in the West, our monasticism has been subject to fragmentation—it has been atomized. We have broken up into different orders, none of which retain the many-sided completeness of the monastic ideal.

The free growth that has been permitted on Athos for a thousand years has extended in all directions and sometimes the branches that should have been pruned have been allowed to wander too far. The fruit has not always been sweet. The branches have not always been strong enough to resist storms. The fact that Athonite monachism has sedulously ignored all modern developments in technology or hygiene is not necessarily in its favor. There should be a reasonable adaptation to the times—though the obvious danger is not lack of adaptation to, but submersion in, the spirit of these times. In the main, the spiritual growth of Athos has been normal, healthy and supremely varied. Such rich variety is a noble, desirable thing. There is room for the weak and the strong. There are all kinds of levels of observance. There are all kinds of opportunities for contemplative perfection. The horizons are not those of one four-walled enclosure. The monk is never shut up within the limits of a rigidly confined outlook. There are always possibilities for unexpected growth; one can always aspire to new—or old directions. However these new directions are always purely contemplative. The monks of Athos have never engaged in any kind of active apostolate, and never even seem to have considered it necessary. Their apostolate of prayer and example has been unexcelled. For centuries the ambition of every devout Orthodox Christian man was to make a pilgrimage to the Holy Mountain—an objective second, in this respect, to Jerusalem alone. Adaptation to the times should not mean abandonment of a contemplative ideal.

What if someday there were to be an Athos for the Western Church, the Western world? Some island, some mountain jutting out into the sea, a "nation" of contemplatives with room for Benedictines and Carthusians and Cistercians and Camaldolese, for cenobites and hermits, for small and large groups with diversified observances, with free access to one another, with reasonable opportunities for mutual stimulation, transit and exchange. Is this a heresy? Is this a dream? Have we reached the point where all dreams are regarded as dangerous and forbidden? When life has no more risk in it and no more dreams, it is no longer life.

Still, though one may dream, one must also be realistic if he hopes to see those dreams come somewhere near actuality. It is evident that with the various contemplative orders structured as they are, and with each one jealous of its own usages, its own intepretations of the Rule, and its own exclusiveness, it would be over-optimistic to expect them to get along together in a monastic "republic" like Athos. They could co-exist, no doubt, and be good friends. But there could never be a real compenetration and mutuality of ideals. One wonders if they could really form a large, homogeneous group, a real intermonastic family. Whatever may be the answer, speculation on the point is perhaps useless. A group of communities and individuals living the monastic life at different levels and with varying tempos could be formed of lay contemplatives, gathered in groups around about a nucleus of one formally established monastic family—say, a community of Primitive Benedictines. Here there would be plenty of flexibility, plenty of opportunity for growth in new directions. Organization ought not be the first and most important consideration. What we really ought to do is what the first monks did: go off somewhere into the wilderness (approved by a qualified director) and see how long and how well we can stand it—with or without companions—and then go on to build upon a foundation of experience.

Each year on the Feast of the Transfiguration of Christ, monks and pilgrims climb to the summit of Athos and there in a small chapel, built upon the peak, the office of the feast is solemnly chanted and the sacred liturgy of the day is celebrated at dawn. Far out at sea, the ships can see the light of a huge fire triumphantly kindled on the Mountain. The flames dancing in the dawn wind and reaching into the purple sky to mingle with the stars speak a far different message from those which we receive from the artificial earth satellites which man has hurled into orbit by the power of his science. It is certainly right and fitting that the mind of man should reach out to explore the cosmos. But in that case, he must be prepared for what he finds there. He must be prepared that the void into which he has projected his mind should in turn take possession of his heart. He must be prepared to find his pseudo-humanism undermined and have it collapse under him while he plunges into the darkness and emptiness of a nominalist abyss. As long as it is only the light of our own mind that peers into infinite spaces, the cosmic depths will reflect nothing but our own vacuity. But when from the heavens come fire and light into our heart—not the light of the sun or of the stars, but the Light that transfigured Christ on Thabor, then man, strong in the love created within him by God, can safely stand as a god upon the earth. Then the light that comes to him from God transfigures and ennobles the whole of creation and all that is in it.

Then the emptiness of man no longer surrounds him and invades him from the outside. On the contrary, his own emptiness, assumed by the God who "emptied Himself" out of love for man, becomes an infinite fulness in which there can be no longer any darkness or any void. Admittedly, faith is still dark. But this is the night of nights, the paschal night, the passage of the Red Sea, in which man follows the Risen Savior through the tomb and the hell in the center of his own being to emerge in the heaven which is the very heart of his own nothingness. The light of Thabor is the light of the Resurrection. The meaning of Athos is the mystery of Easter. The flames that spring up in the summer night, on top of the Holy Mountain, are flames that mutely proclaim the message of God's love for man in Christ: the light that has shone upon us all "in the face of Christ Jesus," the light that dawns in our hearts to the day of eternity. The light of Athos is the light of a daystar that knows no setting. But if, at some future time, the flame of the symbolic bonfire fail to appear on the mountain like the signal that heralded the fall of Troy, then we shall know for certain that the time of battle has come, a dreadful time in which the pillar of fire and cloud must rise in our own hearts to lead us out of the chaos of radioactivity around that other mushroom-like pillar of death with which the world has decided to parody a glorious sign of God, the sign of the passage out of Egypt into the Kingdom of Life.*

* For further details see Appendix B. *A New Book on Mount Athos.*

THE SPIRITUALITY OF SINAI

SAINT JOHN OF THE LADDER

The Oriental Church has no book strictly comparable to the *Imitation of Christ*, a characteristic flowering of medieval Western Christianity, human, tender, devotional, often criticized today as "individualistic." In the Eastern Church, the admirable *Life in Christ* by Nicholas Cabasilas may be a kind of opposite number to the *Imitation*. But it is theological, sacramental, embracing the whole mystery of Christ and of the Church, though lacking nothing in warmth, love, personal devotion. In any case, it never enjoyed the vast popularity of the *Imitation*.

From the point of view of popularity, the most widely read spiritual book in Eastern Christendom, apart perhaps from the *Philokalia*, is the *Holy Ladder* of St. John Climacus, recently published in a new and first-rate English translation.* The influence and the importance of this re-

* *The Ladder of Divine Ascent*, by St. John Climacus, translated by Archimandrite Lazarus Moore, with an introduction by M. Heppell.

markable book makes it the Eastern counterpart of our *Imitation*. And this suggests an interesting comparison between the two.

First of all, the *Ladder* is seldom, if ever, tender. It is a tough, hard-hitting, merciless book. Climacus was a kind of sixth-century desert Hemingway. Except, of course, that he is not entirely disillusioned with everything—he is no victim of *acedia*. But he sees through the weaknesses of men and monks, and cannot resist the temptation to caricature them without mercy. He never stops. Even when he gets to the last, supposedly serene rungs of the *Ladder*, on which all is sweet repose and *hesychia*, he restlessly yields to the same wild reflex and keeps lashing out on all sides. You cannot keep the man quiet. He is an irrepressible fighter.

You will look in vain, in the *Ladder*, for the gentle and affective devotion to Christ Crucified that is the very heart of the *Imitation*. In fact little is said about the Person of the Redeemer—except in one, rare, exceptional little line which is doubtless the most significant in the book, perhaps beyond all awareness and intention on the part of the author. I will postpone discussion of this point to the end of the article.

Meanwhile, if we consider the matter of "individualism," the *Ladder* is certainly as individualistic as the *Imitation*, if not more so. There is scarcely a word about liturgy, sacraments, corporate unity in Christ. Indeed, there is not much explicitly said about charity, though for all his violence, Climacus has a deep undercurrent of friendly and fraternal understanding. The *Ladder* is almost exclusively concerned with the problems, struggles and conquests of the individual monk, seeking his own salvation. And in this it is completely faithful to and characteristic of the desert tradition. Hence we must not be too eager to say that all "individualism" in Christian piety began with the *devotio moderna* and has nothing to do with the Patristic spirit.

Both the *Imitation* and the *Ladder* call for a complete dedication of oneself to the pursuit of spiritual perfection. But in the *Imitation*, the emphasis is all on God's grace and on His merciful help. In the *Ladder* the basic concern is with the will and energy of the monk himself. The spiritual life is a holy war, a death-struggle with the devil, in which one must kill or be killed. One fights desperately under the eye of a severe and, it is implied, somewhat detached Judge. Even the most heroic of penances cannot guarantee to move Him to pity. This is a spirituality as severe, as inflexible, as rugged as the landscape in which it was written.

The desert of Sinai is, of course, the scene of the most dramatic and terrible episode in the history of Israel. The burnt, forbidding cliffs of Djeb-el-Moussa frown pitilessly on a waste of sand, rock and waterless scrub. In this desert, the children of Israel danced madly around the Golden Calf while Moses came down and smashed the Tables of the Law which he had just received from Yahweh in the thundercloud. It is the setting for contradiction, blasphemy, struggle and despair: the despair of man faced with an in-human command, and finding nothing in himself with which to fulfil it. And yet the thunder roars "Thou *shalt*..."

At the same time, the Mountain of God is the great symbol of mystical contemplation. Here Moses saw God in the Burning Bush. Here he spoke to God face to face in darkness, in the cloud, as to a friend. Philo Judaeus, followed by Origen and St. Gregory of Nyssa, had worked out these symbols in a theology of apophatic (dark) contemplation. But to reach that dark vision, the spirit had to be utterly

sinless, perfectly pure, free from all taint of inordinate passion. Brute beasts and defiled sinners were not to touch the
smoking mountain, on pain of death by stoning!

Fugitives from the persecutions of the third and fourth
century made the desert of Sinai a center of eremitical monasticism when Nitria and Scete became the lights of the
Christian world. The fact that Justinian founded a monastery
there in A.D. 527 only proves that Sinai was a famous nation
of monks in his time. The monastery has existed and flourished ever since. It has never been destroyed by the Mos-
lems. Legend ascribes this to the fact that the monks once
gave hospitality to Mohammed. Whether or not they did so
literally, they have never ceased to do so in spirit: the monastery of Sinai has for centuries aided and supported with
alms and medical aid the Moslem nomads of the desert.

St. John Climacus was abbot of this monastery in the
sixth century and here he wrote his famous *Holy Ladder*.
It was addressed to the monks of a nearby monastery of
Raithu. But actually it was to spread from monastery to
monastery all over the Christian world. In the East it exercised a decisive influence in the lives of such important
figures as St. Anthony, founder of the monastery of the
Caves at Kiev, St. Symeon the "New Theologian," and
closer to our time Paissy Velichkovsky, the leader of the
great monastic revival in Russia at the end of the eighteenth
century, which produced the movement of the *stareizki*, or
charismatic, prophetic monks of nineteenth-century Russia.

The *Ladder* has also been well known in the West at least
since the fifteenth century when it was first printed in Ven-
ice. The reformer of La Trappe, Abbot de Rancé, knew it
well and imbibed its spirit, probably from a Greek edition
published in France in 1633. A Trappist monk of Mount
Saint Bernard, England, was the author of the only English

translation in existence before the present text. It is interesting to notice that the Trappist edition highlights the ascetic severity of the original, while suppressing some of the chapter on "solitude," which contains the heart of St. John's doctrine on mystical contemplation. This earlier English edition, published just over a hundred years ago in 1858, was read within the last decade at the Abbey of Gethsemani, in the refectory. In the main, the monks seem to have found it either funny or unpleasant, and some unfledged ascetics openly complained to the present writer that Climacus was nuts. I think this effect was mainly due to the old translation. The new one is much more impressive. It clearly proves that St. John Climacus was no fanatical windbag but a very astute observer of human nature, a man of violent and passionate sanctity, and in his better moments a very fine writer.

II

The *Holy Ladder* is a compilation and popularization of all the spirituality of the Desert. St. John Climacus was not one of the great originators of the monastic tradition. He came three to four centuries after Anthony, Macarius, Evagrius and Cassian. He merely collected what had been taught and lived in the golden age, enlivening the collection with stories from his own experience, with his own caustic observations, and with his sensational style!

It is interesting to compare Climacus with the *Apotheg-mata*—that is with the collection of sayings (*Verba*) of the early Desert Fathers. The contrast is striking. The originators, the first Fathers, were silent, humble men who seemed unable to say anything except in the fewest possible words. Their statements are as laconic, as sober as they can be. And yet they are full of inner life and warmth. They overflow with an inexhaustible spirituality. They are as simple, as direct and as mysterious as the *mondo* of the Zen Masters. And even more charming.

For this laconic charm St. John Climacus has substituted what I am sometimes tempted to regard as repetitious bluster. The reason for this is, I think, that Climacus has a strong and venerable institution behind him. He is speaking with the full support of a powerful monastic organization. The early Fathers had behind them—nothing but the Desert.

The *Ladder*, as its name suggests, starts at the bottom with renunciation of the world and works up to mystical union with God. By far the greater part of the book is concerned with vices, passions, temptations and wiles of the devil, and, of course, with the proper means of unmasking the enemy and busting him in the teeth. It is here that St. John Climacus is his characteristic self, and without doubt this is the aspect of the book that will most impress the modern, casual reader. Even this violent and colorful aspect of the *Ladder* is significant. The book is a literary monument to a very important aspect of religious culture, much too important to be ignored. It throws light on such writers as Dostoievsky, for example. *Crime and Punishment* has a lot to do with the spirituality of St. John Climacus, in a perverse and inverted sort of way. In fact all Russian literature and spirituality is tinged with the ferocity and paradox of Sinai— though it compensates with a tenderness and a depth of human feeling unknown to St. John of the Ladder. You will search the *Ladder* in vain for the compassion of a Staretz Zossima.

The intensity and seriousness of this book's demand for uncompromising battle with sin and with self-indulgence will necessarily frighten modern Christians, always anxious for compromise. That is why Father Georges Florovsky, quoted on the jacket, wisely declares: "The *Ladder* is an invitation to pilgrimage. Only those who have resolved to climb and ascend will appreciate this book." That is true. The others will be fighting it, and if you resist a man like Climacus you get in the way of his flying fists.

At his best, Climacus sometimes suggests Theocritus and La-Bruyère. Here is his pungent description of the "insensible" man—that is, of the man for whom spirituality has become a matter of mere words and routine, rather than of serious practice:

"He talks about healing a wound, and does not stop irritating it. He complains of sickness, and does not stop eating what is harmful. He prays against it, and immediately goes and does it. And when he has done it, he is angry with himself; and the wretched man is not ashamed of his own words. 'I am doing wrong,' he cries, and eagerly continues to do so. His mouth prays against his passion, and his body struggles for it. He philosophizes about death, but he behaves as if he were immortal. He groans over the separation of soul and body, but drowses along as if he were eternal. He talks of temperance and self-control, but he lives for gluttony. He reads about the judgment and begins to smile. He reads about vainglory, and is vainglorious while actually reading. He repeats what he has learnt about vigil, and drops asleep on the spot. He praises prayer, but runs from it as from the plague. He blesses obedience, but he is the first to disobey. He praises detachment, but he is not ashamed to be spiteful and to fight for a rag. When angered he gets bitter, and he is angered again at his bitterness; and he does not feel that after one defeat he is suffering another. Having overeaten he repents, and a little later again gives way to it. He blesses silence, and praises it with a spate of words.

He teaches meekness, and during the actual teaching frequently gets angry. Having woken from passion he sighs, and shaking his head, he again yields to passion."

As might be expected, one of the best chapters in the book deals with *anger*, a subject on which Climacus might be trusted to say the last word. Actually he has some very interesting observations. "Sometimes singing, in moderation, successfully relieves the temper," remarks the hermit in him. And the cenobite and abbot, remembering the monastery choir, hastens to point out that much can be lost in solitude that might have been saved in the cenobium, and his description of the angry hermits, fighting alone like caged partridges, is by all standards a classic:

"When for some reason I was sitting outside a monastery, near the cells of those living in solitude, I heard them fighting by themselves in their cells like caged partridges from bitterness and anger, and leaping at the face of their offender as if he were actually present. And I devoutly advised them not to stay in solitude in case they should be changed from human beings into demons."

However, he is quite impartial. If the angry man should come back to the community and *face* it, the sensual man ought to go into the desert.

III

Like all Oriental Christians, St. John Climacus is a great faster, and he does not hesitate to pour scorn on every form of gluttony. He may shock us, but perhaps this is one of the matters in which we ought to take him a little more seriously, although he is often at his funniest in treating it.

"The preparing of the table exposes gluttons, but the

work of prayer exposes lovers of God. The former dance on seeing the table, but the latter scowl."

He has a subtle and interesting chapter on lust, another on the spirit of blasphemy which is important as a psychological document. The hair-raising description of the monastery prison, and the penitents incarcerated there, reads today like a report on a badly-run mental institution. One can neatly check off symptoms of all the various kinds of schizophrenia and manic depression.

"Others were continually beating their breasts and recalling their past life and state of soul. Some of them watered the ground with their tears; others, incapable of tears, struck themselves. Some loudly lamented over their souls as over the dead, not having the strength to bear the anguish of their heart. Others groaned in their heart, but stifled all sound of their lamentation. But sometimes they could control themselves no longer, and would suddenly cry out.

"I saw there some who seemed from their demeanour and their thoughts to be out of their mind. In their great disconsolateness they had become like dumb men in complete darkness, and were insensible to the whole of life. Their minds had already sunk to the very depths of humility, and had burnt up the tears in their eyes with the fire of their despondency.

"Others sat thinking and looking on the ground, swaying their heads unceasingly, and roaring and moaning like lions from their inmost heart to their teeth . . .

"One could see how the tongues of some of them were parched and hung out of their mouths like a dog's. Some chastised themselves in the scorching sun, others tormented themselves in the cold. Some, having tasted a little water so as not to die of thirst, stopped drinking; others, having nibbled a little bread, flung the rest of it away, and said that they were unworthy of being fed like human beings, since they had behaved like beasts."

However, do not be misled by the gusto with which he lets his pen run away with him. This "Prison" section, always considered one of the most sensational and popular, has in it a deep spiritual truth. Climacus is trying to say that the most spiritual people he knew in the desert were not the ones who thought themselves to be great ascetics and contemplatives but those who were sincerely convinced that they were worthless monks, failures in their vocation. Naturally, this does not mean that spiritual perfection is to be sought in psychotic melodrama. We must pardon the vehement pleasure derived by this saint from pure exaggeration.

Little space is left in which to praise the charm of the last chapters, on solitude and *hesychasm* (contemplation). Here the fiery writer becomes more quiet and even discreet, and deftly, in few words, exposes the mystery of pure prayer— that prayer without thoughts and without words in which the solitary clings to an experience of what cannot be experienced. "The cat keeps hold of her mouse, and the thought of the solitary holds his spiritual mouse. Do not call this example rubbish; if you do, then you do not know what solitude means."

We have said prayer without words. That is not quite accurate. St. John Climacus is not one of those who, like Evagrius and St. Gregory of Nyssa, take us to the heights of obscure *theologia*, the contact with God in darkness, beyond even the purest of concepts. Rather he seems to speak of that contemplative union achieved by the rhythmic repetition of the Holy Name of Jesus, synchronized with deep and controlled breathing, which became the favorite way to contemplation for the monks of Mount Athos. This *hesychasm* came to Athos from Sinai, and one of the chief authorities for it was St. John Climacus himself. Actually, whatever is contained in his *Ladder* on this subject is fairly well hidden and had to be worked out by minds familiar with the more esoteric elements in the Sinaite tradition. The fact remains that the Greeks seem to have been quite justified in their interpretation of that one line which, I said above, turned out to be more influential than all the rest of the book put together: "Let the remembrance of Jesus be present with each breath, and then you will know the value of solitude."

Our just evaluation of St. John Climacus depends on our understanding of a few lines like this. They contain his mystical doctrine, which, by all means, balances the pages of garrulous asceticism. But we have to realize this fact. When we do, we see the real importance of the *Ladder*. Neglect of this truth makes the book little more than a religious and literary curiosity.

PART TWO

THE POWER AND MEANING OF LOVE

1 . Love as a creative force—and its corruptions

Man has lost Dante's vision of that "love which moves the sun and the other stars," and in so doing he has lost the power to find meaning in his world. Not that he has not been able to understand the physical world better. The disappearance of the simple medieval cosmogony upon which Dante built his structure of hell, purgatory, and heaven, has enabled man to break out of the limitations imposed upon his science by that ancient conception. And now he is prepared to fly out into those depths of space which terrified Pascal—and which continue to terrify anyone who is still human. Yet, though man has acquired the power to do almost anything, he has at the same time lost the ability to orient his life toward a spiritual goal by the things that he does. He has lost all conviction that he knows where he is going and what he is doing, unless he can manage to plunge into some collective delusion which promises happiness (sometime in the future) to those who will have learned to use the implements he has now discovered.

Man's unhappiness seems to have grown in proportion to his power over the exterior world. And anyone who claims to have a glib explanation of this fact had better take care that he too is not the victim of a delusion. For after all, this should not necessarily be so. God made man the ruler of the earth, and all science worthy of the name participates in some way in the wisdom and providence of the Creator. But the trouble is that unless the works of man's wisdom, knowledge and power participate in the merciful love of God, they are without real value for the world and for man. They do nothing to make man happy and they do not manifest in the world the glory of God.

Man's greatest dignity, his most essential and peculiar power, the most intimate secret of his humanity is his capacity to love. This power in the depths of man's soul stamps him in the image and likeness of God. Unlike other creatures in the world around us, we have access to the inmost sanctuary of our own being. We can enter into ourselves as into temples of freedom and of light. We can open the eyes of our heart and stand face to face with God our Father. We can speak to Him and hear Him answer. He tells us not merely that we are called to be men and to rule our earth, but that we have an even more exalted vocation than this. We are His sons. We are called to be godlike beings, and, more than that, we are in some sense called to be "gods." "Is it not written in the law, I said you are gods— and they are gods to whom the words of God are spoken?" (John 10:34-35; Ps. 81:6).

This vocation to be sons of God means that we must learn to love as God Himself loves. For God is love, and it is by loving as He loves that we become perfect as our heavenly Father is perfect (Matt. 5:48). Hence, while being called to govern and cultivate the world that God has given us, we are called at the same time to love everything and everyone in it. Nor is this love a matter of mere sentimental complacency. It has a dynamic spiritual meaning, for by this love we are called to redeem and transform the world in that same power which raised up Christ from the dead (Eph. 1:17-23). That power is the infinite love of the Father for His Son.

Love then is not only our own salvation and the key to the meaning of our own existence, but it is also the key to the meaning of the entire creation of God. It is true, after all, that our whole life is a participation in that cosmic liturgy of "the love which moves the sun and the other stars."

But what is love and how do we come to love as sons of God? Surely love is everywhere; man cannot live without it. If everybody loves, or tries to love, why is it that we are not made happy and redeemed by all this constant effort? The answer is that all that seems to be love is not so in reality.

The reality of love is judged, then, by its power to help man get beyond himself, to renew himself in transcending his present limitations. Though the function of natural love is to perpetuate man in time, the function of spiritual love is much greater still—to give man possession of eternity. This it does not merely by "saving man's soul" as an individual, but by establishing in time the eternal kingdom of God. The function of love is to build this spiritual kingdom of unity and peace, and to make man not only the exploiter of creation but truly its spiritual head and king.

A love that merely enables man to "enjoy himself," to remain at peace in a life of inert comfort and to bring into being replicas of himself is not to be regarded as true love. It does not represent a renewal, a progress, a step forward in building the kingdom of God.

True love leads a man to fulfilment, not by drawing things to himself but by forcing him to transcend himself and to become something greater than himself. True spiritual love takes the isolated individual, exacts from him labor, sacrifice, and the gift of himself. It demands that he "lose his life" in order to find it again on a higher level—in Christ.

All true love is a death and a resurrection in Christ. It has one imperious demand: that all individual members of Christ give themselves completely to one another and to the Church, lose themselves in the will of Christ and in the good of other men, in order to die to their own will and their own interests and "rise again" as other Christs. A love that does not tend to this transformation does not fulfil the exacting requirements of true spiritual love, and consequently lacks the power to develop and perpetuate man in his spirituality.

All true love is therefore closely associated with three fundamentally human strivings: with *creative work*, with *sacrifice*, and with *contemplation*. Where these three are present there is reliable evidence of spiritual life, at least in some inchoate form. There is reliable evidence of love. And the most important of the three is sacrifice.

Man's essential mystery is his vocation to be the son of God; but one of the deepest aspects of this mystery is precisely the fact that the fundamental temptation, the one to which Adam owes his fall, is the temptation to be "like unto God."

There is a singular necessity for man to be tried in that which is deepest and most essential about himself. And if we understand the meaning of this testing, we will understand the vital importance of love in the life of man. In the story of the fall of Adam, we see the tempter apparently suggesting that man attain to what he already possessed. *Eritis sicut dii.* But man was already "like unto God." For in the very act of creation God had said: "Let us make man to our image and likeness" (Gen. 1:26). Satan offered man what he already had, but he offered it with the appearance of something that he did not have. That is to say, he offered man the divine likeness as if it were *something more* than God had already given him, as if it were something that could be his apart from a gift of God, apart from the will of God, or even against the will of God.

Satan offered man the power to be like God *without loving Him.* And in this consisted what we call the "fall" and "original sin": that man elected to be "like unto a god" and indeed a god of his own, without loving God his Father and without seeking participation, by love, in the life and power and wisdom of God who is Love.

God wished man His son to be truly divine, to share in His own wisdom, power, providence, justice and kingship. And all this depended on one thing: the love by which alone man could participate in the divine life of his Father. Satan offered man a pseudo-divine life in a wisdom, knowledge, prudence, power, justice and kingship which had some reality in them, indeed, but which were only shadows and caricatures of the reality which is contained in and depends on God who is Love.

Love, then, is the bond between man and the deepest reality of his life. Without it man is isolated, alienated from himself, alienated from other men, separated from God, from truth, wisdom and strength. By love man enters into contact first with his own deepest self, then with his brother, who is his other self, and finally with the wisdom and power of God, the ultimate Reality. But love comes to man in the first place from God. Love is the gift which seals man's being with its fullness and its perfection. Love first makes man fully human, then gives him his divine stature, making him a son and a minister of God.

So necessary is love in the life of man that he cannot be altogether without it. But a love that does not seek reality only frustrates man in his inmost being, and this love that does not act as a bond between a man and reality is called sin. All sin is simply a perversion of that love which is the deepest necessity of man's being: a misdirection of love, a gravitation toward something that does not exist, a bond with unreality.

The difference between real and unreal love is not to be sought in the *intensity* of the love, or in its subjective *sincerity*, or in its *articulateness*. These three are very valuable qualities when they exist in a love that is real. But they are very dangerous when they are associated with a love that is fictitious. In neither case are they any sure indication of the nature of the love to which they belong, though it is true that one might expect man to feel an intense, sincere and articulate love only for a real object and not for an unreal one.

The trouble is that love is something quite other than the mere disposition of a subject confronted with an object. In fact, when love is a mere subject-object relationship, it is not real love at all. And therefore it matters little to inquire whether the object of one's love is real or not, since if our love is only our impulsion towards an "object" or a "thing," it is not yet fully love.

The reality of love is determined by the relationship itself which it establishes. Love is only possible between persons as persons. That is to say, if I love you, I must love you as a person and not as a thing. And in that case my relationship to you is not merely the relationship of a subject to an object, but it is analogous to my relationship to myself. It is, so to speak, a relationship of a subject to a subject. This strange-sounding expression is only another way of saying something very familiar: I must know how to love you *as myself*.

There might be a temptation, under the influence of modern philosophies, to misunderstand this subjective quality in love. It by no means signifies that one questions the real existence of the person loved, or that one doubts the reality of the relationship established with him by love. Such an illusion would indeed make Christian love impossible, or at best only a matter of fantasy. On the contrary, the subjectivity essential to love does not detract from objective reality but adds to it. Love brings us into a relationship with an objectively existing reality, but because it is love it is able to bridge the gap between subject and object and *commune in the subjectivity of the one loved*. Only love can effect this kind of union and give this kind of knowledge-by-identity with the beloved—and the concrete interiority and mystery of this knowledge of the beloved is not adequately described by the scholastic term "connaturality."

When we love another "as an object," we refuse, or fail, to pass over into the realm of his own spiritual reality, his personal identity. Our contact with him is inhibited by remoteness and by a kind of censorship which *excludes* his personality and uniqueness from our consideration. We are not interested in him as "himself" but only as another specimen of the human race.

To love another as an object is to love him as "a thing," as a commodity which can be used, exploited, enjoyed and then cast off. But to love another as a person we must begin by granting him his own autonomy and identity as a person. We have to love him for what he is in himself, and not for what he is to us. We have to love him for his own good, not for the good we get out of him. And this is impossible unless we are capable of a love which "transforms" us, so to speak, into the other person, making us able to see things as he sees them, love what he loves, experience the deeper realities of his own life as if they were our own. Without sacrifice, such a transformation is utterly impossible. But unless we are capable of this kind of transformation "into the other" while remaining ourselves, we are not yet capable of a fully human existence. Yet this capacity is the key to our divine sonship also. For it is above all in our relationship with God that love, considered as a subject-object relationship, is utterly out of the question.

It is true that we have to deal with God most of the time as if He were "an object," that is to say, confronting Him in concepts which present Him objectively to us. Yet, as everyone knows, we only really come to know God when we find Him "by love" hidden "within ourselves"—that is to say, "by connaturality." Yet, paradoxically, we cannot find God "within ourselves" unless we go "out of ourselves" by sacrifice. Only a sacrificial love which enables us to let go of ourselves completely and empty ourselves of our own will can enable us to find Christ in the place formerly occupied by our own selfhood. And in this sacrifice we cease, in a certain manner, to be the subject of an act of knowing and become the one we know by love.

When man acts according to the temptation of Satan to be "like unto God," he places himself as the *unique subject* in the midst of a world of objects He alone is a "person," he alone feels, enjoys, thinks, wills, desires, commands. The manifestations of apparent thought, feeling, and desire on the part of others are of little or no concern to him, except insofar as they represent response to his own acts. He never "becomes" the other. On the contrary, the people around him are only objective manifestations of what goes on subjectively in himself. Hence his relationship with them is, if you like, a relationship with another self, yes, but only in the sense of an *added* self, a *supplementary* self, not in the sense of a different self. The selves of others are nothing except insofar as they are replicas of himself. And when this is carried to its logical extreme (as it is, for example, by the totalitarian dictator), then society at large is made over into the image of the leader. The individuals in such a society cease to have any purpose except that of reflecting and confirming the leader's megalomaniac idea of himself.

Man cannot live without love, and if the love is not genuine, then he must have some substitute—a corruption of real love. These corruptions are innumerable. Some of them are so obviously corrupt that they present no problem to the thinker. The only problem is that of avoiding them in actual behavior. Those which present a problem do so because they can seem, and claim to be, genuine love. These false forms of love base their claim on appeal to an ideal, and their falsity consists precisely in the fact that they tend to sacrifice persons to concepts. And since modern thought has deliberately renounced any effort to distinguish between what exists only in the mind and what exists outside the mind (dismissing the question as irrelevant), love has become more and more mental and abstract. It has become, in fact, a flight from reality and from that interpersonal relationship which constitutes its very essence.

This flight from the personal to the purely mental level

occurs in various ways, two of which can be taken as most typical of our time and of our society. One is what we might call a romantic or liberal approach to love; the other, a legalist or authoritarian approach.

What we call the romantic approach is that love of the good which sacrifices the persons and the values that are present and actual, to other values which are always out of reach. Here a shiftless individualism dignifies itself as the quest for an elusive ideal, whether in politics or art or religion or merely in one's relations with other men. Such love is apparently obsessed with "perfection." It passes from one object to another, examining it superficially, playing with it, tempting it, being tempted by it, and then letting go of it because it is not "the right object." Such love is therefore always discarding the real and actual in order to go on to something else, because the real and actual are never quite right, never good enough to be worthy of love.

Such love is really only an escape from love, because it refuses the obligation of entering into a real relationship which would render love at the same time possible and obligatory. Because it hates the idea of obligation, it cannot fully face even the possibility of such a relationship. Its romanticism is a justification of flight. It claims that it will only begin to love when it has found a worthy object— whether it be a person who can "really be loved," or an ideal that can really be believed in, or an experience of God that is definitive and binding.

In its liberal aspect, this love justifies itself by claiming to dispense everyone else from responsibility to love. It issues a general permission for all to practice the same irresponsibility under the guise of freedom. Romantic liberalism thus declares an open season on "perfect objects," and proceeds comfortably to neglect *persons* and realities which are present and actual, and which, in all their imperfection, still offer the challenge and the opportunity of genuine love.

One who attempts this romantic and liberal fight may entirely avoid commitment to any object, cause, or person; or he may, on the other hand, associate himself with other men in dedication to some social or private purpose. But when he does this his idealism tends to become either an excuse for inertia or a source of repeated demands upon his associates. Such demands are implicit accusations of their unworthiness, and invitations to become more worthy under threat of being rejected. The unworthy object is treated with long-suffering attempts at forgiveness and understanding; but each heroic effort in this direction makes the object more and more of an object. And such, indeed, is the purpose of "love" in this context.

One discovers, on investigation, that this liberal idealism is in fact a way of defending oneself against real involvement in an interpersonal relationship and of keeping other persons subdued and humiliated in the status of objects.

Communal life in this event becomes a shelter which, by providing an all-embracing cover of idealistic vagueness, enables us to take refuge from the present "thou" in the comforting generalizations of the less menacing "they."

The authoritarian and legalist corruption of love is also a refusal to love on the ground that the object is not worthy. But here, instead of undertaking a vast exploration in quest of the worthy object (which can never be found), the presence of the unworthy object becomes the excuse for a tyrannical campaign for worthiness, a campaign to which there is practically no end.

The legalist is perfectly convinced that he is right. In fact, he alone is right. Serene in his own subjectivity, he claims to make everyone else conform to his idea of what is right, obey his idea of the law, and carry out his policies. But since what is loved is the law or the state or the party or the policy, persons are treated as objects that exist in order to have the law enforced upon them, or to serve the state, or to carry out the policy.

Here the objectification of personality and of all spiritual values is carried to the extreme. Here is no longer any romantic compromise with personality as an ideal. Here what matters is the law and the state—or the dialectical process in history. To these the person must always be sacrificed, and there is no question of ever considering him as a person at all except hypothetically. Men are treated as objects who might be capable of being considered as persons if the law should ever come to be perfectly enforced, or if the state should come to be all powerful, or if society should come to be perfectly socialized.

The romantic and liberal error seeks the perfect person, the perfect cause, the perfect idea, the perfect experience. The authoritarian error seeks the perfect society, the perfect enforcement of its own law, in expectation of that perfect situation which will permit objects to turn into persons. Until then, love is a matter of enforcing the law, or stepping up production, and the kindest thing to all concerned is to exterminate everyone who stands in the way of the policy of the moment.

Two things are especially to be noticed when this authoritarian temper is pushed to its logical extreme and becomes totalitarian. Under a totalitarian regime, it is frankly considered more efficient to discount all individual and personal values and to reduce everyone to a condition of extreme objectivization. Whereas the romantic and liberal attitude is that personality should be reverenced at least in theory and as an ideal, here personality is regarded frankly as a danger, and its potentialities for free initiative are brutally discouraged. Not only is man treated as an object in himself, but he is reduced to servitude to material and economic processes, not for his own good but for the sake of "the state" or the "revolution."

This objectivization is justified, implicitly or explicitly, by doctrines which hold either that most races of men are in fact sub-human, or that man has not yet attained his human stature because of economic alienation. In either event, the question of right, of human dignity and other spiritual values of man is altogether denied any consideration.

For a Nazi to treat a Jew as a man, for a Communist to treat a counter-revolutionary as a human being would not only be a weakness but an unpardonable betrayal of the cause. This is all the more cogent when we realize that at any time, any faithful member of the party is liable without reason and without warning to be designated as a counter-revolutionary and thus forced outside the human pale, as something execrable beyond the power of word or thought. All this in order to pay homage to the collective myth. Such is the dignity and greatness of man when he has become "like unto a god."

In these two corruptions of love, error reaches out to affect everything this love attempts to accomplish. For a romantic, "sacrifice" is, in fact, a word which justifies the rejection of the other person as an "imperfect object" in order to pursue the search of an abstract ideal. "Contemplation" becomes a subjective day-dream concerned only with fantasies and abstractions and protected by the stern exclusion of all real claims upon our heart.

For an authoritarian, "sacrifice," "contemplation" and "work" all alike are expressed in ruthless enforcement of the law above all. Everyone, oneself as well as others, must be offered up on the altar of present policy. No other value counts, nothing else is worthy of a moment's concern.

We have seen how these two false forms of love operate in man's secular life. We shall consider, in detail, how they work in the life of the Christian.

II . *Love as a religious force—and its corruptions*

When Christ founded His Church and gave to men His "new commandment" that we should love one another as He has loved us, He made it clear that the Church could never be a mere aggregation of objects, or a collectivity made up of depersonalized individuals.

In all His dealings with men on earth, the Lord acted and spoke in such a way that He appealed always to the deepest and most inviolate recesses of each person. Even those who met Him in the most casual contacts, who cried out to Him from the roadside, asking His help, would be brought before Him and addressed directly, without hedging: "What dost *thou* ask? Canst *thou* believe?" Even a woman who secretly touched the hem of His garment when a thick crowd pressed against Him on all sides was called to speak to Him face to face. She had appealed to Him secretly, perhaps with an intention that had something in it half magical, regarding Him perhaps as a holy thing, a holy force, rather than as a person. But the power that He had felt go out from Him was the power of His love, the power that had been appealed to in His Person, and that demanded to be recognized in a dialogue of "Thou and I."

The Church is, in fact, the united Body of all those who have entered into this dialogue with Christ, those who have been called by their name, or better still, by a new name which no one knows but He who gave it and he who has received it. It is the Body not only of those who know Christ, who have heard of Him, or who have thought about Him: it is the Body of those who know Him in all His mystical dimensions (Eph. 3:18) and who, in union with one another and "all the saints," know the charity of Christ which surpasses all understanding. It is the Body of those who are "filled unto all the fullness of God" (Eph. 3:19). For the Church is the *pleroma* of Christ, the "fullness of Him who is filled all in all" (Eph. 2:23).

This mysterious expression of St. Paul points to the "sacrament" of the Church as the continuation of Christ's incarnation on earth, as a society which is more than any social organization, a spiritual and supernatural unity whose members form one mystical Person, Christ the Lord.

Christ dwells in each one of His members just as truly as He dwells in the whole Church, and that is why He is said to be "all in all." Each one is, in a certain sense, Christ, insofar as Christ lives in him. And yet the whole Church is one Christ.

Each member of the Church, however, "is Christ" only insofar as he is able to transcend his own individual limitations and rise above himself to attain to the level of the Christ-life which belongs to the entire Church. This mystery of plurality in unity is a mystery of love. For "in Christ" we who are distinct individuals, with distinct characters, backgrounds, races, countries, and even living in different ages of the world, are all brought together and raised above our limited selves in a unity of mystical love which makes us "One"—"One Body and one Spirit. . . . One Lord, one faith, one baptism, one God and Father of all who is above all and through all and in us all" (Eph. 4:4-6). "For by

Christ we have access both in one Spirit to the Father"
(*ibid.*, 2:18). "That they all may be one as Thou Father in
Me and I in Thee, that they may be one in Us" (John
17:21).

Those who are one with Christ are also one with one another. But the New Testament shows us how intransigent
the Apostles were in demanding, without compromise, that
this unity be maintained on the highest and most personal
level. It is of course possible for a human being who is not
in the fullest sense a person to be a living and holy member
of the Church—as in the case of children who have not yet
attained the age of reason. But it is by no means the ideal of
the Church that her members should remain at this mental
and spiritual level all their lives. On the contrary, St. Paul
teaches that spiritual immaturity is equivalent to living on
the level of "carnal" men, which is a level of dissension and
division.

The unity of the Mystical Body depends on its members
attaining to maturity in Christ, that is to say, achieving the
full stature of spiritual manhood, of personality and responsibility and of freedom, in Christ Jesus (see 1 Cor. 1 and
2, Eph. 3:13 ff., etc). Failure to attain to this maturity
means inability to "receive the Spirit of Christ" or to "judge
the things of the Spirit." Consequently it means failure to
rise above the limitations of individuals or small groups, and
inability to meet others on a transcendent plane where all
are one in Christ while retaining their individual differences.

One who is not mature, not fully a person "in Christ,"
cannot understand the real nature of the mystery of Christ
as a union of many in one, because he is not yet able to live
on the level of Christ's love. Such love is foolishness to him,
though he may imagine he understands it. It remains a

closed book because he is still not fully a person and he is still not able to enter deeply into that dialogue of love in which he finds himself identified with his brother in the unanimity and love, the "we" which forms the Church, the Mystical Body of Christ.

Those of us today who seek to be Christians, and who have not yet risen to the level of full maturity in Christ, tend unfortunately to take one or other of the corrupt forms of love described above for the action of the Spirit of God and the love of Christ. It is this failure to attain to full maturity in love which keeps divisions alive in the world.

There is a "romantic" tendency in some Christians—a tendency which seeks Christ not in love of those flesh-and-blood brothers with whom we live and work, but in some as yet unrealized ideal of "brotherhood." It is always a romantic evasion to turn from the love of people to the love of love itself: to love mankind more than individual men, to love "brotherhood" and "unity" more than one's brothers, neighbors, and associates.

This corruption of love can be romantic also in its love of God. It is no longer Christ Himself that is loved and sought, but perhaps an objectivized "experience" of Christ, a degree of prayer, a mystical state. What is loved then ceases to be Christ, but the subjective reactions which are aroused in me by the supposed presence of Christ in thought or love or prayer.

The romantic tendency leads to a substitution of aestheticism, or false mysticism, or quietism, for genuine faith and love, and what it seeks in the Church is not so much reality as a protection against responsibility. Failing to establish a true dialogue with our brother in Christ, this fallacy thwarts all efforts at real unity and cooperation among Christians.

It is not necessary to point out that the danger of substituting legalism for Christian love also exists. This danger is perhaps even more actual than that of the romantic error, and tends to become increasingly so in a totalitarian age. Fortunately, the terrible excesses of totalitarian authoritarianism are there to stimulate in us a healthy reaction and a return to the liberty of the sons of God.

The Church must have her structure of law and discipline, like any other visible society of men on earth. In heaven there will be no Law for the elect but God Himself, who is Charity. In heaven, obedience will be entirely swallowed up in love. On earth, unfortunately, not all are able to live without a Law, though as St. Paul says, there should in reality be no need of a Law for the saints. Not all are able to rise to that level of love which, in all things, is a fulfilment of the Law and therefore needs no Law (Gal. 5:13-23).

It is therefore not "legalism" to insist that we must all fulfil the duties of our state and of our proper vocations with all fidelity and in a spirit of humble obedience. There exists in the Church a juridical authority, a hierarchy of ministers through whom the Holy Spirit manifests the will of God in an easily recognizable way. To reject this authority and still claim to love God and the unity of His Church would be a manifest illusion. It has not infrequently happened in the past that some who have believed themselves inspired by charity have in fact rejected obedience and thus done much to dismember the unity of the Body of Christ.

Nothing could be more tragic than a pseudo-mystical enthusiasm which mistakes strong emotion for the voice of God, and on the basis of such emotion claims a "spiritual" authority to break away from communion with the rest of the faithful and to despise legitimate authority. This is not that strong sacrificial love of God which rises above individual interests and cements divergent groups in a transcendent unity. Such errors savor of the romanticism we have discussed above.

Legalism, on the other hand, is another weak form of love which in the end produces dissension, destroys communion, and for all its talk about unity, tends by its narrowness and rigidity to create divisions among men. For legalism, refusing to see truth in anybody else's viewpoint, and rejecting human values *a priori* in favor of the abstract letter of the law, is utterly incapable of "rising above" its own limitations and meeting another on a superior level. Hence the legalistic Christian (like the legalistic Jew who caused so much trouble to St. Paul), instead of broadening his view to comprehend the views of another, insists on bringing everyone else into the stifling confines of his own narrowness.

Legalism is not synonymous with conservatism or traditionalism. It can equally well be found in those social-minded Christians who, by their contact with Communism in the movement for social justice, have unwittingly contracted a spirit of totalitarian narrowness and intolerance. The temptation to legalism arises precisely when the apparent holiness of a *cause* and even its manifest rightness blinds us to the holiness of individuals and persons. We tend to forget that charity comes first and is the only Christian "cause" that has the right to precedence over every other.

Legalism in practice makes law and discipline more important than love itself. For the legalist, law is more worthy of love than the persons for whose benefit the law was instituted. Discipline is more important than the good of souls to whom discipline is given, not as an end in itself but as a means to their growth in Christ.

The authoritarian Christian does not love his brother so much as he loves the cause or the policy which he wants his brother to follow. For him, love of the brother consists, not in helping his brother to grow and mature in love as an individual person loved by Christ, but in making him "toe the line" and fulfil exterior obligations, without any regard for the interior need of his soul for love, understanding and communion. All too often, for the legalist, love of his brother means punishing his brother, in order to force him to become "what he ought to be." Then, when this is achieved, perhaps the brother can be loved. But until then he is not really "worthy of love."

This is in reality a fatal perversion of the Christian spirit. Such "love" is the enemy of the Cross of Christ because it flatly contradicts the teaching and the mercy of Christ. It treats man as if he were made for the sabbath. It loves concepts and despises persons. It is the kind of love that says *corban* (see Mark 7:9-13) and makes void the commandment of God "in order to keep the traditions of men" (*ibid.*).

The reason why this legalism is a danger is precisely because it can easily be a perversion of true obedience as well as a perversion of love. Authoritarianism has a way of becoming so obsessed with the *concept* of obedience that it ends by disobeying the will of God and of the Church in all that is most dear to the Heart of Christ. It is the obedience of the son who says, "Yes, I go" and afterwards does not go to carry out the command of his father. The obsession with law and obedience as *concepts* and *abstractions* ends by reducing the love of God, and of God's will, to a purely arbitrary fiction.

"Obedience" and "discipline" alone cannot guarantee the unity of the Body of Christ. A living organism cannot be held together by merely mechanical and exterior means. It

must be unified by its own interior life-principle. The life of
the Church is divine Love itself, the Holy Spirit. Obedience
and discipline are necessary to prevent us from separating
ourselves, unconsciously, from the guidance of the Invisible
Spirit. But merely bringing people to submit to authority by
external compulsion is not sufficient to unite them in a vital
union of love with Christ in His Church. Obedience without love produces only dead works, external conformity, not
interior communion.

Doubtless there are very few Christians who, in actual
fact, carry this legalism to a dangerous or scandalous extreme. But there remains a taint of legalism in the spirituality of a great many modern Christians, especially among
religious. It is so easy to satisfy oneself with external conformity to precepts instead of living the full and integral
life of charity which religious rules are intended to promote.

Here the danger is not one of a malicious and definitive
perversion of the Christian spirit, but rather of spiritual immaturity. But the danger of this immaturity must nevertheless not be despised, for, as we have said, it frustrates the
spontaneous and fruitful growth of charity in individuals, in
religious communities and in the Church herself.

A sincere and invincible ignorance may often be the cause
of a great deal of this immaturity: the ignorance of those
who lead their Christian lives according to superficial formulas that are poorly understood.

For a great many religious of the present day, "love" and
"obedience" are so perfectly equated with one another that
they become identical. Love is obedience and obedience is
love. In practice, this means that love is cancelled out and
all that remains is obedience—plus a "pure intention"
which by juridical magic transforms it into "love."

The identification of obedience with love proceeds from a

superficial understanding of such dicta as: "Love is a union of wills," "Love seeks to do the will of the beloved." These sayings are all very true. But they become untrue when in practice our love becomes the love of an abstract "will," of a juridical decree, rather than the love of a Person—and of the persons in whom He dwells by His Spirit!

A distinction will be useful here. To say that love (whether it be the love of men or the love of God) is a union of wills, does not mean that a mere external *conformity* of wills is love. The conformity of two wills brought into line with each other through the medium of an external regulation may perhaps clear the way for love, but it is not yet love. Love is not a mere mathematical equation or abstract syllogism. Even with the best and most sincere of intentions, exterior conformity with a regulation cannot be made, by itself, to constitute a union of wills in love. Why? Because unless "union of wills" means something concrete, a union of hearts, a union of spirits, *a communion between persons*, it is not a real enough union to constitute love.

A communion between persons implies interiority and depth. It involves the whole being of each person—the mind, the heart, the feelings, the deepest aspiration of the spirit itself. Such union manifestly excludes revolt, and deliberate mutual rejection. But it also presupposes individual differences—it safeguards the autonomy and character of each as an inviolate and solitary person. It even respects the inevitable ambivalences found in the purest of friendships. And when we observe the real nature of such communion, we see that it can really never be brought about merely by discipline and submission to authority.

The realm of obedience and of regulation, however great its value, however crucial its importance, is something so entirely different that it does little to effect this personal communion one way or the other. It merely removes external obstacles to this communion. But the communion itself implies much more than mere submission or agreement to some practical imperative. Communion means mutual understanding, mutual acceptance, not only in exterior acts to be carried out, but in regard to the inviolate interiority and subjectivity of those who commune with one another. Love not only accepts what the beloved desires, but, above all, it pays the homage of its deepest interior assent to what he *is*. From this everything else follows, for, as we know, the Christian is *Christ*.

Hence, as the Gospel teaches us (Matt. 25:31-46), a Christian loves not simply by carrying out commands issued by Christ, in heaven, in regard to this "object" which happens to be a fellow Christian. The Christian loves his brother because the brother "is Christ." He seeks the mind of the Church because the Church "is Christ." He unites himself in the worship of the Church because it is the worship which Christ offers to His Father. His whole life is lived in the climate of warmth and energy and love and fruitfulness which prevades the whole Church and every member of the Church, because the Church is a Body filled with its own life—filled with the Spirit of Christ.

A good example of the true climate of Christian obedience, a climate most favorable to the growth of love, is found in the Rule of St. Benedict. Benedict of Nursia is not only a lawgiver. More important still is the fact that he is a loving Father. The Rule opens with a characteristically Christian invitation to a dialogue of love between persons, and it is this dialogue which, on every page, elevates Benedictine obedience to the level of charity.

Love is the motive for monastic obedience, not love as

an abstract and lifeless "intention," but love flourishing in
a warm and concrete contact of persons who know, who understand, and who revere one another. Here obedience is not
for the sake of the law but for the sake of Christ. It is not
just "supernaturalized" in the sense of being mentally "offered up." It is totally transfigured by a faith which sees
that Christ lives and acts in the *personal relationship*, the
mutual respect and love, which form the bond between the
spiritual father and his spiritual son. Each, in fact, reveres
Christ in the other. Each realizes that what matters is not
the exact carrying out of an abstract and formal decree that
has no concern for individual cases, but that the important
thing is this relationship, which is a union in the Holy Spirit.
It is for the sake of this sabbath of monastic peace that the
Rule is written. And the sabbath itself exists for the men who
keep the Rule.

Christ came not to destroy the Law. But neither did He
come merely to *enforce* it. He came to *fulfil* the Law.
Everyone knows that this "fulfilment" by Christ means
more than that He simply carried out the Law in a way that
would not have been possible for everyone else. That, of
course, is part of the meaning. Christ satisfied all the exigencies of the Law by "blotting out the handwriting of the decree (the Law) which was contrary to us. And He hath
taken the same out of the way, fastening it to the Cross"
(Col. 2:14). But more than that, He Himself, in His very
Person, is the fulfilment of the Law. That is to say, Christ
in us, Christ in His Church, dwelling in the world in the
unity of charity that makes men one in Him: this is the fulfilment of the Law.

The community of the primitive Church after Pentecost,
in which all the believers were of one heart and of one soul
—this was Christ on earth, and the fulfilment of the Law.

To attempt to satisfy the exigencies of the Law by a quantity of ritual acts and multiple observances, to abide by the countless regulations and decrees of the Torah, this was a futile and hopeless task, rendered all the more ridiculous by the fact that Christ had already "emptied" all these things of their content by dying on the Cross and rising from the dead. Indeed, to return to all these practices was to return to servitude under the "elements of this world," and St. Paul rightly became angry with his "senseless Galatians" who had been "bewitched so that they *should not obey the truth*" (Gal. 3:1).

Obsession with the works of the Law is, then, disobedience to the truth, and a practical contempt for the Cross of Christ (*ibid.*). Obviously the Christian has to be rich in good works, must bring forth fruit. But how does he bring forth fruit? By "remaining in Christ and in the love of Christ" (John 15:1-8). The community of the Church and the life of the Church is then Christ in the world, and the acts of that community are the acts of Christ.

The Christian who no longer has to worry about servitude to the works of the Law need have but one concern: to remain in the community of the faithful, to remain in that love and warmth and spiritual light which pervade the holy society of the Church, to unite himself in simplicity with the holy yet ordinary lives of his brethren, their faith, their worship and their love—this is all. For to live thus, united with the brethren by love, is to live in Christ who has fulfilled the Law. "They were persevering in the doctrine of the apostles and in the communication of the breaking of bread and in prayers . . . and all that were believers were together and had all things in common. Their possessions and goods they sold and divided them to all according as every one had need. And continuing daily with one accord in the temple and breaking bread from house to house, they took their meat with gladness and simplicity of heart, praising God and having favor with all the people" (Acts 2:42-47).

Christ commanded His disciples to love one another, and this commandment summed up all of His will and contained everything else necessary for salvation.

This was not, however, intended to be another commandment of the same kind as the Decalogue—something difficult to be done, a duty to be performed in order to satisfy the demands of God. This is an entirely different kind of commandment. It is like the commandment by which God says, "Let there be light," or says to man, "Stand up, live, be My son." It is not a demand for this or that work, it is a word of life, a creative word, making man into a new being, making his society into a new creation.

The command to love creates a new world in Christ. To obey that command is not merely to carry out a routine duty; it is to enter into life and to continue in life. To love is not merely righteousness, it is transformation from brightness to brightness as by the Spirit of the Lord.

Here, of course, love and obedience are inseparable, not in the sense that obedience is coextensive with love, but in the sense that he who loves fulfills all the commands of the law by loving. To obey is not necessarily to love, but to love is necessarily to obey.

Why does God desire this love from men? Because by it His mercy and His glory are manifested in the world, through the unity of the faithful in Christ. God desires the unity of the Church in order that "men may see what is the dispensation of the mystery which hath been hidden

from eternity in God who created all things. That the manifold wisdom of God may be made known to the principali-
ties and powers in the heavenly places through the Church"
(Eph. 3:9-10).

Love is the key to the meaning of life. It is at the same
time transformation in Christ and the discovery of Christ.
As we grow in love and in unity with those who are loved by
Christ (that is to say, all men), we become more and more
capable of apprehending and obscurely grasping something
of the tremendous reality of Christ in the world, Christ in
ourselves, and Christ in our fellow man.

The transcendent work of Christian love is also at every
moment a work of faith: not only faith in dogmas proposed
to our obedient minds by holy Church, not only faith in abstract propositions, but faith in the present reality of Christ,
faith in the living dialogue between our soul and Christ,
faith in the Church of Christ as the one great and central
reality which gives meaning to the cosmos.

But what does this faith imply? Here again the familiar
phrase "seeing Christ in my brother" is subject to a sadly
superficial interpretation. How many Christians there are,
especially priests and religious, who do not hesitate to assert
that this involves a sort of mental sleight-of-hand, by which
we deftly do away with our neighbor in all his concreteness,
his individuality, his personality with its gifts and limitations, and replace him by a vague and abstract presence of
Christ.

Are we not able to see that by this pitiful subterfuge we
end up by trying to love, not Christ in our brother, but
Christ *instead* of our brother? It is this, in fact, which explains the painful coldness and incapacity for love that are

sometimes found in groups of men or women most earnestly "striving for perfection." It also accounts for so many avoidable failures in the apostolate on the part of those who are so sincere, so zealous, and yet frighten people away from Christ by the frozen rigidity and artificiality of their lives.

Our charity is intended to give glory to God, not by enabling us to multiply meritorious acts on an imaginary "account" recorded for us in a heavenly bank, but by enabling us to see Christ and find Him where He is to be found, in our brother and in the Church.

The purpose of charity is not only to unite us to God in secret but also to enable God to show Himself to us openly. For this we have to resolutely put away our attachment to natural appearance and our habit of judging according to the outward face of things. I must learn that my fellow man, just as he is, whether he is my friend or my enemy, my brother or a stranger from the other side of the world, whether he be wise or foolish, no matter what may be his limitations, "is Christ." No qualification is needed about whether or not he may be in the state of grace. Jesus in the parable of the sheep and the goats did not stop to qualify, or say: "Whenever you did it to one of these My least brethren, *if he was in the state of grace,* you did it to Me." Any prisoner, any starving man, any sick or dying man, any sinner, any man whatever, is to be regarded as Christ—this is the formal command of the Savior Himself.

This doctrine is far too simple to satisfy many modern Christians, and undoubtedly many will remain very uneasy with it, tormented by the difficulty that perhaps, after all, this particular neighbor is a bad man and is foredoomed to hell, and therefore cannot be Christ. The solution of this difficulty is to unite oneself with the Spirit of Christ, to start thinking and loving as a Christian, and to stop being a hair-splitting pharisee.

Our faith is not supposed to be a kind of radio-electric eye which is meant to assess the state of our neighbor's conscience. It is the needle by which we draw the thread of charity through our neighbor's soul and our own soul and sew ourselves together in one Christ. Our faith is given us not to see *whether or not* our neighbor is Christ, but to recognize Christ in him and to help our love make both him and ourselves more fully Christ.

One of the themes that has constantly recurred throughout this article is that corrupt forms of love wait for the neighbor to "become a worthy object of love" before actually loving him. This is not the way of Christ. Since Christ Himself loved us when we were by no means worthy of love and still loves us with all our unworthiness, our job is to love others without stopping to inquire whether or not they are worthy. That is not our business and, in fact, it is nobody's business. What we are asked to do is to love; and this love itself will render both ourselves and our neighbor worthy if anything can.

Indeed, that is one of the most significant things about the power of love. There is no way under the sun to make a man worthy of love except by loving him. As soon as he realizes himself loved—if he is not so weak that he can no longer bear to be loved—he will feel himself instantly becoming worthy of love. He will respond by drawing a mysterious spiritual value out of his own depths, a new identity called into being by the love that is addressed to him.

Needless to say, only genuine love can draw forth such a response, and if our love fails to do this, perhaps it is because it is corrupted with unconscious romanticism or legalism and, instead of loving the brother, is only manipulating and exploiting him in order to make him fit in with our own hidden selfishness.

If I allow the Holy Spirit to work in me, if I allow Christ to use my heart in order to love my brother with it, I will soon find that Christ loving in me and through me has brought to light Christ in my brother. And I will find that the love of Christ in my brother, loving me in return, has drawn forth the image and the reality of Christ in my own soul.

This, then, is the mystery of Christ manifesting Himself in the love which no longer regards my brother as an object or as a thing, which no longer treats him merely as a friend or an associate, but sees in him the same Lord who is the life of my own soul. Here we have a communion in a subjectivity that transcends every object of knowledge, because it is not just the climate of our own inner being, the peculiar silence of our own narrow self, but is at once the climate of God and the climate of all men. Once we know this, then, we can breathe the sweet air of Christ, a divine air, which is the breath of Christ.

This "air" is God Himself—the Holy Spirit.

CHRISTIANITY AND
TOTALITARIANISM

The task of the Christian in our time is the same as it has always been: to build the Kingdom of God in this world. To manifest Christ in individuals and in society—or rather to allow the Savior to manifest His hidden presence in the world by the charity and unity, in one Body, of those He came to save. "That they all may be one as Thou Father in me and I in Thee, that they also may be one in us: that the world may believe that Thou hast sent me." This task is of course ultimately spiritual and eschatalogical, for the earthly manifestation of the Kingdom of God is still only a shadow of the eternal Kingdom that is to come. However, the spiritual character of the Kingdom cannot be made into a pretext for ignoring the temporal happiness and welfare of man in this present life. This may have been a temptation in the past. Those who yielded to it may perhaps have been excusable in their day. But it is no longer permitted to us to close our eyes to the danger of so grave an error. We must plainly and courageously face the fact that "building the Kingdom of God in this world" in preparation for the ultimate and eschatalogical revelation of the Kingdom in eternity means in fact *building a better world here and now:*— a better world for man to live in, and thus save his immortal soul.

Why is this so? Because man is not a pure spirit: his life in the world is a bodily life. He needs food, shelter, protection, comradeship and work. He lives as a member of a visible society. His interior and spiritual life, in a word, his salvation, depends in large measure on his ability to provide a normal and reasonable standard of living for himself and his family, to take part freely in the political, artistic and intellectual life of the world, and above all to serve and love his God.

The Kingdom of God is the Kingdom of Love: but where freedom, justice, education, and a decent standard of living are not to be had in society, how can the Kingdom of Love be built in that society? A starving man has little capacity to think about love. It is true, great saints can live and thrive in conditions that would be impossible for the average man. But the Kingdom of God is not made up exclusively of great saints: it is a living, Mystical organism made up of *average* men, with their weaknesses, their limitations, their good will, their talents, their deficiencies—all taken up and divinized by the Holy Spirit, so that Christ lives and manifests Himself in one and all. We who have been called, as average men, to live in this great mystery of the One Christ, must take care to see that we build for one another a world of justice, decent living, honest labor, peace and truth, fully recognizing that without these conditions we can only with great difficulty protect our weakness against sin, loss of faith, and ultimate despair.

Christians are not the only ones in the world who are faced with this need to build a new and better society. Indeed, it must be said to our confusion that we have not even been the first to undertake this most pressing task of our century. Others, whose good will we cannot doubt, have rushed ahead and taken upon themselves the responsibility which we ourselves had been perhaps slow to assume. Yet their good will cannot permit us to ignore the terrible blunders which they have committed in their attempts to build a better world without love, without Christ, and without God.

It is true that Love and Religion tend to lose their meaning and become mere words in a world where Justice, Peace, and Humanity have been so often and so cynically betrayed. But it is even more true that a society that attempts to create Justice, Peace and Humane living without God, ends without fail by falling headlong into an even greater injustice, an even more terrible addiction to war, cruelty and violence.

Those who seek to build a better world without God are those who, trusting in money, power, technology and organization, deride the spiritual strength of faith and love and fix all their hopes on a huge monolithic society, having a monopoly over all power, all production, and even over the minds of its members. But to alienate the spirit of man by subjecting him to such monstrous indignity is to make injustice and violence inevitable. By such means we may indeed increase economic production but in doing so we will only make the world worse.

The fact that the Church is the Mystical Body of Christ immediately sets it apart from every form of "aggregation," or "collectivity." If the Church were merely a moral body, a social organization, there would be no spiritual mystery about the union of her many members into one body. They would simply be united by common interests and a common purpose. But the Church is something far greater and more mysterious than this. The unity of the members of Christ is such that together they form one Person, One Christ, and yet each one personally "is Christ."

Christ the Lord is all in all, and present in each one of His members. Christ is not Head of the Church in the same way that a Dictator is Head of a Totalitarian State. By his authority and power, the Dictator imposes his policies on every individual in the state, controlling them in and through a vast political organization. Christ rules His faithful first of all from within, with the power and authority of supernatural life and of grace. It is because of the inner movement of the Holy Spirit the "believers" unite themselves freely with one another in the Church, under the authority of a visible head who represents Christ on earth. The Church as a visible society has, of course, her organization, laws and discipline. But these are all secondary, and relatively unimportant compared with the principle of inner and spiritual unity which is the charity of Christ. Charity can only be exercised among free individual men. Charity is the mark of a *person*, not of an organization.

The Church therefore is not an army or a mass-movement in which the individual loses himself. When the prophets preached the Messianic Kingdom of Peace, they based their preaching on justice and mercy which implied a profound respect for the rights and integrity of the human person. And when Christ, in the New Testament, preached the Kingdom of God, He opened the way only to individuals. No one can enter the Kingdom except by his own personal decision.

We are not saved *en masse*. Masses indeed may be called, but only individuals are chosen because only individuals can respond to a call by a free choice of their own. The Church is not, and has never been merely for the mass-man, the passive, inert man who drifts with the crowd and never decides anything for himself.

The mass-man is material for a mass-movement because he is easily transformed into a fanatic. That is why the mass-movement is so congenial to fanatics, and seeks to keep the fanaticism of its members at a high pitch. Indeed, when the members of a mass-movement begin to lose their fanatical hatred of everything that is *not* the movement, then that movement itself begins to die. This is a truth which Hitler openly admitted, and it explains the frantic insistence of the Russians on maintaining an iron curtain and preaching virulent hatred of the unknown world that lies beyond it.

In spite of this, there are as we know many Russians who instinctively realize that outside the Iron Curtain are millions of persons who, like themselves, love peace and do not want war. This instinct of love, and identification of oneself with the foreigner and stranger, this ability to find oneself in another, which alone can preserve world peace, is a fundamentally Christian instinct. Its continued presence in the Western World is due to the influence of our Christian past. Woe to us if this heritage is ever lost!

Nothing is so harmful to the Church as fanaticism. And it is harmful precisely because it produces an *ersatz* of Christian fervor and unity. The fanaticism of a mass-movement has the semblance of a unanimous spiritual front—the dedication of members to a common purpose to resist error and stamp out evil. It is precisely this semblance of spirituality and dedication that makes fanaticism deadly.

Fanaticism is never really spiritual because it is not *free*. It is not free because it is not enlightened. It cannot judge between good and evil, truth and falsity, because it is blinded by prejudice. Faith and prejudice have a common need to rely on authority and in this they can sometimes be confused by one who does not understand their true nature. But faith rests on the authority of love while prejudice rests on the pseudo-authority of hatred. Everyone who has read the Gospel realizes that in order to be a Christian one must give up being a fanatic, because Christianity is love. Love and fanaticism are incompatible. Fanaticism thrives on aggression. It is destructive, revengeful and sterile. Fanaticism is all the more virulent in proportion as it springs from *inability* to love, from incapacity to reciprocate human understanding.

Fanaticism refuses to look at another man as a person. It regards him only as a thing. He is either a "member" or he is not a member. He is either part of one's own mob, or he is outside the mob. Woe to him, above all, if he stands outside the mob with the mute protest of his individual personality! That was what happened at the Crucifixion of Christ. Christ, the Incarnate Son of God, came as a Person, seeking the understanding, the acceptance and the love of free persons. He found Himself face to face with a compact fanatical group, that wanted nothing of His Person. They feared His disturbing uniqueness. It was necessary, as Caiphas said, that this "one man should die for the nation"— that the individual Person, and above all *this* Person, should be sacrificed to the collectivity. From its very birth, Christianity has been categorically opposed to everything that savors of the mass-movement.

A mass-movement always places the "cause" above the individual person, and sacrifices the person to the interests of the movement. Thus it empties the person of all that is his own, takes him out of himself, casts him in a mold which endows him with the ideas and aspirations of the group rather than his own. There is nothing wrong in the person sacrificing himself for society: there can be times when this is right and necessary, and in the sacrifice the person will find himself on a higher level. But in the case of a mass-movement the emptying of the individual turns him into a husk, a mask, a puppet which is used and manipulated at will by the leaders of the movement. The individual ceases to be a person and becomes simply a "member," a "thing" which serves a cause, not by thinking and willing, but by being pushed about like a billiard ball, in accordance with the interests of the cause.

Contrast this with the teaching of Christ, for whom the soul of the individual was more important than the most sacred laws and rites, since these exist only for the sake of persons, and not vice versa. "The sabbath was made for man and not man for the sabbath." (Mark 2:27) Christ even placed the bodily health and well being of individuals before the law of the sabbath. One of the bitterest complaints made against Him was that He cured on the sabbath.

A mass-movement readily exploits the discontent and frustration of large segments of the population which for some reason or other cannot face the responsibility of being persons and standing on their own feet. But give these persons a movement to join, a cause to defend, and they will go to any extreme, stop at no crime, intoxicated as they are by the slogans that give them a pseudo-religious sense of transcending their own limitations. The member of the mass-movement, afraid of his own isolation and his own weakness as an individual, cannot face the task of discovering within himself the spiritual power and integrity which can be called forth only by love. Instead of this, he seeks a movement that will protect his weakness with a wall of anonymity and justify his acts by the sanction of collective glory and power. All the better if this is done out of hatred, for hatred is always easier and less subtle than love. It does not have to respect reality, as love does. It does not have to take account of individual cases. Its solutions are simple and easy. It makes its decisions by a simple glance at a face, a colored skin, a uniform. It identifies the enemy by an accent, an unfamiliar turn of speech, an appeal to concepts that are difficult to understand. And then fanaticism knows what to do. Here is something unfamiliar. This is not "ours." This must be brought into line—or destroyed.

Here is the great temptation of the modern age, this universal infection of fanaticism, this plague of intolerance, prejudice and hate which flows from the crippled nature of man who is afraid of love and does not dare to be a person. It is against this temptation most of all that the Christian must labor with inexhaustible patience and love, in silence, perhaps in repeated failure, seeking tirelessly to restore, wherever he can, and first of all in himself, the capacity of love and understanding which makes man the living image of God.

In the Old Testament, the Chosen People followed Moses as a group toward the Promised Land. As a community they entered with Josue into the Kingdom of Promise. It was sufficient to be part of the community that kept God's law, and the rest was taken care of. But in the New Testament, the message of salvation is addressed not to a group or a totality but to individuals. *Si quis vult* . . . "If any man, any person, decides and wills to follow me . . ." In the New Testament salvation is a matter of a free personal decision to accept and to follow Christ, to do the will of Christ, to please Him, to be His friend. The ritual of baptism is sufficient evidence of the care the Church takes to treat her children as individual persons, and to show a supreme respect for their freedom. Only a person can say "volo" "I will." The Christian is not saved as a member of a mob, by joining in mass acclamations and allowing himself to be lost and submerged in the vast anonymous exultation of a totality. The *Alleluia* of the victorious Church of Christ is indeed the acclamation of a "great multitude which no man can number" (Apoc. 7:9) but it is made up of the "*Volo*," the declaration of each one that he is a member of Christ, a friend of Christ. And this witness may often be sealed by the Christian's own blood in martyrdom. Religious vows are not merely the individual's consecration of himself to the service of a good cause, not merely a matter of immersing oneself in the anonymity of an Order—religious profession is the act by which one declares that he is before all else a friend, even a spouse, of Christ. It is not a renunciation of personality, but like martyrdom, its highest affirmation.

The members of a mass-movement may perhaps choose to become units in the totalitarian community: more often they are dragged into it or they drift into it passively, without too definite a decision. In any case, membership in a mass-movement is too often merely an "escape from freedom," a renunciation of personal responsibility, in order to live not by one's own mind and one's own freedom but by the thought and decisions of the group: the party line, the will of the leader. The disastrous consequences of this renunciation of moral responsibility on the part of the individual has been made clear by the unbelievable atrocities committed in police states all over the world in the last thirty years. These things have been done "with a good conscience" by people who have ceased to think and decide for themselves, carried away by the hypnotic effect of feeling themselves lost in a huge entity vastly more powerful and more effective in its actions than an individual could ever be. The member of the mass-movement loses his sense of limitation, weakness, fallibility, in the unlimited power and infallibility of the group.

When Christ called the "poor in spirit" blessed, He did not preach the abdication of our human dignity, He did not preach flight from individual responsibility and from the risks and limitations it implies. On the contrary, who is more poor in spirit than the man who takes the risk of standing on his own feet, who tries to realize his own fallibility and struggles to decide in his own conscience what is the will of God? From the moment that we break away from the reassuring passivity and confusion which surrounds us on all sides as we drift with the stream of the world, we become aware of our own insecurity, our fallibility, and we "work out our salvation in fear and trembling."

Take the moral teaching of St. Paul to the Ephesians or Corinthians, as an example. The life of the pagan world, with its idolatry, its comfortable, accepted rituals and superstitions, its drunkenness, its luxury and its self-indulgence, created an atmosphere of warm, delusive irresponsibility in which the individual could drift along without worrying too much. This is not hard for us to visualize since our present day society is just about the same. We too feel the risk and insecurity that comes when we nerve ourselves to break away from this passivity, to resist those who try to "deceive us with vain words" (Ephesians 5:6) to "be not partakers with them" (id. 7) and "to be no more children tossed to and fro with every wind of doctrine by the wickedness of

men . . . who walk in the vanity of their mind, having
their understanding darkened, being alienated from the
life of God . . . who despairing have given themselves up
to lasciviousness . . . and covetousness" (Ephesians 4:14-19).

It is the man who identifies himself with a powerful
group, glories in its display of might and fills his mouth and
his head with its jargon, who ceases to be poor in spirit because he no longer has to take the responsibility of thinking
and willing as a fallible person.

Personality means at once glory and lowliness, power and
risk. When he is called upon to answer for his actions, the
person who stands alone is weak and helpless indeed if he
finds himself faced with a group that does not approve of
his action. And yet he is in possession of great spiritual power
if his personal decision has been made in the light of truth,
with the testimony of a good conscience, as the act of a
child of God. "What then shall we say to these things? If
God be for us, who is against us? . . . Who shall accuse
against the elect of God? God that justifieth." (Romans
8:31-33)

The individual Christian does not stand absolutely alone.
He who has in his heart the testimony of Christ and of the
Holy Spirit, who stands firm in the love of God and of his
truth, who clings to the truth not because of a temporal
power and glory that are seen, but because of the invisible
glory of God in the inmost depths of his being, in faith—
such a one is united with all who share the same hope, the
same faith, the same love. He is one with those who are
filled with the same Spirit. His unity with them is expressed
by an exterior confession of faith, by fidelity to the same
laws, by participation in the same liturgical worship of the
All Holy One. He is a member of the visible Church, the

Mystical Body of Christ. But these things alone do not constitute the essence of his unity with his brethren and with Christ, which is interior and spiritual. Of the Christian's interior union with Christ and his brethren, his faith and obedience and worship are only the outward sign not the whole spiritual essence.

Hence there must be something more in the Christian life and apostolate, than merely persuading Christians to adhere to the same doctrinal propositions, to obey the same laws, and frequent the same sacraments. If we are content with merely exterior practice of our religion we will tend to make Christianity another of the mass-movements that cover the face of the earth. Then the Christian, rather than a free man, humbled by the consciousness of his responsibility, tends to become another fanatic who allows himself the worst excesses and excuses them easily on the ground that he is "defending the faith" or "fighting for the Church." A timely example: the readiness some Christians might have today to accept the idea of an all-out atomic surprise attack on Russia, and their approval of the most drastic and cruel methods in order to "stamp out communism." Such things are complacently "justified" by the argument that the communists are atheists, enemies of God, and hence "outside the law." The example may seem a gratuitous supposition. Let us hope there are few such Christians in the world, or none at all. Yet we cannot forget the frightful barbarities perpetrated by the Western Crusaders in Constantinople, desecrating Greek Churches, sacking monasteries and committing all sorts of other crimes, confident that these were acts proper to a holy war! Such incomprehension of the law and love of Christ seems almost unbelievable. Yet the study of history shows us these things and others like them repeated over and over again. By such actions the Kingdom of God is not built, it is destroyed: or would be if the gates of hell could prevail against it.

The union that binds the members of Christ together is not the union of proud confidence in the power of an organization. The Church is united by the *humility* as well as by the charity of her members. Hers is the union that comes from the consciousness of individual fallibility and poverty, from the humility which recognizes its own limitations and accepts them, the meekness that cannot take upon itself to condemn, but can only forgive because it is conscious that it has itself been forgiven by Christ. The union of Christians is a union of friendship and mercy, a bearing of one anothers' burdens in the sharing of divine forgiveness. Christian forgiveness is not confined merely to those who are members of the Church. To be a Christian one *must* love all men, including not only one's own enemies but even those who claim to be the "enemies of God." "Whosoever is angry with his brother shall be in danger of the judgment . . . Love your enemies, do good to them that hate you, pray for them that persecute and calumniate you, that you may be the children of your Father who is in heaven." (Matt. 5:22, 44, 45). The solidarity of the Christian community is not based on the awareness that the Church has authority to cast out and to anathematize, but on the realization that Christ has given her the power to forgive sin in His Name and to welcome the sinner to the banquet of His love in the Holy Eucharist. More than this, the Church is aware of her divine mission to bring forgiveness and peace *to all men*. This means not only that the sacraments are there for all who will approach them, but that Christians themselves must bring love, mercy and justice into the lives of their neighbors, in order to reveal to them the presence of Christ in His Church. This can only be done if all Christians strive generously to love and serve all men with whom they come into contact in their daily lives.

It has been repeatedly pointed out that the Mystical Body of Christ is not an organization but an organism. However, if this is to be an intuition that has meaning, and not just a verbal formula, we must realize that an organism is a living thing, and that it is ruled by the laws of life. Life is subject to its own laws. It does not allow itself to be governed by anything outside itself. The life which Christ came to give to the world is His own life, His love, and His freedom. He Himself is the "way, the truth and the life" both of the Christian and of the Church. Our task as Christians is to continue on earth that same life which Christ lived among us. Each individual Christian embarks upon a life in which he will govern his conduct by the pattern of the Gospels, and on the Christ-likeness of the saints. But in order to understand both the Gospels and the example of the saints, he must be not only guided exteriorly by the Church but also interiorly formed and taught by the Holy Spirit. Such a life cannot be reduced to mere external conformity to the patterns and norms of a given social group, no matter how Christian may be its intentions. Each Christian must work out his own salvation, as a member of Christ, and work it out in union with others. But the new circumstances of each age in the life of the Church confronts each new generation of Christians with problems and solutions for which the past offers no fully satisfactory example.

This means that each Christian has a truly creative mission in the society of his time. He has to begin anew, under new conditions, the great task of helping to redeem mankind by love. This does not mean simply applying formulas that were good in the 13th Century—though these are not necessarily out of place either. But we must discover new solutions for problems that are entirely new in our age The discovery is not the work of science only, but above all the work of love.

The history of the Church is a confusion of successes and apparent failures of Christianity. It is in fact an ever-repeated series of attempts to begin constructing the Kingdom of God on earth. This is not surprising, nor is it something Christ Himself failed to foresee. The parable of the cockle sown among the wheat shows clearly that He had this in mind, and that it accords with His Father's plan.

The life of the Church in history as well as the life of the individual Christian is a constantly repeated act of starting over again, of good intentions ending in achievements and in mistakes: of errors that have to be set right, of failings that have to be utilized, of lessons that are learned poorly and have to be learned over again. There have been hesitations and false starts in Christian history. There have even been grave errors, but these are imputable to Christian secular societies rather than to the Church. The Church alone has never lost her way. But the thing that keeps her on the right way is not power, not human wisdom, not political dexterity, or diplomatic foresight. There are times in the history of the Church when these things became, for Christian leaders, stones of stumbling and sources of delusion. The thing that keeps the Church and the Christian on the right way is love. And this is necessary, because love is the highest expression of personality and of freedom.

The Kingdom of God is, then, not the Kingdom of those who merely preach a doctrine or follow certain religious practices: it is the Kingdom of those who love. To build the Kingdom of God is to build a society that is based entirely on freedom and love. It is to build a society which is founded on respect for the individual person, since only persons are capable of love.

One cannot help getting the impression that this is not sufficiently well understood in our day. Love is a word that has been emptied of content by our materialistic society. In our world "love" is reduced to the infatuation celebrated in popular songs. Genuine love cannot be taken for granted, and least of all today. But we Christians seem to take it for granted. We seem to feel that we "love one another" and that we know very well what love is. We tend to act as if things were so well regulated by love in our own house-hold that we could safely forget about it and go out to preach to others. Hence we are not worried about love, so much as about doctrine. At all costs we want to get every-body to agree with us, and to accept our beliefs.

In this way we tend to become proselytizers rather than apostles. That is to say that we are looking for "members" who, by their numbers and their material support will bol-ster up our own faith and give us more confidence in the doctrine that we preach.

The true Apostle is not preaching a doctrine or leading a movement or recruiting for an organization: he is preaching Christ, because he loves other men and knows that thus he can bring them happiness, and give meaning to their lives. The proselytizer is selling his doctrine because he needs proselytes. The Apostle is preaching Christ because men need the mercy of God and because only in the love of Christ can they find happiness. The proselytizer is bitter and impatient when his ambitions are thwarted: and when they are successful he only communicates his own bitterness and restlessness to those whom he has "converted" into a replica of himself. The Apostle has no ambitions for himself, and his faith is so deep that it does not depend on being preached with great exterior success: even if no one were to believe him, the Apostle would continue quietly and patiently to preach the love of God for man in Christ, without hackneyed slogans, without arrogance and without the salesman's insufferable insistence.

The spirit of proselytism grows out of human cupidity and ambition, and it is this which endangers the purity of the Christian faith in our age, by making Christianity sometimes too like the mass movements that are springing up everywhere. For proselytism, not being "rooted and grounded in charity" (Ephesians 3:17) but springing rather from a hidden anxiety for domination and power, is overanxious to imitate the techniques and the policies of politicians and business men.

It is quite true that the Church must make use of the great new inventions of our age in order to preach the Gospel far and wide. But the Christian apostle must learn how to use these things in a different spirit and with different techniques from the man of the world. The radio and newspaper publicity that surrounds for example the death of a Pope, his burial, and the election and coronation of his successor, can immensely debase the dignity and significance of the Church's symbolic rituals by presenting them in the senseless clichés of journalese.

Christianity loses its meaning when it is described in the language of those whose mind is a constant series of uninterpreted sensations. Filtered through this tepid medium and reduced to the same formless neutrality that emasculates every other truth as soon as it becomes "news," the realities of Christianity and the Church have nothing whatever to gain and everything to lose by mere "publicity." Unless we strive to develop a greater spirit of self-criticism and discretion in our use of the mass-media that have been developed by business and politics, we run a serious risk of becoming, in spite of ourselves, a "party" of parades, slogans and mass demonstrations.

There *must* of course be huge concourses of the faithful in witness of the glories of our faith, but no matter how large a congregation of Christians may be, if it is fully Christian it is never merely a crowd, never merely a mass meeting. The individual is always more important than the collectivity. This is manifested in a rather striking way by the cures that take place, at times, during great demonstrations at Lourdes. The important thing is not that there is a huge crowd singing or praying, but that *one person* who was crippled gets up and goes away whole. The joy of all is simply the amplification of the joy of that one.

It is deeply significant that in any gathering of Christians, each individual person present is so important that a spiritual or temporal favor granted to him can burst into a thousandfold increase of joy in the whole multitude praising God.

A mass-movement is a pyramid at whose summit a few powerful men thrive and grow stronger on the labors of the huge anonymous mass which sacrifices itself in adoration of them. The Kingdom of God is just the opposite: it is the Kingdom of One who being equal to God took the form of a servant and suffered the death of the Cross that the love and life of God might descend and reach out into the lowest depths and bring light to all who are sitting in darkness, poverty, hopelessness and the shadow of death. In the Kingdom of God those who are higher exist for those who are below them. As Christ said:

> The princes of the gentiles lord it over them and they that are greater exercise power upon them. It shall not be so among you: but whosoever will be the greater among you, let him be your minister, and he that will be first among you shall be your servant.
>
> (Matt. 20:25-27)

No matter how gigantic the Christian congregation may sometimes become in its zeal to bear massive witness to its faith in Christ, the type of the Christian gathering will always remain not the parade of thousands of loyal members of a "cause" but the family of the faithful reunited peacefully for the breaking of Bread in the Holy Eucharist, the Lord's Supper. The supreme manifestation of Christian unity is always the relatively small group that gathers around the altar for Mass. The Holy Sacrifice is indeed magnificently impressive when it is offered before an enormous multitude in a stadium, at a Eucharistic congress. Yet it is far more truly itself when it simply unites the members of a parish in the parish Church early on a Sunday morning. By way of analogy, the daily meal which unites families and friends together in the evening, at home, is much more truly significant and human in its ordinariness and genuine warmth than the elaborate formal banquet where a hundred strangers get together in a hotel to nibble at strange cooking and listen to a series of speeches.

Karl Marx's basic charge against religion was that it engineered a systematic *alienation* of the human spirit. It took man away from himself, and from his own spirit. It emptied his life of its personal content to make him a "thing" belonging to something and someone else. It reduced him from the status of an individual person living his own life and forging his own future, to that of a "believer," an anonymous cipher in a religious organization, a worshipper of invisible powers, who devotes his energies and his income to the service of a fiction which he himself creates: a fiction whose existence is encouraged and abetted by the economic rulers of his world.

There is no doubt a certain crudity in Marx's conception. It represents an analysis of religion *from the outside*, by one whose religious instincts had remained frustrated. Marx was not a man without religion: he was a man whose religious development had been thwarted by the practical bourgeois indifferentism and hypocrisy in the midst of which he lived. But his hidden religious energies certainly found a devious outlet in the obvious messianism of his philosophy. In any case, his idea of man's alienation by religion, economics, politics and philosophy is his most genial contribution to the history of human thought. There is no need for Christianity to fear this sharp instrument of Marxian criticism. It becomes indeed one of our own most potent weapons if we turn it against those who claim to be the inheritors of Marx's thought.

Where has man's spirit ever reached such a pitch of alienation as in the mass movements of the twentieth century, and especially in the Soviet Union? The intellectual, spiritual, artistic and religious life of the Soviet citizen has been systematically drained at its source by communist indoctrination. The pseudo-scientific "organization" of man's life in all its departments, not for his benefit but for the benefit of the "revolution" (that is for the heads of the communist Party) has completely emptied man's life of personal meaning and enterprise. The present disturbances and re-actions among Russian youth (hooliganism and stilyagism), bear eloquent witness to the sense of futility aroused by this emptying and de-personalization of man's life. The most ironical fact about the twentieth century is that Atheistic Communism has finally realized, in its ultimate perfection, the economic alienation of man which Karl Marx ascribed in part to religion.

We may be tempted, for a moment, to smile at this strange confirmation of all that our faith teaches us of the ways of God with man—that the most effective way in which man is "punished" on this earth is to let his errors take their course and work themselves out to their logical conclusion. Yet we are in no position to sit back and enjoy a complacent triumph. These same errors are all too likely to be our own.

We are living in an age of universal alienation and mass movements. Christian circles are by no means immune from the contagion of totalitarianism. It is all too easy for us to seek a kind of massive, monolithic strength in discipline, publicity, and proselytism. It is all too easy for us to lose sight of Christ and His charity, and to exchange the basic truths of the Gospel for new slogans that promise to be "more effective" in rallying thousands to our cause. Let us beware. The blaring of loudspeakers, the roaring of slogans, the tramp of marching thousands, will never produce any-thing but alienated fanatics. Christianity can never be al-lowed to savor of a mass-movement. Christians can never, with a good conscience, yield to the lure of totalitarianism. Even when a political system promises a strong arm with which to defend the Church, if that arm ends in a mailed fist, and if the "protection" offered is that of a secret police and concentration camps, we cannot accept its protection.

If that system offers to "defend the faith" by the atomic bombing of defenseless civilians, we cannot accept its protection. Such defense is a mockery and a desecration of God in His image. It is a renewal of the crucifixion of Christ, in those for whom He died.

Our mission in the world is the same as it has always been, to build the Kingdom of God, which is a Kingdom of Love. Love cannot exist except between persons. For there to be love, we must first of all safeguard the liberty and integrity of the human person. We must provide an education that strengthens man against the noise, the violence, the slogans and the half-truths of our materialistic society.

Our duty to preserve the human person in his integrity, his freedom and his individuality, and to arm him spiritually against the peril of totalitarianism, is not just something it would be nice for us to discuss and perhaps to study. It is an urgent task which demands insistently to be carried out wherever there is a Catholic parish, a Catholic school, and especially a Catholic university or seminary. It is the most important duty of the Catholic intellectual. It is not an easy task. It is a very delicate one, precisely because our zeal against one type of mass-movement can so easily plunge us head first into another and worse kind of which we are less afraid.

The experience of the past ten years has shown, or should have shown, that it is not enough to be anti-communist to preserve freedom in America. What will the next ten years bring? There is unfortunately all too great a danger that it will see the rise of a fatal mass movement for which the moral and cultural disorder of twentieth-century America have prepared the way only too well.

PART THREE

SACRED ART AND THE SPIRITUAL LIFE

We live in an age of confusion and of extremes. On the one hand, ours is a time of mass-civilization, of totalitarian and passive comformities. On the other, we see futile gestures of individualistic rebellion, and exhibitionism. We are invited to sympathize with protests that are little more than pose or declamation. This same confusion affects the arts and the spiritual life as much, perhaps more, than anything else. On the whole it is a disquieting feature of modern religion that it tends more and more to dilute faith and to substitute for it "togetherness"—passive conformity with the group—as if the "obedience of faith" of which St. Paul speaks were nothing more than the refusal to think for oneself and the renunciation of all loyalty to one's inmost spiritual aspirations. As a result of this distortion, there arises a temptation to go to the other extreme, to seek attention and consolation by non-conformist rebellion. Hence the Church tends to be divided between a large mass of passive and inert conventionalists who cling blindly to what is familiar, and a small minority of eccentric faddists who are in love with anything new just because it is new.

In the realm of sacred art we see these two trends at work. Both of them produce bad art, and it is difficult to say which one has worse effects. In quanitity, of course, the dead conventionalism of conformist piety can certainly be said to be most productive. But the fact that new shapes are in fashion means that pseudo-modern sacred art has more of an impact. Between them, the two trends produce greater and greater confusion. And it is hard even for the discriminating to detect, in the midst of all this, the really solid and inspired work that is being done, everywhere, by capable, honest and dedicated talent. There *are* good artists and craftsmen. Sacred art *is* alive, and really developing. There has been, and continues to be, much healthy and creative thought. There has been intelligent writing on the subject of art, work, the life of the spirit. All this has not however been produced by the men who receive the greatest publicity. I might mention two names in this connection: Eric Gill and Ananda Coomaraswamy. Both are now dead but their work remains. Anyone who wants to get a good perspective by which to judge art, in its relation to the life of the spirit, ought to study Gill's essays (for instance, *Sacred and Secular*) and Coomaraswamy's lucid conferences on art (for instance, *The Christian and Oriental or True Philosophy of Art*). This Indian thinker, so sympathetic to traditional Christian values and so deeply immersed in that Catholic thought in which he recognized the western counterpart to Oriental contemplative spirituality, has left us at least one definitive full-length book on the philosophy of art: his *Transformation of Nature in Art*. This book should be studied and loved in all Catholic colleges and seminaries.

But how many people, outside of specialists in the field, have heard of Coomaraswamy? How many remember Eric Gill? How many know such followers of Gill as Peter Watts, for example? The artist who considers himself obliged, first of all, to do "good work," who has a profound respect for his craft, his materials, his vocation, is no longer the object of much interest. Such values do not attract the eye of the camera or the notice of publicists. Without condescending to the philistine fashion of laughing on principle at abstract and experimental art, we may be permitted to wonder if the people who "create" blindly by throwing blobs of paint at the canvas, or dripping paint aimlessly about, really deserve the interest they have aroused or the money they have accumulated. Experimentalism is certainly a healthy phenomenon, in itself. But not a cult of experiment for its own sake, without regard for its fruitfulness.

The function of this essay, originally addressed to teachers and others engaged in the formation of Catholic religious and lay persons, is not to decry modern art or to condemn pious conventionalism, but simply to make a more fundamental appeal: that people may learn to open their eyes and *see*, instead of thinking that they see, looking only at what they have been told to see, or at what they imagine they ought to see. This may sound too simple, but in fact the problem is enormous. We are a generation of men who have eyes and see not, ears and hear not, because we have let ourselves be so completely and abjectly conditioned by words, slogans and official pronouncements.

Because of this inability to look, to see, to admire, to contemplate, we allow ourselves to be passively deluged with all kinds of pious and artistic tripe, content if it is approved by our own group, uneasy if it is approved only by "experts" whom we don't quite trust, and miserable if it appears to be the kind of thing that is approved by a group or a faction to which we feel hostile. But in any case, if the productions in question have the sanction of fashion or of business, in a word if they are the work of successful and popular artists— or if they are widely accepted by "right thinking men,"— we accept them without trying to see what it is we have accepted.

It might be well to remark here, in parenthesis, that conventionalism in art has been carried to its logical extreme in the totalitarian countries. Many of the Soviet visitors to the Vatican Pavilion in the Brussels Exposition were shocked by the examples of modern liturgical art they saw there: shocked by that more than by anything else. In all matters of art, culture and spirituality it can certainly be said that communism has succeeded in producing bourgeois complacency in all its final and exquisite perfection. Such is the effect of blind conformity, and the refusal to use one's eyes for the purpose for which they were created: to see and enjoy God's beauty in creation, and to seek Him in and through that beauty.

In a word, then, it is our inability to really use our sense faculties, our imagination, our creative intelligence, that makes us the slaves of slogans, arbitrary pronunciamentos, and party lines in art. And this servility, which is a rank infidelity to God the Creator and to the Sanctifying Spirit of Truth, has brought about the corruption of sacred as well as non-sacred art. It has also enfeebled the spirit of man, and dulled his intelligence. It has paralyzed his meditation and his interior prayer. That is why there is so little thought given to the influence of bad art in Christian life. Teachers, priests and parents seem very little aware of the fact that bad art is harmful, and that truly Christian sacred art—the art which is traditional and genuinely spiritual art—exercises a powerful formative influence on the Christian soul. This influence is in some ways completely irreplaceable. But *bad* art exercises an equally powerful influence for *de*formation.

The prevalence of bad so-called sacred art everywhere constitutes a really grave spiritual problem, comparable, for example, to the analogous problem of polluted air in some of our big industrial centers. One breathes the bad air, aware only of a slight general discomfort, headache, stinging of the eyes; but in the long run the effect is grave. One looks at the bad art, in Church, in pious magazines, in some missals and liturgical books, on so called "holy" pictures; one is aware of a vague spiritual uneasiness and distaste.

Or perhaps, worse still, one *likes* the cheap, emotional, immature and even sensual image that is presented. To *like* bad sacred art, and to feel that one is *helped* by it in prayer, can be a symptom of real spiritual disorders of which one may be entirely unconscious, and for which perhaps one may have no personal responsibility. The disease is there— and it is catching!

Those of us who have the obligation of forming Christian and religious souls, whether in schools, colleges, novitiates, or seminaries, ought to reflect on this as well as on so many other dangers. Or rather—since it is bad psychology to see nothing but dangers and evils all around us—let us be aware of the dynamic and vitalizing spiritual effect of a purer and more traditional artistic sense. Let us realize that desire for a more living liturgy, a keener appreciation of theology and scripture, a greater awareness of the spiritual depth and of the contemplative possibilities of Christian life, cries out for the help that will be afforded by a sane and spiritual formation in sacred art.

All these things go together. Man is a living unity, an integrated whole. He is not sanctified just in his mind, or in his will. The whole man must be made holy, body and soul together, imagination and senses, intelligence, heart and spirit.

Sacred art is theology in line and color, and it speaks to the whole man: to his eye first of all, but also to his mind and to his heart. A sacred picture or statue, is an artistic symbol of the Christian victory of spirit over flesh. It is a witness to the power of the divine Spirit at work to transfigure the whole of creation and to "recapitulate all things in Christ," restoring all material creation to the spiritual and transforming rule of divine love. In a sacred image, material things recover a spiritual harmony that was lost when the whole world fell with Adam; and in so doing, the material elements of the image become as it were the vehicle of the Holy Spirit, and furnish Him with an occasion to reach souls with His hidden, spiritual power.

For this spiritual effect to be realized, certain important conditions are essential. The work of art must be genuinely spiritual, truly traditional, artistically alive. In other words it must possess a combination of religious and artistic qualities which is very rarely found today.

Where a work of religious art lacks these fundamental qualities, it remains spiritually dead. To contemplate and to enjoy such a work of art is like eating spoiled food, and has a bad spiritual effect. I do not mean to suggest that we must all now become spiritual and artistic hypochondriacs, and start worrying about the possible bad effect of some picture we have just looked at. But there is a healthy reaction to bad food: you get rid of it. And there is a healthy reaction to bad art: you throw it out. Instead of passively accepting bad art, let us learn actively to reject it. Let us learn to say *no* to false piety, faddism, and pretense.

The problem, of course, is in the formation of artistic taste, and in developing the capacity to judge between good and bad—an exceedingly difficult problem for some people. But at all events, it should be possible for most of us still in our right minds to agree that there is a certain type of "holy" picture that is genuinely unholy because, if one shrugs off his mental bad habits and really *looks* at the thing, it will be seen to be in reality a monstrous caricature of our Lord, or of the Blessed Virgin, or one of the saints.

I am not now speaking of that modern art in which deformity seems to be adopted as a matter of principle, but of the widely accepted sentimental and pseudo-realistic presentation of the Lord and His saints which is, in fact, both shocking and absurd and which sometimes plumbs the very depths of hideous vulgarity. The conscientious Catholic teacher or parent should learn to quietly destroy, hide, or otherwise get rid of such things rather than put them in the hands of children who, because the pictures are presented as "beautiful" and "holy," will cultivate a compulsive attitude of reverence toward them. I wonder how many of the young Catholics who have fallen away from their faith after leaving school might not perhaps trace this defection, in part, to the hidden and instinctive revulsion they felt for the kind of piety represented by such pictures.

It will do no good to protest that one cannot argue about matters of taste. *De gustibus non est disputandum.* It is true of course that individual preferences are the privilege of all those who have enough sense and taste to choose. But when it comes to the distinction between good taste and bad, then certainly we must argue. *De gustibus* est *disputandum.* Artistic taste is a gift of God, a talent that must not be allowed to be lost or destroyed. On the contrary, it must be developed. No one has the right to sit by passively and allow vulgarity, ugliness, and sham to usurp the place that belongs to art and spiritual truth. But obviously, this presupposes that one has had training, and that he has enough Christian humility to take his own judgment with a grain of salt.

St. John Damascene once said: "If a pagan comes and asks you to show him your faith, take him to the Church and let him see the sacred ikons." These words were uttered, as a matter of course, in the great age of Byzantine art. Times, and art, have changed. It would be superfluous to comment on the fact that these words are no longer as true as they used to be. In fact, some of us would instinctively be ashamed to let a non-Catholic friend see some of the statues or stained glass windows that are found in our Churches.

Even those who are sincerely proud of the picture of the Sacred Heart in their living room, may perhaps intuitively realize that their Protestant neighbor respects the sincerity of their faith, but deplores the quality of their art. The sentimental, feminine character of the picture may, indeed, only confirm the neighbor in a secret antipathy for our faith. Yet what visitor to Rome is not in awe at the frescoes of the Sistine chapel, or the great Byzantine mosaics in the other Roman basilicas? It is not the *content* of our holy pictures that antagonizes the non-Catholic, but their *style.*

But let us be on our guard against fads. A craze for everything that appears to be modern, whether good, bad or indifferent, is no cure for the sentimental bad taste of a past age. We must, rather, learn to see that there is much the same vulgarity and unconscious impiety in pseudo-modern sacred art as there was in the sentimental pious picture of a couple of generations ago. In fact, the progressive degeneration of popular pious art seems to be intensified by the addition of a little streamlining. While in the older popular pictures of the Blessed Virgin she at least appeared sweet and inoffensive, we now see her made up with lipstick and mascara, Hollywood style, and, at the same time, elongated and launched into space as if she were jet-propelled. Perhaps I am crazy, but I find it impossible to see anything either holy or beautiful in such pictures as these.

So much for the bad. Where are we to look, to find something good? It would certainly be wrong, in the first place, to cultivate a habit of prejudice and callow snap-judgments.

It is equally wrong to condemn all modern art simply because it is "modern" and to approve of it all because it seems new and "different." In art, as in everything else, vitality is not synonymous with mere newness. Each work of art must be judged on its own merits and not by the light of preconceived ideas or of prejudice, whether favorable or unfavorable. Let us never be snobs. Let us try to recognize real merit wherever it is found, even in the most unexpected places.

Let us be willing to admit, for instance, that Henri Matisse is a great artist and that his experiment with the chapel of the Dominican nuns at Vence is in many ways interesting and effective. This does not mean that we have to regard it as completely perfect. It is only a worthwhile experiment. It is deficient in a certain "sacredness." As for the shrine of Ronchamp, designed by Le Corbusier, let us not condemn it without first understanding *why* he did the things that were done. Perhaps he was not simply being provocative.

Remember, Gothic architecture was once something entirely new and unheard of! But remember also that the age of Gothic architecture is past.

There has never been so much shallow and ignorant snobbery in the world of art and letters as we have today: all kinds of snobbery, the intellectual snobbery of the highbrow, the political snobbery of the radical, the bourgeois snobbery of the solid business man who wants everything to "look *real.*" There is a danger of liturgical snobbery in certain quarters, and of a snobbery in reverse among the ascetically inclined minority who want to get along without any art or literature at all. The best thing we can do is to keep our skins safe in this war of moods, tastes and fashions, and cultivate our own judgment, forming it by a patient and humble study of Christian tradition. And let us be broad minded—for that is one of the meanings of the word "Catholic."

There are fortunately plenty of excellent reproductions of all the best art. The fact that we never enter a museum is of no importance. We do not need to go to Assisi and see Giotto on the walls which he actually painted. We may perhaps get a much more adequate idea of him from an inexpensive magazine. But what we have to do is open our eyes and look at the right things.

Is there any simple, certain and "unsnobbish" way of finding out what are the "right things"? Certainly no one will debate that for a Christian, there are definite schools and traditions that are universally acceptable. The first and most important of these is the Byzantine tradition. This is the tap root of the great tree of Christian art, both in the Eastern and in the Western Church. What is the Byzantine style? Think of the well known picture of our Lady of Perpetual Help: this is a popular western adaptation of an ancient oriental ikon. The average reproduction of this picture may not be distinguished for high quality or genius, but it is at least a pardonable imitation of a genuinely Christian and spiritual artistic style. One might express a desire that such pictures, good in themselves, might always be reproduced with good taste. As for the ancient original ikons still venerated in the Eastern Church, they include some of the finest and most "Sacred" works of Christian art.

Then there are the Italian primitives—especially Fra Angelico, explicitly praised by Pope Pius XII as an artist and a saint. Giotto, the great painter of the early Franciscans, Cimabue, who is still essentially Byzantine, and so on. These painters have a purity and innocence of vision that is sublimely spiritual and contemplative.

The great artists of the Christian renaissance and counter-reformation are popular enough and need no introduction: Raphael, Michelangelo, Leonardo da Vinci, and so on. The most interesting artists of this period are perhaps the ones who are less well known—for instance Paolo Uccello.

We must remember, too, that with the end of the renaissance there began a great decline in sacred art which led to the atrocities of recent centuries. It was during the baroque era that the saints in art began to strike operatic attitudes and found themselves surrounded by rosy clouds of infant cherubim. It was then that the only distinguishing mark separating male from female sanctity was to be sought in the clothing of the holy ones. (Sometimes not even a beard was a reliable indication. There *are* bearded ladies.)

Here a mention of El Greco is called for. A contemporary of St. Teresa and St. John of the Cross, El Greco has aroused special interest in our own day because he was a forerunner of the modern expressionist painters. And it must be admitted that El Greco is a great, though perhaps some-times overrated, religious artist. He has been called a "mys-tic"—but let us not exaggerate the "mystical" content of his paintings. In studying his canvases, one can quickly come to appreciate how a certain liberty, taken by the artist in his treatment of human forms, has resulted in some very suc-cessful expressions of *spiritual realities.*

From this we learn the very important truth that photo-graphic realism is no asset in sacred art, but on the contrary a liability. Sacred art is not meant to be slavishly realistic. It is not meant merely to provide an accurate representation of material forms. It is not just a *copy* of visible reality. On the contrary, sacred art has as its mission the difficult task of *conveying a hidden and invisible spiritual reality.* In fulfill-ing this task, the sacred artist must be careful that he does not render his work too opaque and impenetrable to the spiritual light. He must take care not to be too concerned with matter and with sensual appearances. Consequently one of the tasks of the sacred artist is to convey hidden realities by *suggesting* them rather than by trying to *repre-sent* them.

That is why those who seek to portray spiritual emotions and feelings on the faces of the saints often end up with such fatuous results. Even El Greco himself does not alto-gether escape this pitfall. Let us make up our minds once for all that genuinely spiritual realities cannot be "copies," they can only be suggested. Then we will be able to free our-selves from our captivity to realism and theatrical falsity. We will understand the reasons for expressionism in sacred art.

One need only add that a sophisticate like El Greco will, like oysters, always be an acquired taste, and I offer no sub-stantial guarantees that he will be popular with the fourth grade.

Among modern sacred artists I might mention the late Georges Rouault, both because he is quite well known and because his work, like that of El Greco, bears witness to the effectiveness of expressionism in sacred art. Not all will be able to like Rouault immediately. He is violent, like most modern artists. But he is also a deep and poignant, and authentic witness to the somewhat grim spiritual temper of our times. An example of his work? Look at the cover of Guardini's *The Lord* published several years ago. An *"Ecce Homo"* of Rouault was reproduced here, in full color.

In spite of the overwhelming flood of bad "holy cards," there are some very good ones to be had. Perhaps the best work in this field has been done by the Benedictines of Marialaach, in Germany. Their *Ars liturgica* press has printed hundreds of beautiful reproductions of ikons, of medieval manuscript paintings, primitive and Byzantine works, and modern sacred art. It is incredible that these things are not better known and spread about everywhere. Everyone who has at heart the significance of sacred art in relation to the Christian life and worship ought to spend a couple of dollars, once in a while, for a hundred of these cards and give them away on all sides. It would be a real, though very modest, apostolate!

In America, excellent reproductions of ikons may be obtained from *Jubilee* magazine, 377, 4th Avenue, New York 16.

Let us be convinced of the importance of *good taste* in everything related to Christian life and worship, and let us be animated with a certain zeal for the beauty of God's house which forbids us to be indifferent to vulgarity, cheapness, showiness and worldly sensuality in Christian art. We do not have to be experts on art, or know all the names and dates of "famous masterpieces." We have no obligation to lecture others on aesthetic theory, or convince the Philistine that he does not know art when he sees it. But it would certainly be desirable if we had that genuine sense of proportion and beauty which is gradually being destroyed in our materialistic society. Christian art should be an oasis of beauty and spiritual truth in a world of ugliness, falsehood and sin.

But in an age of concentration camps and atomic bombs, religious and artistic sincerity will certainly exclude all "prettiness" or shallow sentimentality. Beauty, for us, cannot be a mere appeal to conventional pleasures of the imagination and senses. Nor can it be found in cold, academic perfectionism. The art of our time, sacred art included, will necessarily be characterized by a certain poverty, grimness and roughness which correspond to the violent realities of a cruel age. Sacred art cannot be cruel, but it must know how to be compassionate with the victims of cruelty: and one does not offer lollipops to a starving man in a totalitarian death-camp. Nor does one offer him the messages of a pitifully inadequate optimism. Our Christian hope is the purest of all lights that shines in darkness, but it shines in darkness, and one must enter into darkness to see it shining.

Let us be willing to admit that perhaps some of our modern artists, with all their shortcomings and poverty (which they themselves will be the first to admit) are instinctively trying to be true to their place in history. Unfortunately, even where sacred art is concerned, credit for such sincerity does not belong to the many, but only to the few.

A RENAISSANCE HERMIT:
BL. PAUL GIUSTINIANI

Just as the Church of God can never be without martyrs, so too she can never be without solitaries, for the hermit, like the martyr, is the most eloquent witness of the Risen Christ. It was on the night of Easter that the Risen Savior breathed upon His Apostles, that they might receive of His Spirit, Who had not been given before because Christ was not yet glorified. St. Paul has told us that all who are sons of God are activated and moved by the Spirit of God. They have the Spirit of Christ because they belong to Christ. Having His Spirit, they live no longer according to the flesh but according to the Spirit. *Qui vero secundum Spiritum sunt, quae sunt Spiritus sentiunt.*[1] Therefore they are of one mind and one Spirit with Jesus Christ.

Now at the beginning of His public life, Jesus was led into the desert by the Spirit, that He might engage in single

[1] Romans 8:5.

combat with the devil. The struggle in the desert was the prelude to the struggle in the Garden of the Agony. This last was the exemplar and meritorious cause of the charity of all the martyrs and all the hermits who would be tested, like Christ Himself, in the furnace of tribulation because they were pleasing to God. The Church of God, triumphing in her martyrs and ascetics, would thus be able to declare with Christ Himself: "The prince of this world indeed comes, and he has no part in me: but he comes that the world may know that I love the Father!" [2]

There must, therefore, be hermits. Nor is this only because there will always be men who desire solitude. The Christian hermit is one who is led into the desert by the Spirit, not by the flesh, even though he may well have a natural inclination to live alone. Our own time has seen hermits like the Dominican, Père Vayssière, who entered the Order of Preachers knowing that he wanted to preach the Gospel, and completely unaware that he would spend most of his life in solitude at La Sainte Baume. Nor must there always be hermits merely because there are always contemplative souls, or because the contemplative naturally seeks physical solitude: (For without the efficacious desire of exterior solitude, interior solitude will always remain a fantasy or an illusion.) The true reason for the persistence of hermits even in ages which are most hostile to the solitary ideal is that the exigencies of Christian life *demand* that there be hermits. The Kingdom of God would be incomplete without them, for they are the men who seek God alone with the most absolute and undaunted and uncompromising singleness of heart. If we have forgotten that the Fathers of the Church assigned to the hermit a high, even the highest place among all Christian vocations, a modern

[2] John, 14:30-31.

theologian, Dom Anselm Stolz, is there to remind us of the fact.[3] And now another Benedictine, Dom Jean Leclercq, has added an important volume to the slowly growing collection of works on the solitary life appearing in our own time.[4]

This book is all the more important because it introduces us to a hermit as interesting as he is unknown—a surprising figure, rising up almost unaccountably in the Italy of Raphael and Macchiavelli, Castiglione and Michelangelo Buonarotti. Paul Giustiniani became a novice at Camaldoli in 1510. That is to say that he entered the most ancient of the eremitical Orders that have survived in the Western Church. Camaldoli goes back to the tenth century and Saint Romuald. Less famous than the Chartreuse, Camaldoli nevertheless has retained more of the aspect of an ancient "laura" than we would find in any Charterhouse. The Camaldolese idea is simply to apply the Rule of St. Benedict to the eremitical life. St. Benedict declared, of course, that his Rule was written for cenobites. Therefore, the Camaldolese idea presupposes, first of all, a *cenobium*, a monastery where the monks live and work and pray in community. But St. Benedict also holds the solitary life in high honor, and suggests that certain monks, after a long probation in the monastery, may be called by God to a hermitage. St. Romuald made it possible for monks to have solitude without losing anything of the *bonum obedientiae* which is the treasure of monastic life, and without departing from that life in common, the life of fraternal charity, which is the security of all who do not feel themselves equal to the hero-

---

[3] Dom A. Stolz, O.S.B. *L'Ascèse Chrétienne*, Chevetogne, 1948, c. 1.
[4] *La Vie Erémitique d'après la Doctrine du Bienheureux. Paul Giustiniani*, Paris, 1955. (The present essay was written as a preface to this book by Dom Leclercq.)

ism of another Anthony. The *Sacro Eremo* of Camaldoli is therefore a community of hermits, a village of ancient cells hidden in a pine forest several thousand feet above sea level in the Appenines behind Arrezzo.

Paul Giustiniani entered Camaldoli at a time when the eremitical fervor had lost some of its ancient heat, and he left it for a stricter solitude. Eventually he was to start a new eremitical congregation of his own, the Hermits of Monte Corona, who still have a community at Frascati outside Rome and several others in Italy, Spain, and Poland. News has even been received of a recent foundation in the United States, in Ohio. Giustiniani bears the same relation to Camaldoli as the Abbé de Rancé does to the Order of Citeaux, and, in another sense, as Dom Innocent Lemasson does to the Chartreuse. Like each of these great men, Paul Giustiniani seeks to rekindle the ancient fire that is burning low in an age that has no love for asceticism, for contemplation or for solitude. It is therefore the greatest interest to have at our disposal a volume that brings together from his various works, most of which are inaccessible, a complete doctrine of the solitary life.

Let us now turn to the doctrine of Blessed Paul, whose name recalls to our minds the half legendary figure of the "first hermit" whom St. Anthony is supposed to have discovered in a cave where he had lived for over a hundred years unknown to men.

The eremitical life is above all solitary. St. Romuald chose to settle in the once inviolable forests of Camaldoli and to seek God in a solitude that was *sacred*, that is to say entirely consecrated to Him. The inviolable character of "holy solitude" is a witness to the infinite transcendence of Him Whose holiness elevates Him above all things. In order to seek Him Who is inaccessible the hermit himself becomes inaccessible. But within the little village of cells centered about the Church of the *Eremo* is a yet more perfect solitude: that of each hermit's own cell. Within the cell is the hermit himself, in the solitude of his own soul. But—and this is the ultimate test of solitude—the hermit is not alone with himself: for that would not be a sacred loneliness. Holiness is life. Holy solitude is nourished with the Bread of Life and drinks deep at the very Fountain of all Life. The solitude of a soul enclosed within itself is death. And so the authentic, the really sacred solitude is the infinite solitude of God Himself, Alone, in Whom the hermits are alone.

From this obligation to seek interior solitude flow all the other demands made upon the hermit, the other essential obligations of his state: silence, stability, recollection, mortification, labor, fasting, vigils and prayer. These detach the soul from all that is not God. They are not peculiar to the hermit. They belong to the monastic life wherever it is found. But the hermit has a very special obligation to practice them, without however departing from discretion which is one of the most important virtues of the solitary. After all, it is discretion which teaches us to live by the interior guidance of the Holy Spirit. It is discretion which teaches us to distinguish between the voice of the Spirit and the voice of the flesh or of the evil one. Discretion does not permit us to be cowards, but neither does it allow us to fall headlong into the abyss of vanity, pride, or presumption. Without discretion, the solitary life ends fatally in disaster.

In the true spirit of St. Benedict, Paul Giustiniani declares that even in the hermitage the best mortifications are those which are not of our own choice, and that even the hermit should seek to please God more by great fidelity in his ordinary duties than by extraordinary feats of ascetic heroism. The life of the solitary will be a continual warfare, in which the flesh fights not only against the spirit but against the flesh itself and in which the spirit also fights not only against the flesh but even against the spirit.

It is here, in this inexpressible rending of his own poverty, that the hermit enters, like Christ, into the arena where he wages the combat that can never be told to anyone. This is the battle that is seen by no one except God, and whose vicissitudes are so terrible that when victory comes at last, the total poverty and emptiness of the victor are so absolute that there is no longer any place in his heart for pride.

Such is the *eremitica puritas* which opens the way for contemplation. Without this "annihilation" the solitary might perhaps be tempted to seek rest in the consolations of God for their own sake. He might enjoy a selfish and self-complacent solitude in which he was delivered from responsibilities and inundated with supernatural favors. In words that remind us of St. John of the Cross, Paul Giustiniani speaks of the false contemplatives who "are displeased by everything that deprives them of the rest they think they have found in God but which they seek, really, in themselves. Their only care is to seek after peace, not in things below them, not in themselves, but in God; however they desire this peace not for the glory of God, but out of love for themselves."

Nor does the sacredness of solitude and the true eremitical purity allow the hermit to become absorbed in a zeal that does not extend beyond the welfare or reputation of his own monastery and his own Order, still less beyond his own progress and his own virtues. A life alone with God is something too vast to include such limited objectives within its range. It reaches up to God Himself, and in doing so embraces the whole Church of God.

Meanwhile the hermit supports this interior poverty of

spirit with the greatest exterior poverty. He must live like the poorest of the poor, *Eremitica puritas* is the peace of one who is content with bare necessities. Such peace is impossible where poverty is a mere matter of exterior form. The hermit is not one who, though deprived of the right to possess them, actually has the use of better objects and enjoys more plentiful comforts than could ever be afforded by the materially poor. The eremitical community itself must be a poor community. And although this simplicity guarantees the hermit a high place in the Church, he himself will remember that his elevation is in reality a matter of humility and abjection. He takes no part in the active affairs of the Church because he is too poor to merit a place in them. For him to accept prelacy would be an infidelity because it would be an act of presumption. Paul Giustiniani pursues this subject of poverty into the most remote corners of the hermit's soul. The solitary will not even pride himself on his strict observances, or compare himself with religious of other Orders. He will avoid the supreme folly of those who, having nothing in the world but their humility, lose even that by boasting of it! By this perfect forgetfulness of himself, the hermit merits to be called the successor of the martyrs.

There is a positive side to all this. Solitude is not sought for its own sake. If the eremitical life is the highest form of Christianity it is because the hermit aspires more than anyone else to perfect union with Christ. Jesus Himself is the living Rule of the hermit, just as He is the model of every religious. It is Christ Himself who calls us into solitude, exacting of us a clean break with the world and with our past, just as He did of St. Anthony. Perhaps more than any other the solitary life demands the presence of the Man Christ Who lives and suffers in us. Even if we worshipped the one true God in the desert, without the Incarnate Word our solitude would be less than human, and therefore far short of the divine: without Him no one comes to the Father. Without Jesus we all too easily fulfil the words of Pascal—"qui veut faire l'ange, fait la bête." Solitude must therefore translate itself into the three words: "Cum Christo Vivere"—to live with Christ. Solitude is a fortress that protects the heart against all that is not Christ, and its only function is to allow Christ to live in us. Solitude spiritualizes the whole man, transforms him, body and soul, from a carnal to a spiritual being. It can only do so in the Spirit of Christ Who elevates our whole being in God, and does not divide man's personality against itself like those false asceticisms which St. Paul knew to be enemies of the Cross of Christ.

In a hymn to this solitude which is "too unknown," Giustiniani says: "It is thou that announcest the coming of the Holy Spirit: and not only announcest Him, but bringest Him into the human heart just as the dawn, which announces the day, brings to our eyes the brightness of the sun."

This brings us to the mystical doctrine of Paul Giustiniani who, like the Fathers of the Church, believed that the eremitical life was ordered exclusively to contemplation and was the only purely contemplative life. Like the Fathers, also, when he speaks of contemplation he means mystical contemplation. This is without doubt the most interesting and important part of the book. In pages that remind us now of St. Catherine of Genoa, now of St. Bernard, now even of John Ruysbroeck, Paul Giustiniani teaches us a doctrine elevated but sure since his whole emphasis is on the coincidence of humility and greatness in the experience of union. The way of contemplation is never exalted, and the hermit must aspire to be "lifted up" in no other way than on the Cross, with Christ. He does not reach the Father except through the abjection of Christ, Who lives again in the hermit that *exinanivit semetipsum* by which He merited for us a share in His sonship and in His divine glory. Reading the pages of Giustiniani on annihilation we are reminded of St. John of the Cross, who describes the soul that is purified and ready for union with God in these terms:

"In this detachment the spiritual soul finds its quiet and repose; for, since it covets nothing, nothing wearies it when it is lifted up, and nothing oppresses it when it is cast down, for it is in the center of its humility; since, when it covets anything, at that very moment it becomes wearied." [5]

The whole purpose of the solitary life is to bring the soul into the "center of her humility" and to keep it there. The hermit does not pretend to have acquired any esoteric secret or any exalted technique by which he penetrates into the mystery of God. His only secret is the humility and poverty of Christ and the knowledge that God lifts up those who have fallen: *Dominus erigit elisos*. Without this humility, the contemplatives can be a prey to "all the illusions." For "the true servants of Christ love God with all their being, and do not love themselves at all. They keep themselves so perfectly under the guardianship of humility as to be known by God alone, but unknown to men."

But once he is perfectly united with the poverty and humility of Christ crucified, the solitary lives entirely by the life and Spirit of Christ. He can therefore be transformed and elevated to the perfection of selfless love for God, that love in which he no longer knows himself or anything else, but only God alone. This is the culmination of mystical love in which the contemplative "loves God in God." It is here that we detect interesting resonances from the doctrine of

[5] Ascent of Mt. Carmel—Vol. I, ch. 1, #13, p. 63 (Complete Works of Saint John of the Cross; Newman Press, 1949).

Ruysbroeck. Whether or not Giustiniani knew the Flemish mystic, a comparison between them might be interesting. This is not the place for it. What is more important here is to notice that this love for God in God, which is the highest perfection of the solitary and contemplative life is also the perfect justification of the hermit's utility to the rest of the Church.

The hermit is not to be considered a "dynamo" of apostolic power in the crude sense of a machine actively producing a great quantity of prayers and works of penance for the salvation of souls. We have seen that quantity becomes a negligible factor in the life of *eremitica puritas*. The solitary should not seek to replace his lost possessions by merely numerical accumulation of prayers and good works over which he can gloat like a happy miser at the end of each day. In praying to God for souls, he realizes it is not so important to know the souls for whom he is praying, as *Him to Whom* he is praying. But the perfect love of God teaches him to find souls in God Himself. He discovers that the soul which is on fire with love for God actually loves herself and other men more in proportion as she thinks about herself and them less. Hence the paradox that the less the contemplative seems to love others and himself, the more he forgets them in order to direct all his love to God, the more he actually loves them and the better he serves their spiritual interests. Loving God in God, the solitary is perfectly united to that infinite Love with which God loves all things in Himself. Loving all things in Him, the hermit powerfully cooperates with the action of His love, drawing them to Himself. Thus he fulfils most efficaciously the purpose of his divine vocation which is to restore all things in Christ. Consequently the fruitfulness of the hermit in the Church of

God depends on his fidelity to the call to solitude, obscurity and abjection in Christ.

The doctrine of Paul Giustiniani is therefore a striking testimony to the primacy of contemplation and of the contemplative life in the Church.

It does not follow from this that everyone who aspires to perfection should therefore seek to become a hermit. The eremitical life is a charism reserved for few. Most monks will remain in the cenobium. Nevertheless, the fact that cenobitic life is safer and of wider appeal does not imply that the eremitical life is unsafe and has no appeal. The cenobium and the hermitage complete each other. If the cenobium disdains and repudiates the hermitage, it dooms itself to mediocrity. When the windows of the monastery no longer open out upon the vast horizons of the desert, the monastic community inevitably becomes immersed in vanity. All that is accidental, trivial, and accessory tends to assume a rank of high importance and to become the sole end of the monastic life. It is where monks have forgotten their potential destiny to solitude that they allow themselves to run to seed in bickering about curiosities, or squandering their contemplative leisure in material cares.

The doctrine of Paul Giustiniani should remind us all of the monk's true destiny as a man of God. True, Paul Giustiniani lacks the freshness of Cassian and the Desert Fathers, the luminous simplicity of St. Benedict, or St. Gregory, even more the sober enthusiasm of St. Bernard or the Greek Fathers. There is something in him of dryness which he contracted from the stoics and from scholastic philosophy. But the genuine spirit of the desert is there, and the contemplation which brightens his pages is unmistakably true.

In closing this preface, I might observe that it is perhaps

something altogether new and unusual for a book on an Italian hermit to appear, written by a Benedictine in Luxemburg and prefaced by a Cistercian in the southern United States. This joining together of Camaldoli, Monte-Corona, Clervaux and Gethsemani is surely significant. I dare to hope that it speaks very well for the union of the sons of St. Benedict with one another in our time—a union in prayer and deep charity and mutual understanding. If it be true, as I think it is, then our monasticism indeed has a function in the world. And it proclaims to all who will hear it the solemn affirmation of Christ who said: "Behold I am with you all days, even to the consummation of the world." [6]

[6] Matthew, 28:19.

NOTES FOR A PHILOSOPHY
OF SOLITUDE*

"Un cri d'oiseau sur les récifs. . . ."
St John Perse.

ONE . *The tyranny of diversion*

1.   Why write about solitude in the first place? Certainly not in order to preach it, to exhort people to become

---

* This could also properly be called a "Philosophy of Monastic Life" if it be understood that a monk is, etymologically, a *monachos* or one who is isolated, alone. However since "monastic" now suggests not so much the man as the institution, I have seldom used the word "monk" in these pages. I am speaking of the solitary spirit which is really essential to the monastic view of life, but which is not confined to monasteries. Nor is it limited to men and women who have consecrated their lives to God by vow. Therefore, though I am treating of the traditional concept of the *monachos*, or solitary, I am deliberately discarding everything that can conjure up the artificial image of the monk in a cowl, dwelling in a medieval cloister. In this way I intend obviously, not to disparage or to reject the monastic institution, but to set aside all its accidentals and externals, so that they will not interfere with my view of what seems to me to be deepest and most essential. But by that same token, the "solitary" of these pages is never necessarily a "monk" (juridically) at all. He may well be a layman, and of the sort most remote from cloistered life, like Thoreau or Emily Dickenson.

solitary. What could be more absurd? Those who are to become solitary are, as a rule, solitary already. At most they are not yet aware of their condition. In which case, all they need is to discover it. But in reality, all men are solitary. Only most of them are so averse to being alone, or to feeling alone, that they do everything they can to forget their solitude. How? Perhaps in large measure by what Pascal called "divertissement"—diversion, systematic distraction. By those occupations and recreations, so mercifully provided by society, which enable a man to avoid his own company for twenty-four hours a day.

Even the worst society has something about it that is not only good, but essential for human life. Man cannot live without society, obviously. Those who claim they would like to do so, or that they might be able to do so, are often those who depend most abjectly upon it. Their pretense of solitude is only an admission of their dependence. It is an individualistic illusion.

Besides protecting man's natural life, enabling him to care for himself, society gives each individual a chance to transcend himself in the service of others and thus to become a person. But no one becomes a person merely by diversion—in the sense of *divertissement*. For the function of diversion is simply to anesthetize the individual as individual, and to plunge him in the warm, apathetic stupor of a collectivity which, like himself, wishes to remain amused. The bread and circuses which fulfil this function may be blatant and absurd, or they may assume a hypocritical air of intense seriousness, for instance in a mass movement. Our own society prefers the absurd. But our absurdity is blended with a certain hard-headed, fully determined seriousness with which we devote ourselves to the acquisition of money, to the satisfaction of our appetite for status, and our justification of ourselves as contrasted with the totalitarian iniquity of our opposite number.

2.   In a society like ours, there are obviously many people for whom solitude is a problem or even a temptation. I am perhaps in no position to resolve their problem or to exorcise their temptation. But it is possible that—knowing something at least of interior solitude—I might be able to say something of it which will reassure those tempted ones. At least I can suggest that if they have not been able to rest in the fervid consolations which are lavished upon them by society itself, that they do not need to seek such rest as that. They are perhaps perfectly capable of doing without such reassurance. They ought possibly to realize that they have less need of diversion than they are told, with such dogmatic self-complacency, by the organization men. They can confidently detach themselves from the engineers of the human soul whose talents are devoted to the cult of publicity Such an influence in their life is truly, as they tend to suspect, as unnecessary as it is irritating. But I do not promise to make it unavoidable.

Nor do I promise to cheer anybody up with optimistic answers to all the sordid difficulties and uncertainties which attend the life of interior solitude. Perhaps in the course of these reflections, some of the difficulties will be mentioned. The first of them has to be taken note of from the very start: the disconcerting task of facing and accepting one's own absurdity. The anguish of realizing that underneath the apparently logical pattern of a more or less "well organized" and rational life, there lies an abyss of irrationality, confusion, pointlessness, and indeed of apparent chaos. This is what immediately impresses itself upon the man who has renounced diversion. It cannot be otherwise: for in renouncing diversion, he renounces the seemingly harmless pleasure of building a tight, self-contained illusion about himself and about his little world. He accepts the difficulty of facing the million things in his life which are incomprehensible, instead of simply ignoring them. Incidentally it is only when the apparent absurdity of life is faced in all truth that faith really becomes possible. Otherwise, faith tends to be a kind of diversion, a spiritual amusement, in which one gathers up accepted, conventional formulas and arranges them in the approved mental patterns, without bothering to investigate their meaning, or asking if they have any practical consequences in one's life.

3.   One of the first essentials of the interior solitude of which I speak is that it is the actualization of a faith in which a man takes responsibility for his own inner life. He faces its full mystery, in the presence of the invisible God. And he takes upon himself the lonely, barely comprehensible, incommunicable task of working his way through the darkness of his own mystery until he discovers that his mystery and the mystery of God merge into one reality, which is the only reality. That God lives in him and he in God—not presicely in the way that words seem to suggest (for words have no power to comprehend the reality) but in a way that makes words, and even attempts to communicate, seem utterly illusory.

The words of God, the words which unite in "One Body" the society of those who truly believe, have the power to signify the mystery of our loneliness and oneness in Christ, to point the way into its darkness. They have the power, also, to illuminate the darkness. But they do so by losing the shape of words and becoming—not thoughts, not things, but the unspeakable beating of a Heart within the heart of one's own life.

4.   Every man is a solitary, held firmly by the inexorable

limitations of his own aloneness. Death makes this very clear, for when a man dies, he dies alone. The only one for whom the bell tolls, in all literal truth, is the one who is dying. It tolls "for thee" in so far as death is common to all of us, but obviously we do not all die at one and the same moment. We die *like* one another. The presence of many living men around the deathbed of one who is in agony may unite them all in the mystery of death, but it also unites them in a mystery of living solitude. It paradoxically unites them while reminding them acutely—and beyond words—of their isolation. Each one will have to die, and die *alone*. And, at the same time (but this is what they do not want to see) each one must also *live* alone. For we must remember that the Church is at the same time community and solitude. The dying Christian is one with the Church, but he also suffers the loneliness of Christ's agony in Gethsemani.

Very few men are able to face this fact squarely. And very few are expected to do so. It is the special vocation of certain ones who dedicate their whole lives to wrestling with solitude. An "agony" is a "wrestling." The dying man in agony wrestles with solitude. But the wrestling with one's solitude is also a life-work—a "life agony." When a man is called to be a solitary—(even if only interiorly)—he does not need to be anything else, nor can anything else be demanded of him except that he remain physically or spiritually alone fighting his battle which few can understand. His function in the Church—a social function and a spiritual one—is to remain in the "cell" of his aloneness, whether it be a real cell in the desert, or simply the spiritual cell of his own incomprehensible emptiness: and, as the desert fathers used to say, his "cell will teach him all things."

5.   The true solitary is not one who simply withdraws

from society. Mere withdrawal, regression, leads to a sick solitude, without meaning and without fruit. The solitary of whom I speak is called not to leave society but to transcend it: not to withdraw from the fellowship with other men but to renounce the appearance, the myth of union in diversion in order to attain to union on a higher and more spiritual level—the mystical level of the Body of Christ. He renounces that union with his immediate neighbors which is apparently achieved through the medium of the aspirations, fictions and conventions prevalent in his social group. But in so doing he attains to the basic, invisible, mysterious unity which makes all men "One Man" in Christ's Church beyond and in spite of natural social groups which, by their special myths and slogans, keep a man in a state of division.

The solitary, then has a mysterious and apparently absurd vocation to supernatural unity. He seeks a spiritual and simple oneness in himself which, when it is found, paradoxically becomes the oneness of all men—a oneness beyond separation, conflict and schism. For it is only when each man is one that mankind will once again become "One." But the solitary realizes that the images and myths of a particular group—projections of the interests, ideals and sins of that group—can take possession of him and divide him against himself.

The illusions and fictions encouraged by the appetite for self-affirmation in certain restricted groups, have much to be said for them and much to be said against them. They do in practice free a man from his individual limitations and help him, in some measure, to transcend himself. And if every society were ideal, then every society would help its members only to a fruitful and productive self-transcendence. But in fact societies tend to lift a man above himself only far enough to make him a useful and submissive instrument in whom the aspirations, lusts and needs of the group can function unhindered by too delicate a personal conscience. Social life tends to form and educate a man, but generally at the price of a simultaneous deformation and perversion. This is because civil society is never ideal, always a mixture of good and evil, and always tending to present the evil in itself as a form of good.

6.   There are crimes which no one would commit as an individual which he willingly and bravely commits when acting in the name of his society, because he has been (too easily) convinced that evil is entirely different when it is done "for the common good." As an example, one might point to the way in which racial hatreds and even persecution are admitted by people who consider themselves, and perhaps in some sense are, kind, tolerant, civilized and even humane. But they have acquired a special deformity of conscience as a result of their identification with their group, their immersion in their particular society. This deformation is the price they pay to forget and to exorcise that solitude which seems to them to be a demon.

7.   The solitary is one who is called to make one of the most terrible decisions possible to man: the decision to disagree completely with those who imagine that the call to diversion and self-deception is the voice of truth and who can summon the full authority of their own prejudice to prove it. He is therefore bound to sweat blood in anguish, in order to be loyal to God, to the Mystical Christ, and to humanity as a whole, rather than to the idol which is offered to him, for his homage, by a particular group. He must renounce the blessing of every convenient illusion that absolves him from responsibility when he is untrue to his deepest self and to his inmost truth—the image of God in his own soul.

The price of fidelity in such a task is a completely dedicated humility—an emptiness of heart in which self-assertion has no place. For if he is not empty and undivided in his own inmost soul, the solitary will be nothing more than an individualist. And in that case, his non-conformity is nothing but an act of rebellion: the substitution of idols and illusions of his own choosing for those chosen by society. And this, of course, is the greatest of dangers. It is both futility and madness. It leads only to ruin.

For to forget oneself, at least to the extent of preferring a social myth with a certain limited productiveness, is a lesser evil than clinging to a private myth which is only a sterile dream. And so, as Heraclitus said long ago, "We must not act and speak like sleepers . . . The waking have one common world, but the sleeping turn aside each into a world of his own." Hence the vocation to solitude is not a vocation to the warm narcissistic dream of a private religion. It is a vocation to become *fully awake*, even more than the common somnolence permits one to be, with its arbitrary selection of approved dreams, mixed with a few really valid and fruitful conceptions.

8.　　　　It should be clear from the start then that the solitary worthy of the name lives not in a world of private fictions and self-constructed delusions, but in a world of emptiness, humility, and purity beyond the reach of slogans and beyond the gravitational pull of diversions that alienate him from God and from himself. He lives in unity. His solitude is neither an argument, an accusation, a reproach or a sermon. It is simply itself. It *is*. And therefore it not only does not attract attention, or desire it, but it remains, for the most part, completely invisible.

9.　　　　It should be quite clear then, that there is no question in these pages of the eccentric and regressive solitude that clamors for recognition, and which seeks to focus more pleasurably and more intently on itself by stepping back from the crowd. But unfortunately, however often I may repeat this warning, it will not be heeded. Those who most need to hear it are incapable of doing so. They think that solitude is a heightening of self-consciousness an intensification of pleasure in self. It is a more secret and more perfect diversion. What they want is not the hidden, metaphysical agony of the hermit but the noisy self-congratulations and self-pity of the infant in the cradle. Ultimately what they want is not the desert but the womb.

The individualist in practice completely accepts the social fictions around him, but accepts them in such a way that they provide a suitable background against which a few private and favored fictions of his own can make an appearance. Without the social background, his individual fictions would not be able to assert themselves, and he himself would no longer be able to fix his attention upon them.

TWO . *In the sea of perils*

1.   There is no need to say that the call of solitude (even though only interior) is perilous. Everyone who knows what solitude means is aware of this. The essence of the solitary vocation is precisely the anguish of an almost infinite risk. Only the false solitary sees no danger in solitude. But his solitude is imaginary, that is to say built around an image. It is merely a social image stripped of its explicitly social elements. The false solitary is one who is able to imagine himself without companions while in reality he remains just as dependent on society as before—if not more dependent. He needs society as a ventriloquist needs a

dummy. He projects his own voice to the group and it comes back to him admiring, approving, opposing or at least adverting to his own separateness.

Even if society seems to condemn him, this pleases and diverts him for it is nothing but the sound of his own voice, reminding him of his separateness, which is his chosen diversion. True solitude is not mere separateness. It tends only to *unity*.

2.   The true solitary does not renounce anything that is basic and human about his relationship to other men. He is deeply united to them—all the more deeply because he is no longer entranced by marginal concerns. What he renounces is the superficial imagery and the trite symbolism that pretend to make the relationship more genuine and more fruitful. He gives up his lax self-abandonment to general diversion. He renounces vain pretenses of solidarity that tend to substitute themselves for real solidarity, while masking an inner spirit of irresponsibility and selfishness. He renounces illusory claims of collective achievement and fulfilment, by which society seeks to gratify and assuage the individual's need to feel that he amounts to something.

The man who is dominated by what I have called the "social image" is one who allows himself to see and to approve in himself only that which his society prescribes as beneficial and praiseworthy in its members. As a corollary he sees and disapproves (usually in *others*) mostly what his society disapproves. And yet he congratulates himself on "thinking for himself." In reality, this is only a game that he plays in his own mind—the game of substituting the words, slogans and concepts he has received from society, for genuine experiences of his own. Or rather—the slogans of society are felt to rise up within him as if they were his own, "spontaneous experience." How can such a man be really "social"? He is imprisoned in an illusion and cut off from real, living contact with his fellow man. Yet he does not feel himself to be in any way "alone!"

3.   The solitary is first of all one who renounces this arbitrary social imagery. When his nation wins a war or sends a rocket to the moon, he can get along without feeling as if he personally had won the war or hit the moon with a rocket. When his nation is rich and arrogant, he does not feel that he himself is more fortunate and more honest, as well as more powerful than the citizens of other, more "backward" nations. More than this: he is able to despise war and to see the futility of rockets to the moon in a way quite different and more fundamental from the way in which his society may tolerate these negative views. That is to say, he despises the criminal, bloodthirsty arrogance of his own nation or class, as much as that of "the enemy." He despises his own self-seeking aggressivity as much as that of the politicians who hypocritically pretend they are fighting for peace.

4.   Most men cannot live fruitfully without a large proportion of fiction in their thinking. If they do not have some efficacious mythology around which to organize their activities, they will regress into a less efficacious, more primitive, more chaotic set of illusions. When the ancients said that the solitary was likely to be either a god or a beast, they meant that he would either achieve a rare intellectual and spiritual independence, or sink into a more complete and brutish dependence. The solitary easily plunges into a cavern of darkness and of phantoms more horrible and more absurd than the most inane set of conventional social images. The suffering he must then face is neither salutary nor noble. It is catastrophic.

5.   I do not pretend, in these pages to establish a

clear formula for discerning solitary vocations. But this much needs to be said: that one who is called to solitude is not called merely to imagine himself solitary, to live as if he were solitary, to cultivate the illusion that he is different, withdrawn and elevated. He is called to emptiness. And in this emptiness he does not find points upon which to base a contrast between himself and others. On the contrary, he realizes, though perhaps confusedly, that he has entered into a *solitude that is really shared by everyone*. It is not that he is solitary while everybody else is social: but that everyone is solitary, in a solitude masked by that symbolism which they use to cheat and counteract their solitariness. What the solitary renounces is not his union with other men, but rather the deceptive fictions and inadequate symbols which tend to take the place of genuine social unity—to produce a façade of apparent unity without really uniting men on a deep level. Example—the excitement and fictitious engagement of a football crowd. This is to say, of course, that the Christian solitary is fully and perfectly a man of the Church.

Even though he may be physically alone the solitary remains united to others and lives in profound solidarity with them, but on a deeper and mystical level. They may think he is one with them in the vain interests and preoccupations of a superficial social existence. He realizes that he is one with them in the peril and anguish of their common solitude: not the solitude of the individual only, but the radical and essential *solitude of man*—a solitude which was assumed by Christ and which, in Christ, becomes mysteriously identified with the solitude of God.

6.　　　The solitary is one who is aware of solitude in himself as a basic and inevitable human reality, not just as something which affects him as an isolated individual. Hence his solitude is the foundation of a deep, pure and gentle sympathy with all other men, whether or not they are capable of realizing the tragedy of their plight. More—it is the doorway by which he enters into the mystery of God, and brings others into that mystery by the power of his love and his humility.

7.   The emptiness of the true solitary is marked then by a great simplicity. This simplicity can be deceptive, because it may be hidden under a surface of apparent complexity, but it is there nevertheless, behind the outer contradictions of the man's life. It manifests itself in a kind of candor though he may be very reticent. There is in this lonely one a gentleness, a deep sympathy, though he may be apparently unsocial. There is a great purity of love, though he may hesitate to manifest his love in any way, or to commit himself openly to it. Underneath the complications that are produced in him by his uneasiness with social images, the man tends to live without images, without too much conceptual thought. When you get to know him well—which is sometimes possible—you may find in him not so much a man who seeks solitude as one who has already found it, or been found by it. His problem then is not to find what he already has, but to discover what to do about it.

8.   One who has made the discovery of his inner solitude, or is just about to make it, may need considerable spiritual help. A wise man, who knows the plight of the new solitary, may with the right word at the right time spare him the pain of seeking vainly some long and complex statement of his case. No such statement is necessary: he has simply discovered what it means to be a man. And he has begun to realize that what he sees in himself is not a spiritual luxury but a difficult, humiliating responsibility: the obligation to be spiritually mature.

9.   The solitary condition also has its jargon and its

conventions: these too are pitiful. There is no point in consoling one who has awakened to his solitude by teaching him to defile his emptiness with rationalizations. Solitude must not become a diversion to itself by too much self-justification. At least allow the lonely one to meet his emptiness and come to terms with it: for it is really his destiny and his joy. Too many people are ready to draw him back at any price from what they conceive to be the edge of the abyss. True, it is an abyss: but they do not realize that he who is called to solitude is called to walk across the air of the abyss without danger, because, after all, the abyss is only himself. He should not be forced to feel guilty about it, for in this solitude and emptiness of his heart there is another, more inexplicable solitude. Man's loneliness is, in fact, the loneliness of God. That is why it is such a great thing for a man to discover his solitude and learn to live in it. For there he finds that he and God are one: that God is alone as he himself is alone. That God wills to be alone in him.

When this is understood, then one sees that his duty is to be faithful to solitude because in this way he is faithful to God. Fidelity is everything. From it the solitary can expect truth and strength, light and wisdom at the right time. If he is not faithful to the inner anonymity and emptiness which are the secret of his whole life, then he can expect nothing but confusion.

10.   Like everything else in the Christian life, the vocation to spiritual solitude can be understood only within the perspectives of God's mercy to man in the Incarnation of Christ. If there is any such thing as a Christian hermit, then he must be a man who has a special function in the mystical body of Christ—a hidden and spiritual function, and perhaps all the more vital because more hidden. But this

social function of the solitary contemplative, precisely because it has to be invisible, cannot be allowed in any way to detract from his genuinely solitary character. On the contrary, his function in the Christian community is the paradoxical one of living outwardly separated from the community. And this, whether he is conscious of it or not, is a witness to the completely transcendental character of the Christian mystery of our unity in Christ.

The hermit remains to put us on our guard against our natural obsession with the visible, social and communal forms of Christian life which tend at times to be inordinately active, and often become deeply involved in the life of secular, non-Christian society. It is true to say of every Christian that he is in the world but not of it. But in case he might be likely to forget this—or worse still in case he might never come to know it at all—there must be men who have completely renounced the world: men who are neither in the world nor of it. In our day, when "the world" is everywhere, even in the desert where it makes and proves its secret weapons, the solitary retains his unique and mysterious function. But he will fulfil it perhaps in many paradoxical ways. Wherever he does so, even where he is unseen, he testifies to the essentially mystical bond of unity which binds Christians together in the Holy Spirit. Whether he is seen or not, he bears witness to the unity of Christ by possessing in himself the fullness of Christian charity.

In fact, the early Christians who went into the desert to see the hermits of Nitria and Scete admired in them not so much their extreme asceticism as their charity and discretion. The miracle of the Desert Fathers was precisely that a man could live entirely separate from the visible Christian community with its normal liturgical functions, and still be full of the charity of Christ. He was able to be so only because he was completely empty of himself. The vocation to solitude is therefore at the same time a vocation to silence, poverty and emptiness. But the emptiness is for the sake of fulness: the purpose of the solitary life is, if you like, contemplation. But not contemplation in the pagan sense of an intellectual, esoteric enlightenment, achieved by ascetic technique. The contemplation of the Christian solitary is the awareness of the divine mercy transforming and elevating his own emptiness and turning it into the presence of perfect love, perfect fulness.

Hence a Christian can turn his back on society, even on the society of his fellow Christians, without necessarily hating society. This is because of the spiritual and mystical character of the Christian Church—the same spiritual character which accounts for the fact that one who renounces marriage in order to be a priest or a monk can thereby, if he is faithful, attain to a higher and more spiritual fruitfulness. So a Christian hermit can, by being alone, paradoxically live even closer to the heart of the Church than one who is in the midst of her apostolic activities. The life and unity of the Church are, and must be, visible. But that does not mean that the invisible and spiritual activities of men of prayer are not supremely important. On the contrary, the invisible and more mysterious life of prayer is *essential* to the Church. Solitaries, too, are essential to her!

11.   Withdrawal from other men can be a special form of love for them. It should never be a rejection of man or of his society. But it may well be a quiet and humble refusal to accept the myths and fictions with which social life cannot help but be full—especially today. To despair of the illusions and façades which man builds around himself is certainly not to despair of man. On the contrary, it may be a sign of love and of hope. For when we love someone,

we refuse to tolerate what destroys and maims his personality. If we love mankind, can we blind ourselves to man's predicament? You will say: we must do something about his predicament. But there are some whose vocation it is to realize that they, at least, cannot help in any overt social way. Their contribution is a mute witness, a secret and even invisible expression of love which takes the form of their own option for solitude in preference to the acceptance of social fictions. For is not our involvement in fiction, particularly in political and demagogic fiction, and implicit confession that we despair of man and even of God?

12.   Christian hope in God and in the world to come is inevitably also hope in man, or at least *for* man. How can we despair of man when the Word of God was made man in order to save us all? But our Christian hope is, and must remain, inviolably pure. It must work and struggle in the chaos of conflicting policy which is the world of egotism: and in order to do so it must take on visible, symbolic forms by which to declare its message. But when these symbols become confused with other secular symbols, then there is danger that faith itself will be corrupted by fictions, and there is a consequent obligation, on the part of some Christians, to affirm their faith in all its intransigent purity.

At such a time, some men will seek clarity in isolation and silence, not because they think they know better than the rest, but because they want to see life in a different perspective. They want to withdraw from the babel of confusion in order to listen more patiently to the voice of their conscience and to the Holy Spirit. And by their prayers and their fidelity they will invisibly renew the life of the whole Church. This renewal will communicate itself to others who remain "in the world" and will help them also to regain a clearer vision, a sharper and more unpromising appreciation of Christian truth. These will give themselves to apostolic work on a new level of seriousness and of faith. They will be able to discard fictitious gestures of zeal in favor of genuine self-sacrificing love. So when, as in our time, the whole world seems to have become one immense and idiotic fiction, and when the virus of mendacity creeps into every vein and organ of the social body, it would be abnormal and immoral if there were no re-action. It is even healthy that the reaction should sometimes take the form of outspoken protest, as long as we remember that solitude is no refuge for the rebellious. And if there is an element of protest in the solitary vocation, that element must be a matter of rigorous spirituality. It must be deep and interior, and intimately personal, so that the solitary is one who is critical, first of all, of himself. Otherwise he will divert himself with a fiction worse than that of all the others, be-coming a more insane and self-opinionated liar than the worst of them, cheating no one more than himself. Solitude is not for rebels like this, and it promptly rejects them. The desert is for those who have felt a salutary despair of conventional and fictitious values, in order to hope in mercy and to be themselves merciful men to whom that mercy is promised. Such solitaries know the evils that are in other men because they experience these evils first of all in themselves.

Such men, out of pity for the universe, out of loyalty to mankind, and without a spirit of bitterness or of resent-ment, withdraw into the healing silence of the wilderness, or of poverty, or of obscurity, not in order to preach to others but to heal in themselves the wounds of the entire world.

13.   The message of God's mercy to man must be preached. The word of truth must be proclaimed. No one can deny this. But there are not a few who are beginning to feel the futility of adding more words to the constant flood of lan-guage that pours meaninglessly over everybody, everywhere,

from morning to night. For language to have meaning, there must be intervals of silence somewhere, to divide word from word and utterance from utterance. He who retires into silence does not necessarily hate language. Perhaps it is love and respect for language which impose silence upon him. For the mercy of God is not heard in words unless it is heard, both before and after the words are spoken, in silence.

14.   There have always been, and always will be, men who are alone in the midst of society without realizing why. They are condemned to their strange isolation by temperament or circumstance, and they get used to it. It is not of these that I am speaking, but of those who having led active and articulate lives in the world of men, leave their old life behind and go into the desert. The desert does not necessarily have to be physical—it can be found even in the midst of men. But it is not found by human aspirations or idealism. It is mysteriously designated by the finger of God.

15.   There have always been solitaries who, by virtue of a special purity, and simplicity of heart, have been destined from their earliest youth to an eremitical and contemplative life, in some official form. These are the clear, uncomplicated vocations, and I do not speak explicitly of them here either. They have known from an early age that their destination was a Charterhouse or a Camaldolese cell. Or they have found their way, as though by unerring instinct, into the place where they will be alone. The Church has welcomed these without question and without trouble into the "shadowy" (*umbratilis*) life of peace which she has reserved for her most favored children. There, in the peace and silence of a solitude fully recognized, protected and approved by the Highest Authority of the Church, they live their lives, not without the sufferings and the complexities

which in solitude are unavoidable, but in a peace and assurance which are a rare guarantee of a truly special vocation.

It is not of these that I speak but of the paradoxical, tormented solitaries for whom there is no real place; men and women who have not so much chosen solitude as been chosen by it. And these have not generally found their way into the desert either through simplicity or through innocence. Theirs is the solitude that is reached the hard way, through bitter suffering and disillusionment.

To say that they have been "found" and chosen by solitude is a metaphor that must not be taken to mean that they have been drawn into it entirely passively. The solitude of which I speak is not full grown and true until it has been elected by a deep interior decision. Solitude may choose and select a man for herself, but he is not hers unless he has accepted. On the other hand no amount of deciding will do any good, if one has not first been invited to make the decision. The door to solitude opens only from the inside. This is true of both solitudes, the exterior and the interior. No matter how alone one may be, if he has not been invited ot interior solitude and accepted the invitation with full consciousness of what he is doing, he cannot be what I call a *monachos*, or solitary. But one who has made this choice and kept to it is always alone, no matter how many people there may be around him. Not that he is withdrawn from them, or that he is not one of them. His solitude is not of that order at all. It does not set him apart from them in contrast and self-affirmation. It affirms nothing. It is at the same time empty and universal. He is one, not by virtue of separation but by virtue of inner spiritual unity. And this inner unity is at the same time the inner unity of all. Needless to say, such unity is secret and unknown. Even those who enter it, know it only, so to speak, by "unknowing."

It should therefore be clear that one who seeks to enter into this kind of solitude by affirming himself, and separating himself from others, and intensifying his awareness of his own individual being, is only travelling further and further away from it. But the one who has been found by solitude, and invited to enter it, and has entered freely, falls into the desert the way a ripe fruit falls out of a tree. It does not matter what kind of a desert it may be: in the midst of men or far from them. It is the one vast desert of emptiness which belongs to no one and to everyone. It is the place of silence where one word is spoken by God. And in that word are spoken both God Himself and all things.

16.   Often the lonely and the empty have found their way into this pure silence only after many false starts. They have taken many wrong roads, even roads that were totally alien to their character and vocation. They have repeatedly contradicted themselves and their own inmost truth. Their very nature seems itself to be a contradiction. They have perhaps few "clear signs" of *any* vocation. But they end up nevertheless alone. Their way is to have no way. Their destiny is poverty, emptiness, anonymity.

17.   Of course, everyone with any sense sees, from time to time, in a lucid moment, the folly and triviality of our conventionalized attitudes. It is possible for anyone to dream of liberty. But to undertake the wretched austerity of living in complete honesty, without convention, and therefore without support, is quite another matter. That is why there exist communities of beatniks, of esoteric thinkers and cultists, of quasi-religious faddists, of western followers of oriental religions. The break with the big group is compensated

by enrollment in the little group. It is a flight not into solitude but into a protesting minority. Such a flight may be more or less honest, more or less honorable. Certainly it inspires the anger of those who believe themselves to be the "right thinking majority" and it necessarily comes in for its fair share of mockery on that account. Perhaps this mockery is so welcome as to contribute, negatively, to the process of falsification and corruption which these groups almost always undergo. They abandon one illusion which is forced on everyone and substitute for it another, more esoteric illusion, of their own making. They have the satisfaction of making a choice, but not the fulfilment of having chosen reality.

18.   The true solitary is not called to an illusion, to the contemplation of himself as solitary. He is called to the nakedness and hunger of a more primitive and honest condition. The condition of a stranger (*xeniteia*) and a wanderer on the face of the earth, who has been called out of what was familiar to him in order to seek strangely and painfully after he knows not what.

And in demanding "honesty" of the hermit, let us not be too hypocritically exacting. He too may have his eccentricities. He may rely heavily on certain imperfect solutions to problems which his human weakness does not allow him to cope with fully. Let us not condemn him for failing to solve problems we have not even dared to face.

The solitary life is an arid, rugged purification of the heart. St. Jerome and St. Eucherius have written rhapsodies about the flowering desert, but Jerome was the busiest hermit that ever lived and Eucherius was a bishop who admired the hermit brethren of Lerins only from afar. The *eremi cultores*, the farmers of the desert sand, have had less to say about the experience. They have been washed out by dryness, and their burnt lips are weary of speech.

19.   The solitary who no longer communicates with other men except for the bare necessities of life is a man with a special and difficult task. He is called to be, in some way, invisible. He soon loses all sense of his significance for the rest of the world. And yet that significance is great. The hermit has a very real place in a world like ours that has degraded the human person and lost all respect for that awesome loneliness in which each single spirit must confront the living God.

20.   In the eyes of our conformist society, the hermit is nothing but a failure. He has to be a failure—we have absolutely no use for him, no place for him. He is outside all our projects, plans, assemblies, movements. We can countenance him as long as he remains only a fiction, or a dream. As soon as he becomes real, we are revolted by his insignificance, his poverty, his shabbiness, his total lack of status. Even those who consider themselves contemplatives, often cherish a secret contempt for the solitary. For in the contemplative life of the hermit there is none of that noble security, that intelligent depth, that artistic finesse which the more academic contemplative seeks in his sedate respectability.

21.   It has never been either practical or useful to leave all things and follow Christ. And yet it is spiritually prudent. Practical utility and supernatural prudence are sometimes flatly opposed to one another, as wisdom of the flesh and prudence of the spirit. Not that the spirit can never allow itself to accomplish things in a practical, temporal way. But it does not rest in purely temporal ends. Its accomplishments belong to a higher and more spiritual order—which is of course necessarily hidden. Practical utility has its roots in the present life. Supernatural prudence lives for the world to come. It weighs all things in the balance of eternity. Spiritual things have no weight for the "practical" man. The

solitary life is something that cannot even tip his scales. It is "nothing," a non-entity. Yet St Paul says: "The foolish things of the world hath God chosen that He may confound the wise, and the weak things of the world hath God chosen that He may confound the strong. And the base things of the world, and the things that are contemptible hath God chosen, and things that are not, that He might bring to nought things that are." (I Corinthians, 1:27,28)

And why is this? "That no flesh should glory in His sight." It is the invisible glory that is real. The empty horizons of the solitary life enable us to grow accustomed to a light that is not seen where the mirage of secular pursuits fascinates and deludes our gaze.

22.   The hermit remains there to prove, by his lack of practical utility and the apparent sterility of his vocation, that cenobitic monks themselves ought to have little significance in the world, or indeed none at all. They are dead to the world, they should no longer cut a figure in it. And the world is dead to them. They are pilgrims in it, isolated witnesses of another kingdom. This of course is the price they pay for universal compassion, for a sympathy that reaches all. The monk is compassionate in proportion as he is less practical and less successful, because the job of being a success in a competitive society leaves one no time for compassion.

The monk has all the more of a part to play in our world, because he has no proper place in it.

THREE . *Spiritual poverty*

1.   One of the most telling criticisms of the solitary may well be that even in his life of prayer he is less "productive." You would think that in his solitude he would

quickly reach the level of visions, of mystical marriage, something dramatic at any rate. Yet he may well be poorer than the cenobite, *even in his life of prayer*. His is a weak and precarious existence, he has more cares, he is more insecure, he has to struggle to preserve himself from all kinds of petty annoyances, and often he fails to do so. His poverty is spiritual. It invades his whole soul as well as his body, and in the end his whole patrimony is one of insecurity. He enjoys the sorrow, the spiritual and intellectual indigence of the really poor. Obviously such a vocation has in it a grain of folly. Otherwise it is not what it is meant to be, a life of direct dependence on God, in darkness, insecurity and pure faith. The life of the hermit is a life of material and physical poverty without visible support.

2.   Of course, one must not exaggerate or be too absolute in this matter. Absolutism itself can become a kind of "fortune" and "honor." We must also face the fact that the average human being is incapable of a life in which austerity is without compromise. There comes a limit, beyond which human weakness cannot go, and where mitigation itself enters in as a subtle form of poverty. Maybe the hermit turns out, unaccountably, to have his ulcer just like the next man. No doubt he has to drink large quantities of milk and perhaps take medicines. This finally disposes of any hope of him becoming a legendary figure. He, too, worries. Perhaps he worries even more than others, for it is only in the minds of those who know nothing about it that the solitary life appears to be a life free from all care.

3.   We must remember that Robinson Crusoe was one of the great myths of the middle class, commercial civilization of the eighteenth and nineteenth centuries: the myth not of eremitical solitude but of pragmatic individualism. Crusoe is a symbolical figure in an era when every man's

house was his castle in the trees, but only because every man was a very prudent and resourceful citizen who knew how to make the best out of the least and could drive a hard bargain with any competitor, even life itself. Carefree Crusoe was happy because he had an answer to everything. The real hermit is not so sure he has an answer.

4.   It is true that the solitary life must also be a life of prayer and meditation, if it is to be authentically Christian. For the *monachos* in our context is purely and simply a man of God. This should be clear. But what prayer! What meditation! Nothing more like bread and water than this interior prayer of his! Utter poverty. Often an incapacity to pray, to see, to hope. Not the sweet passivity which the books extol, but a bitter, arid struggle to press forward through a blinding sandstorm. The solitary may well beat his head against a wall of doubt. That may be the full extent of his contemplation. Do not mistake my meaning. It is not a question of intellectual doubt, an analytical investigation of the theological, philosophical or some other truths. It is something else, a kind of unknowing of his own self, a kind of doubt that questions the very roots of his own existence, a doubt which undermines his very reasons for existing and for doing what he does. It is this doubt which reduces him finally to silence, and in the silence which ceases to ask questions, he receives the only certitude he knows: The presence of God in the midst of uncertainty and nothingness, as the only reality but as a reality which cannot be "placed" or identified.

Hence the solitary man says nothing, and does his work, and is patient, (or perhaps impatient, I don't know) but generally he has peace. It is not the world's kind of peace. He is happy, but he never has a good time. He knows where he is going, but he is not "sure of his way," he just knows by going there. He does not see the way beforehand, and when he arrives, he arrives. His arrivals are usually departures from anything that resembles a "way." That is his way. But he cannot understand it. Neither can we.

5.   Beyond and in all this, he possesses his solitude, the riches of his emptiness, his interior poverty but of course, it is not a possession. It is simply an established fact. It is there. It is assured. In fact, it is inescapable. It is everything. It contains God, surrounds him in God, plunges him in God. So great is his poverty that he does not even see God: so great are his riches that he is lost in God and lost to himself. He is never far enough away from God to see Him in perspective, or as an object. He is swallowed up in Him, and therefore so to speak, never sees Him at all.

6.   All that we can say of this indigence of the lonely life must not make us forget the fact that this man is happy in his solitude, but especially because he has ceased to regard himself as a solitary in contradistinction to others who are not solitary. He simply is. And if he has been impoverished and set aside by the will of God, this is not a distinction, but purely and simply a fact. His solitude is sometimes frightening, sometimes a burden, yet it is more precious to him than anything else because it is for him the will of God,—not a thing willed by God, not an object decreed by a remote power, but simply the pressure, upon his own life, of that pure actuality which is the will of God, the reality of all that is real. His solitude is, for him simply reality. He could not break away from this will even if he wanted to. To be prisoner of this love is to be free, and almost to be in paradise. Hence the life of solitude is a life of love without consolation, a life that is fruitful because it is pressed down

and running over with the will of God: and all that has his will in it is full of significance, even when it appears to make no sense at all.

7.   The terror of the lonely life is the mystery and uncertainty with which the will of God presses upon our soul. It is much easier, and gentler, and more secure to have the will of God filtered to us quietly through society, through decrees of men, through the orders of others. To take this will straight in all its incomprehensible, baffling mystery, is not possible to one who is not secretly protected and guided by the Holy Spirit and no one should try it unless he has some assurance that he really has been called to it by God. And this call, of course, should be made clear by Directors and Superiors. One has to be born into solitude carefully, patiently and after long delay, out of the womb of society. One cannot rashly presume to become a solitary merely by his own will. This is no security outside the guidance of the Church.

8.   The lone man remains in the world as a prophet to whom no one listens as a voice crying in the desert, as a sign of contradiction. The world necessarily rejects him and in that act, rejects the dreaded solitude of God Himself. For that is what the world resents about God: His utter otherness, His absolute incapacity to be absorbed into the context of worldly and practical slogans, His mysterious transcendency which places Him infinitely beyond the reach of catchwords, advertisements and politics. It is easier for the world to recreate a god in its own image, a god who justifies its own slogans, when there are no solitaries about to remind men of the solitude of God: the God Who cannot become a member of any purely human fellowship. And yet this Solitary God has called men to another fellowship, with Himself, through the Passion and Resurrection of Christ—

through the solitude of Gethsemani and of Cavalry, and the mystery of Easter, and the solitude of the Ascension: all of which precede the great communion of Pentecost.

9.   The lonely man's function is to remain in existence as solitary, as poor and as unacceptable as God Himself in the souls of so many men. The solitary is there to tell them, in a way they can barely understand, that if they were able to discover and appreciate their own inner solitude they would immediately discover God and find out, from His word to them, that they are really persons.

10.   It is often said that exterior solitude is not only dangerous, but totally unnecessary. Unnecessary because all that really matters is interior solitude. And this can be obtained without physical isolation.

There is in this statement a truth more terrible than can be imagined by those who make it, so readily and with so little awareness of the irony implicit in their words.

11.   Indeed there is a special irony about solitude in community: that if you are called to solitude by God, even if you live in a community your solitude will be inescapable. Even if you are surrounded by the comfort and the assistance of others, the bonds that unite you with them on a trivial level break one by one so that you are no longer supported by them, that is, no longer sustained by the instinctive, automatic mechanisms of collective life. Their words, their enthusiasms become meaningless. Yet you do not despise them, or reject them. You try to find if there is not still some way to comprehend them and live by them. And you find that words have no value in such a situation. The only thing that can help you is the deep, wordless communion of genuine love.

At such a time it is a great relief to be put in contact with others by some simple task, some function of the ministry.

Then you meet them not with your words or theirs, but with the words and sacramental gestures of God. The word of God takes on an ineffable purity and strength when it is seen as the only way in which a solitary can effectively reach the solitudes of others—the solitudes of which these others are unaware.

Then he realizes that he loves them more than ever: perhaps that he now loves them really for the first time. Made humble by his solitude, grateful for the work that brings him into contact with others, he still remains alone. There is no greater loneliness than that of an instrument of God who realizes that his words and his ministry, even though they be the words of God, can do nothing to change his loneliness: and yet that, beyond all distinction between mine and thine, they make him one with everyone he encounters.

12.   What then is the conclusion? That this solitude of which we have been speaking, the solitude of the true *monachos*, of the lone one, is not and cannot be selfish. It is the opposite of selfish. It is the death and the forgetfulness of self. But what is self? The self that vanishes from this emptiness is the superficial, false social self, the image made up of the prejudices, the whimsey, the posturing, the pharisaic self-concern and the pseudo dedication which are the heritage of the individual in a limited and imperfect group.

There is another self, a true self, who comes to full maturity in emptiness and solitude—and who can of course, begin to appear and grow in the valid, sacrificial and creative self-dedication that belong to a genuine social existence. But note that even this social maturing of love implies at the same time the growth of a certain inner solitude.

Without solitude of some sort there is and can be no maturity. Unless one becomes empty and alone, he cannot give himself in love because he does not possess the deep self which is the only gift worthy of love. And this deep self, we immediately add, cannot be *possessed*. My deep self is not "something" which I acquire, or to which I "attain" after a long struggle. It is not mine, and cannot become mine. It is no "thing"—no object. It is "I."

The shallow "I" of individualism can be possessed, developed, cultivated, pandered to, satisfied: it is the center of all our strivings for gain and for satisfaction, whether material or spiritual. But the deep "I" of the spirit, of solitude and of love, cannot be "had," possessed, developed, perfected. It can only *be*, and *act* according to deep inner laws which are not of man's contriving, but which come from God. They are the Laws of the Spirit, who, like the wind, glows where He wills. This inner "I," who is always alone, is always universal: for in this inmost "I" my own solitude meets the solitude of every other man and the solitude of God. Hence it is beyond division, beyond limitation, beyond selfish affirmation. It is only this inmost and solitary "I" that truly loves with the love and the spirit of Christ. This "I" is Christ Himself, living in us: and we, in Him, living in the Father.

LIGHT IN DARKNESS

THE ASCETIC DOCTRINE OF ST. JOHN
OF THE CROSS

In understanding the sanctity and Doctrine of St. John of
the Cross, the first thing we must do is to see them in the
clear perspectives of the New Testament, the Sermon on the
Mount, the profound discourses in the Gospel of St. John,
and particularly the mystery of the Passion and the Resurrection of the Son of God. In this way, we will be preserved
from the danger of giving the writings of the Carmelite Doctor a kind of stoical bias which makes his austerity seem
pointlessly inhuman, and which, instead of opening our
hearts to divine grace closes them in upon themselves in
fanatical rigidity.

There are plenty of "hard sayings" in St. John of the
Cross, just as there were hard sayings in the Gospel. Our
Lord said that we must "hate our Father and Mother . . .
and even our own life." But we know that the hard sayings
in the Gospel need to be properly qualified and understood.
The command to "hate" father and mother, which at times

seems so scandalous, does not interfere with the commandment to love and revere them. It is simply a strong statement of the hierarchy of value for the Christian—in which
the salvation of his own soul comes before everything else,
and in which, *if there arises a choice* between the love of
parents and the love of truth, or the love of one's own life
and fidelity to the word of God, then one's natural love
must be sacrificed.

This same principle will serve to explain many of the
seemingly harsh and extreme statements of St. John of the
Cross. His whole asceticism is basically a question of choice,
of preference. And we cannot understand what he is talking
about if we do not see what the choice really is. On the one
hand, the love and the will of God: on the other, the love
and the gratification of self. But what do these alternatives
mean *in practice?* If we merely take them in the abstract,
then the asceticism of St. John of the Cross becomes something mechanical, cold, soulless and inhuman: a kind of
mathematical exclusion of all spontaneity in favor of dreary
and rigid self-punishment. But if we see what he is talking
about in the concrete, it is quite a different matter. For on
the one hand, we have the confused, dissipated, and unruly
urges of our indisciplined desire, which draw us into a state
of blindness, weariness, distraction and exile from God. On
the other hand there are the very real and very urgent in-
spirations of the Holy Spirit of Divine Wisdom, that "loving, tranquil, lonely and peaceful sweet inebriator of the
spirit. Hereby the soul feels itself to be gently and tenderly
wounded and ravished, knowing not by whom, nor whence,
nor how." (*Living Flame of Love,* iii, 38 Vol III p. 181)
One who does not genuinely experience in himself the
reality of these two alternatives cannot fully appreciate the
ascetic teaching of St. John of the Cross. However, even

those who are not themselves mystics can profit by reading his works, if only they remember to see them in perspective.

When St. John of the Cross says, for instance, that we must treat our companions in the monastery as if they were not there, he can be tragically misunderstood by anyone who does not know precisely what the saint is aiming at. He certainly does not mean that we could simply stifle our spontaneous love and live like creatures without sensibility or affection. This would, in fact, be a sin not only against charity but even against temperance. (Insensibility is a sin against temperance, says St. Thomas: II II Q. 142 a.1) On the contrary, St. John *presumes* a very special situation: a community of contemplatives in which all have a definite call to "enjoy" the much higher and more spiritual form of love that we have suggested above. This secret, silent, contemplative union with God does not in fact exclude fraternal union but on the contrary it contains it within itself. Those who live the contemplative life on this level, are all the more closely united with one another in proportion as they grow in spiritual union with God. Therefore St. John of the Cross is certainly very wise in warning them against the temptation to become too preoccupied with one another on a more exterior, more conventional level, which would in fact keep them from growing in true delicacy of love. Experience in the contemplative life shows us that spiritual confusion awaits those who yield to foolish and sentimental impulse under the guise of charity, and allow themselves to lose their first fruits of prayer in an absurdly useless preoccupation with the lives of those around them. They become nothing else but sentimental busybodies, interfering with the order of the community, the peace of their companions, and the secret action of the Holy Spirit. Sometimes this false charity procedes from a hidden sensuality, and in other cases it is an expression of latent activism, an attempt to escape from the interior solitude of the contemplative with the deprivations it implies. Such temptations are quite natural, of course: but a spirituality that is basically active and extraverted will not help one to meet the problem in a contemplative way. St. John of the Cross firmly and resolutely sticks to his viewpoint. His way may seem drastic, but it can lead one to the interior detachment and tranquility without which a fully contemplative life is impossible.

Seen in this light, the *Cautions*, addressed to the community of nuns which the saint directed at Beas in Andalusia, is likely to be interpreted more wisely. The same things would not be said in the same way either to people in the world, or to religious living the active life. Incidentally, notice the obvious human tenderness with which St. John of the Cross writes in his letters to these nuns. It is well known that he had a special preference for this community (headed by the saintly Anne of Jesus) and he made no effort to disguise the fact that the nuns were a great consolation to him. But his love was simple and supernatural. It was not based on merely superficial considerations, but on a deep sharing of ideals and love "in the Spirit." In any case, we can see that the saint practiced what he preached and was able at the same time to love these souls who had been confided to his direction by the Lord, and to be perfectly detached in his love for them. This "reconciliation of opposites" is the mark of true sanctity. Needless to add, it gives the soul of the saint a perfectly Christ-like character, for every page of the Gospel shows us, in Christ Our Lord, a supreme harmony between well-ordered human feelings and the demands of a divine nature and personality.

All the doctrine of St. John of the Cross is aimed at this ideal balance of the human and the divine: a balance that is to be attained, however, not on a humanistic level, but "in the Spirit." Now if our human nature is to be brought under the complete and exclusive control of the Spirit of Light, then there is only one way: to follow Christ in His passion and to rise with Him from the dead. The "passion" in our life is our crucifixion by asceticism and by passive purification, especially by mystical trials. Our resurrection is the joy and the peace of contemplative prayer, and union with the Divine Spouse in mystical love.

Just as we can never separate asceticism from mysticism, so in St. John of the Cross we find darkness and light, suffering and joy, sacrifice and love united together so closely that they seem at times to be identified. It is not so much that we come through darkness to light, as that the darkness itself is light.

> Never was fount so clear, undimmed and bright;
> From it alone, I know, proceeds all light,
>   Although 'tis night.

Hence the essential simplicity of his teaching: enter into the night and you will be enlightened. "Night" means the "darkening" of all our natural desires, our natural understanding, our human way of loving; but this darkening brings with it an enlightenment. The greater our sacrifice, the deeper the night into which we plunge, the more promptly and more completely will we be enlightened. But the point to be carefully remembered is that we are *not enlightened by our own efforts, our own love, our own sacrifice.* These, on the contrary, are darkness. Even our highest spiritual abilities are darkness in the sight of God. All must be "darkened" that is to say forgotten, in order that God Himself may become the light of our soul.

The "darkness" which St. John teaches is not a pure negation. Rather it is the removal and extinguishing of a lesser light in order that pure light may shine in its place. It is like putting out a candle which is no longer of any use in the full light of day. The problem, of course, is that we *do not see* the spiritual daylight of God's presence all around us, we only see the candlelight of our own desires and judgments. This is of course familiar doctrine, common to all ascetic theologians. But one special point is emphasized by St. John of the Cross. He would extinguish not only the "light" of sensual and inordinate passions, but even certain desires, judgments and illuminations which appear to be good and holy. Indeed, he precedes by the "darkening" even of those good and helpful notions of God, those lights and consolations of prayer which have an important positive part to play in the beginnings of the spiritual life. But as we go on, if we become attached to these thoughts, ideas and images of God, and remain concerned with our selves and our spiritual progress, we will not be able to "see" the purer and more spiritual light of God Himself. Hence, as the saint says:

It is clear that, in order perfectly to attain to union in this life through grace and through love, a soul must be in darkness with respect to all that can enter through the eye, and to all that can be received through the ear, and can be imagined with the fancy, and understood with the heart, which here signifies the soul. And thus a soul is greatly impeded from reaching this high estate of union with God when it clings to any understanding or feeling or imagination or appearance or will or manner or its own, or to any other act or to anything of its own, and cannot detach and strip itself of all these. For, as we say, the goal which it seeks is beyond all this, yea, beyond even the highest thing that can be known or experienced; and thus a soul must pass beyond everything to unknowing. (Ascent of Mount Carmel, II IV, Vol. I, p. 76)

This enables us to understand the peculiar emphasis in the *Maxims* upon quietness, silence, solitude, and the "absence of business and bustle" in the interior life.

> On the road to life there is very little bustle and business, and it requires mortification of the will rather than much knowledge. He that cumbers himself least with things and pleasures will go farthest along that road. (Maxim 55)

> Since God is inaccessible, see that thou concern not thyself with how much thy faculties can comprehend and thy senses can perceive, that thou be not satisfied with less and that thy soul lose not the swiftness that is needful for one that would attain to Him. (Maxim 52)
> As one that drags a cart uphill, even so does that soul journey toward God, that shakes not off anxiety and quenches not desire. (Maxim 53)

Finally, this gives us an insight into the reason why St. John of the Cross tells his penitents to welcome darkness and spiritual trial as a great good, and assures them that when they are without consolation and light in prayer, and are fully aware of their own poverty, God is probably closer to them than ever before. Of course, this is not a universal principle for all, but it applies to those who are called to the way of contemplative prayer.

If we read the saint carefully, and take care to weigh every word, we will see that he is preaching a doctrine of pure liberty which is the very heart of the New Testament. He wants us to be free. He wants to liberate us not only from the captivity of passion and egoism, but even from the more subtle tyranny of spiritual ambition, and preoccupation with methods of prayer and systems for making progress. But of course, one must first be *called* to this contemplative freedom. The way St. John of the Cross prescribes is not fully intelligible outside of this special call to contemplative prayer. Here is what he says:

> Wherefore in this state the soul must never have meditation imposed upon it, nor must it perform any acts, nor strive after sweetness of fervor; for this would be to set an obstacle in the way of the principal agent, who . . . is God. For God secretly and quietly infuses into the soul loving knowledge and wisdom without any intervention of specific acts, although he sometimes produces them in the soul for some length of time. And the soul has then to walk in loving awareness of God, without performing specific acts, but conducting itself as we have said passively, and having no diligence of its own, but possessing this pure, simple and loving awareness, as one that opens his eyes with an awareness of love.
>
> (*Living Flame of Love* iii, 32, Vol. iii, p. 77.)

Most of the maxims and teachings collected here point to this special kind of interior peace, detachment and emptiness. St. John of the Cross strives to liberate the soul from trivial and exterior concerns, and even from lesser, more busy forms of active asceticism, in order that it may rest in detached unconcern, and yield in all simplicity to the secret action of God. The great thing is to be delivered from useless desires, desires which though they appear to be very profitable and efficacious, in reality lead us off the right road because they emphasize our own action more than the action of grace. This is St. John's main concern: that contemplatives should not waste their time and their efforts in doing work that only has to be undone by God and done over again, if they are to come to union with Him.

> It is very needful, my daughters, to be able to withdraw the spirit from the devil and from sensuality, for otherwise without

knowing it we shall find ourselves completely failing to make progress and very far removed from the virtues of Christ, and afterwards we shall awaken and find our work and labour inside out. Thinking that our lamp was burning, we shall find it apparently extinguished, for when we blew upon it, and thought thereby to fan its flame, we may rather have put it out.

(*Letter vi, to the nuns of Beas*)

St. John was no quietist. On the contrary few saints make more insistent demands for the right kind of work: but this work is all interior. It consists in love and suffering, not in external projects that make much noise and raise a lot of dust but, in the end, leave us no further advanced than we were before. The same letter we have just quoted insists, a few lines further down: "It is impossible to continue to make progress save by working and suffering with all virtue, *and being completely enwrapped in silence.*"

The last phrase is what is most important, and most characteristic of St. John of the Cross. It is the key to his asceticism of light in darkness, which seeks in all things to bring the soul into the *interior depths* where love is invisible, and to rescue it from the triviality of the obvious and showy forms of spiritual life which are good only for those who remain on the surface.

Any one of the maxims of St. John of the Cross is an inexhaustible mine of spiritual truth for the reader who really, sincerely and humbly seeks to renounce himself and abandon himself, in faith, to the mercy of God.

The ascetic teaching of St. John of the Cross is part and parcel of his mysticism and cannot be separated from it. That is why the poems of St. John happily complete the aphorisms and cautions, and incite the reader to go on to the saint's great mystical treatises which are nothing but commentaries on his poems. The remarkable beauty of his poems shows that his asceticism, far from destroying his creative genius, had liberated and transformed it by dedicating it to God.

THE PRIMITIVE CARMELITE IDEAL

1 . *The prophetic spirit*

When we approach the question of the origins of the Carmelite Order and of its primitive spirituality, we must first of all make a clear-cut distinction between this new form of life and the ancient monastic tradition of the west. If we make the mistake that has been made by some historians and view the Carmelites as another expression of the same movement of monastic renewal that brought into being the Camaldolese, the Cistercians, the Carthusians, the Vallombrosans, the Grandmontines and so many others in the 11th and 12th centuries, we will be doomed to confusion and ambiguity from the start. We will be forced to explain what cannot be explained: the evolution of a monastic order into an order of mendicant preaching friars.

The problem is actually far more subtle. The first Carmelites had initiated something quite original and unique: a loose-knit community of hermits with an informal, occasional apostolate. Neither the eremitical nor the apostolic aspects of this new life were systematically organized and neither was the subject of a formal program such as we would envisage at the present time, when starting "something new." But the fact is, that in abandoning this original plan and conforming to the successful and more highly organized institution of the mendicants, with a special apostolic purpose, the Carmelites of the second generation had perhaps let go of something quite unique and quite characteristically their own, in order to follow something that was successfully working, but had been devised by others for a considerably different purpose. It remains open to question, of course, to what extent the originality of the first Carmelites was lost in the process of this transformation. To say that it disappeared altogether would not fit the facts. But to say that it was considerably modified is only to bring to mind the source of the contentions and divisions which plagued the early history of the Order.

The Carmelites were originally hermits. And of course their life was the traditional hermit life known to the east from the earliest centuries of the Church. They lived as the desert fathers had lived eight hundred years earlier. They began as an offshoot of the ancient, informal, charismatic monachism of Syria and Palestine. But they were not monks in the western sense, and they never were. They were originally not cenobites. They had no liturgical office in common. They did not live in monasteries or cloisters. They were in fact simple laymen, living as solitaries in a loosely connected group, in caves and huts on the side of Mount Carmel. Their manner of life was not yet institutionalized, and even when they first asked for a Rule, from the hands of the Patriarch of Jerusalem, that Rule was, as we shall see, deliberately kept simple and uncomplicated. Its formal prescriptions were left at the bare minimum. There was just enough "legislation" to preserve the primitive simplicity and purpose of the life. What was that purpose? In the words of the Rule itself, it was: "Let each one remain in his cell or near it, meditating day and night on the Law of the Lord, and vigilant in prayer, unless he is legitimately occupied in something else."

Nothing could be simpler. The purpose of the life was solitude and contemplation, but within a framework that allowed complete liberty for the individual development of each one under the guidance of the Holy Spirit. It was a kind of informal "lay-monasticism" of a solitary type. To say that meditative prayer came first of all was to make clear that contemplation was the primary and indeed the unique purpose of the life. But at the same time it was not to be considered as something that rigidly excluded every other activity whatever. On the contrary, room was left for other legitimate activities, within due proportion. And apparently, even at the very beginning, a certain apostolate was conceded to be a normal and legitimate overflow from this life of prayer. Of course this apostolate would be extremely restricted. It would undoubtedly be a matter less of preaching than of other works of mercy since only a few of the hermits were priests. Yet preaching was most certainly included in the Carmelite life even in its earliest beginnings. What is important however is not the fact that preaching was considered part of the life, but that the life itself was left free and informal so that the hermits could do anything that conformed to their ideal of solitude and free submission to the Holy Spirit. The primitive Carmelites could preach, as they could also engage in any other work of mercy. What were the conditions? We would say today, these works were legitimate as long as they remained subordinate to a life of contemplation. But this abstract formula is itself misleading. To put it more concretely, they could do whatever good work was compatible with a life of which most was spent in the solitude of the cell, meditating on the Law of the Lord.

Even the inexorable defender of solitude and opponent of the life led by Carmelites in the cities of the west, the General of the Order called Nicholas the Frenchman, admitted willingly that the preaching apostolate was an integral part of the purest and most primitive tradition of the Order, the tradition which he himself defended. But it had to be an apostolate of solitaries and contemplatives, not of friars living in a busy city. He wrote:

> Conscious of their imperfection, the hermits of Carmel persevered for a long time in the solitude of the desert, but as they intended to be of service to their neighbor, in order not to be guilty of infidelity to their way, they went sometimes, but rarely, down from their hermitage. That which they had harvested with the sickle of contemplation, in solitude, they went to thresh it on the threshing floor of preaching, and to sow it abroad on all sides.[1]

What is the explanation of this? It is probably to be sought in the symbolic adoption by the Carmelites of the prophet Elias as their "Founder." It is quite true that the hermits living on the slopes of Mount Carmel, near the "spring of Elias," where the prophet himself had prayed and dwelt alone, and where the "sons of the prophets" had

---

[1] From the French translation of the ancient text known as the *Ignea Sagitta* (Burning Arrow) in *Les Plus Vieux Textes du Carmel*, Paris 1944, p. 173.

had a "school," [2] could themselves claim to be descendants
of the ancient prophets. It is quite true that Elias, in a broad
sense, was the "founder" of this way of life since he had in
fact been the inspiration of those countless generations that
had lived there in the places hallowed by his memory and
stamped with his indelible character.

The first Carmelites then were not only hermits and descendants of the early desert fathers, but they were also very
conscious of a certain *prophetic* character about their vocation. This meant of course that they were inclined to give
precedence to what we would call the "mystical" side of
their vocation over the ascetic, never of course neglecting
or excluding the latter. For in the truly contemplative life,
contemplation and asceticism necessarily go hand in hand.
You cannot really have the first without the second, though
it is not impossible for a monastic life to consist of asceticism without contemplation, except in a formal and exterior
sense of the word.

A prophet in the traditional sense is not merely a man
who foretells the future under spiritual inspiration. That is
in fact quite accidental. He is above all a "witness," just as
the martyr is a witness. (The Greek word martyr means
witness.) But he is a witness in a different way than the martyr. The martyr suffers death. The prophet suffers inspiration, or vision. He shoulders the "burden" of vision that
God lays upon him. He bows under the truth and the
judgments of God, sometimes the concrete, definite historical judgment pronounced on a given age, sometimes
only the manifestation of God's transcendent and secret
holiness, which is denied and opposed by sin in general.

[2] *Schola* not only in the sense of a place where one learns, but in the
more original and etymological sense of a place of leisure, quiet and
retirement, where one can think deeply.

But above all the prophet is one who bears the burden of the divine mercy—a burden which is a gift to mankind, but which remains a burden to the prophet in so far as no one will take it from him. In this connection, we can see that St. Therese of Lisieux was a true descendant of the early, prophetic saints of her Order when she took upon herself the burden of victimhood of the merciful love of God. This consecration of our modern saint is not fully understandable unless it is seen in the light of the early prophetic tradition of Carmel. In fact, she realized this ideal most perfectly in herself, and for that reason she became in our time the patroness of the Catholic missions. For the missionary too needs to realize that he is a prophet bearing a burden, a burden of mercy and of truth which too often men are unable to receive. He is not merely an official, or a teacher, who comes to organize a Christian community and to disseminate doctrinal truths. He bears with him, in his sacramental power, not merely news about Christ, but the presence of the Redeemer and the fact of Redemption.

If we are to understand the true notion of the prophetic spirit which Carmel concretized around the symbolic figure of Elias, we must recall to mind all the meaning of the prophetic vocation in Old Testament times. A prophet is one who lives in direct submission to the Holy Spirit in order that, by his life, actions and words, he may at all times be a sign of God in the world of men. Christ the Incarnate Word was of course the supreme Prophet, and all sanctity participates in this prophetic quality. Their submission to God is not merely a matter of charismatic accident but of perfect fidelity to grace.

The prophet is a man of God not only in the sense that he is seized and controlled passively by God, but much more truly in the sense that he is consciously and

freely obedient to the Holy Spirit, no matter what the price
may be. And this presupposes fidelity in all the obscure mysterious trials by which his soul is purified so that he may become a divine instrument. The great prophets of Israel were
men of God, divine instruments, whose function it was to
keep alive the spirit of equality, theocratic independence
and spiritual autonomy which had characterized the life of
Israel in the desert. The Lord had liberated Israel "with a
strong arm" from Egypt that they "might sacrifice to Him
in the desert." (Exodus 5: 1-4) This was necessary for several reasons: not only that Israel might be free to follow a
special and divine call, but also because God would not accept, from His people, a sacrifice consisting of the "abomi-
nation" of the Egyptians. It was not His plan that Israel
should simply resign itself to slavery under Pharaoh with its
hardships and "offer up" the toil of making bricks without
straw, thereby giving an example of virtue to the Egyptians!

The forty years in the desert came to be regarded as the
golden age of the history of Israel, the age of Israel's nup-
tials with the Lord—the pattern of all future perfection. For
after settling in the Promised Land, Israel was tempted to
leave the austere, unseen yet ever-present and all merciful
Lord of the desert, and ally herself in adulterous union with
the visible, dramatic and sometimes licentious gods of the
fertile Canaanite land. She would be recalled to order by the
prophets, and always in the same terms: return to the spirit
of your days in the desert! Recovery of the spirit of the
desert meant a return to fidelity, to charity, to fraternal
union; it meant the destruction of the inequalities and op-
pressions dividing rich and poor; conversion to justice and
equity meant the return to the true sabbath. For the law of
the desert was the law of the sabbath, of peace, direct dependence on the Lord, silence and trust, forgiveness of

debts, restoration of unity, purity of worship. This spiritual sabbath had been corrupted by the levitical jurists into a vast complex of legalistic problems and moral cases. The prophets, like Isaias inveighed against this perversion of the true spirit. Always, with Osee, they summoned Israel back to the fidelity of the desert. "Behold I will allure her" says Yaweh to Osee, "and lead her into the wilderness, and will speak to her heart." (Osee 2:14) In the days of King Achab, when Jezabel the queen was filling the land with priests of Baal, Yaweh raised up His prophet Elias as a witness and a messenger to Israel. The first public act of the prophet was to declare that there would be a three years' drought, a symbolic punishment and purification—a reminder of the desert.

And Elias the Thesbite of the inhabitants of Galaad said to Achab: as the Lord liveth, in whose sight I stand, there shall not be dew nor rain these years but according to the words of my mouth.

(3 Kings, 17:1)

The early Carmelite Fathers read much meaning into these words of the prophets and into their context, finding here an allegory of the whole Carmelite vocation. To stand in the presence of the living God, first of all. Then to "go toward the east and hide thyself in the torrent of Carith . . . and there thou shalt drink of the torrent: and I have commanded ravens to feed thee there." (id. 3-4)

The author of that moving ancient text on the spirit of Carmelite prayer and contemplation, the *Institution* of the first Fathers, interprets the retirement of Elias in typical medieval style. To hide in the torrent of Carith is to embrace the ascetical life, which leads to the perfection of charity by one's own efforts, aided by the grace of God. To drink of the torrent is to passively receive the secret light of contemplation from God and to be inwardly transformed by His wisdom:

> . . . to taste, in a certain manner, in our heart, and to experience in our spirit the power of the divine presence and the sweetness of the glory from on high, not only after death but even in this mortal life. That is what is really meant by drinking from the torrent of the joy of God . . . It is in order to accomplish this twofold end (asceticism and contemplation) that the monk must enter upon the eremitical way, according to the testimony of the prophet: "In a desert land, where there is no way, and no water so in the sanctuary have I come before thee, to see thy power and thy glory." [3]

The Carmelite, then, is the successor of the prophets as witness to the desert vocation of Israel, that is of the Church: a reminder that we do not have on this earth a lasting city, and that we are pilgrims to the city of God. But, more specifically, the Carmelite seeks, by his preaching and by the witness of his contemplative life, not merely to bring the Gospel message to the people at large, but above all, and in a special way, to lead others in the ways of prayer, contemplation and solitude. The Carmelite Apostolate has, ideally speaking, this very special modality of its own. It is a contemplative apostolate to other potential contemplatives. It is an apostolate of interior prayer. It is a "school of prophets." It teaches, indeed, but what it teaches above all is the way of the hidden life. And here above all, *nemo dat quod non habet*. No one can give something which he does not himself have.

[3] *Les Plus Vieux Textes*, p. 114. The *Institution* is by an unknown author, probably of the 14 century. The Biblical quote is from Psalm 62:3.

If Elias stands as the model of all Carmelites, there is another and more ideal figure than that of the prophet: the figure of the Blessed Virgin of Mount Carmel who, even more than Elias, embodies in herself the perfection of the Carmelite ideal. Where in Elias we see at once the zeal and the weaknesses of the prophet, his greatness and his imperfections, his conflicts and inner contradictions, in Mary we see a sanctity that is beyond prophecy and beyond conflict, hidden in perfect humility and in ordinariness. It would therefore be a tragic mistake to look at the Carmelite ideal too exclusively from the prophetic viewpoint. This would lead to distortion and dramatization, to violence and ultimately to a kind of pharisaical pretense. But the example and influence of the Queen of prophets are there to heal these divisions. The sanctity of Our Lady was great indeed, but so great that it cannot adequately be expressed in anything other than the ordinary ways of human existence. In this, as in so many other things, she resembles her Divine Son. Like Him, she was in all things human and ordinary, close to her fellow men, simple and unassuming in her way of life, without drama and without exaltation. The true, sure instinct of the Carmelite saints has gone direct to the heart of this truth. The mysticism of St. Theresa is rooted in a life of ordinariness and common sense, because it accepts the wholeness of human nature just as it is. The doctrine of St. John of the Cross goes to the greatest lengths to exclude everything that savors of heroic show and mystical display, discarding all visions, revelations, locutions and ecstasies in favor of "dark faith." For "in order for the understanding to be prepared for divine union, it must be pure and void of all that pertains to sense, and detached and freed from all that can clearly be perceived by the understanding, profoundly hushed and put to silence, and leaning upon faith which alone is the proximate and proportionate means whereby the soul is united to God." [4]

The "little way" of St. Therese of Lisieux is predominantly a Marian way. The whole spirit and ideal of Carmel is, at least implicitly, a re-living of that great mystery of faith in the Blessed Virgin who was "blessed because she believed" (Luke 1:45) and who, by her faith, brought the Lord of Majesty into the world in human form.

It can be said that the Carmelite spirit is essentially a "desert" spirit, a prophetic ideal. And that Elias represents the exterior, the more material aspect of that ideal. But that the Virgin Mary is the symbol and source of the interior spirit of Carmel. Which means that in the long run, the desert spirit and prophetic ideal of Carmel are understood most perfectly by those who have entered into the "dark night" of Marian faith.

II . *Carmelite origins*

Who were the first Carmelites? It would be very interesting to know more about them. They were pilgrims and Crusaders from the west who, in the 12th century, renounced the world with its ambitions and its wars—even its "holy wars"—in order to consecrate their lives to God in solitude on Mount Carmel. The first Carmelites were men whom the spirit of Elias had rescued from the awful shipwreck that was the second Crusade, preached by St. Bernard of Clairvaux. They were men who had been launched into war by a cenobite, the holiest and greatest prophet of their time. It is certain that Bernard himself must first have communi-

[4] Ascent of Mount Carmel, Bk. ii, c. 9, vol. i. (Peers trans.) p. 98.

cated to them something of that spirit and power of Elias, the burning and shining light that was in him.

A Greek monk, John Phocas, on pilgrimage to the Holy Land, gives the following description of the westerners living as hermits on Carmel. The text, written about 1185, undoubtedly refers to events going back ten or twenty years before the writing.

At the end of the point that looks out over the sea, we find the cave of the prophet Elias. This extraordinary man there lived an altogether angelic life, before being taken up into heaven. In this place there was once a big building whose ruins are still there today . . . For some time, now, a white-haired monk, invested with the priestly dignity and a native of Calabria, has made his dwelling in the ruins of this monastery, as a result of a vision in which the prophet Elias appeared to him; he has built a little wall and a tower, with a chapel, and about ten brethren have gathered about him. He is living there still today.[5]

It is thought by some historians that this hermit was not a Calabrian, but a Frenchman, St. Berthold of Malifay, a native of the Limousin in west-central France. He was the predecessor of Saint Brocard, generally considered the founder of the Order as he received the rule from the Patriarch.

The "Rule of St. Albert" as the primitive Carmelite legislation is called, was not written by a Carmelite at all. The original hermits, laymen gathered around one or two simple priests, felt that they ought to receive some definite code of life from the Church. They applied to the Patriarch of Jerusalem, Albert of Avogardo, an Augustinian canon. This prelate, with great discretion, drew up a simple set of monastic usages covering the essentials of the solitary life. To

[5] Les Plus Vieux Textes p. 59.

give them a firm and reliable structure, he had them elect a
Prior whom they would obey, traced out the broad lines of
their life of poverty in solitude, reminding them of their
chief obligation: to spend their days in solitary prayer, working and praying alone in their cells.

In the preamble to this rule, St. Albert recalled to their
minds that all religious life is first and foremost the service
of the Lord and "dependence on Jesus Christ, serving Him
faithfully with a pure heart and a good conscience." A simple and seemingly obvious sentence, which nevertheless
contains in it the principles of a truly interior and spiritual
life of prayer. Without such a spirit as this, no life at all,
however contemplative, however sacrificial, has any deep
Christian significance.

It also goes without saying that, like every other form of
Christian ascetical life, the life of the hermits of Mount Carmel was above all a life of charity, of fraternal unity in
Christ. Not of course that it was cenobitic: but the hermits
too, though, solitaries, lived in deep spiritual communion
and fraternal solidarity with one another. When, later, Nicholas the Frenchman so vehemently lamented what he
thought was the decline of the Order, when the Carmelites
moved to western Europe and began to live in cities, he
did this not only because they had apparently lost their ideal
of solitude, but also because it seemed to him that they were
losing their charity and their union in Christ. And it is true
that the crisis of adaptation to life in the west as mendicants did severely threaten the original unity of the Order.

Few facts are known about the early history of the Carmelites in the east. In 1187, after the defeat of the Christian
armies, St. Berthold built a monastery near the fountain of
Elias. This was not a step towards the common life, but
rather a way of providing a refuge for the hermits in case of

attack. However the Carmelites did have establishments even in towns, at this early date. They maintained a hospice in Jerusalem, a chapel at Sareptha (presumably for pilgrims), a monastery at Acre and another in the city of Tyre. They also had a monastery called Beaulieu, on Mount Lebanon. There were other eremitical colonies of Carmelites including one across the Jordan on the Mountain of the Forty Days' Fast.

At first the Carmelites were not troubled by the Saracens. The more remote colonies of hermits were however devastated in 1240. Already in 1238, a group of hermits had taken refuge in Cyprus, another in Sicily, while a third was established at Les Aygalades, near Marseilles. In 1241 some Carmelites went to England, and St. Louis, visiting the holy mountain in 1254, took six of them with him to Paris. After the fall of Acre in 1291, the last Carmelites in the east were exterminated. They died, we are told, singing the *Salve Regina*.

The fact that the Carmelites moved west in small groups, and settled in places distant from one another, in divergent situations, meant that the unity of the Order was gravely threatened from the very start. What is surprising is not the fact that history of the Order now became a long series of misunderstandings and divisions, but rather the fact that it survived at all. In brief, the source of the trouble was this: those who led the way to Europe, though they at first settled in out of the way places, also began to live in towns and to engage in the active apostolate. They met with great opposition, particularly on the part of the secular clergy. But they were convinced that the only way in which they could gain a solid footing in the west and thus perpetuate the Order, was to present themselves as Mendicant Friars like the Dominicans and Franciscans.

In 1265, when Nicholas the Frenchman came west from
Carmel to attend the General Chapter of the Order,—at
which he was elected Prior General to succeed St. Simon
Stock—he found this situation which was to him incomprehensible and deeply disturbing. Unable to change matters,
he denounced the trend away from solitude and retired to
a hermitage, as we shall see in detail.

St. Simon Stock is mainly credited for the transformation
of the Order of Mount Carmel into a mendicant and
apostolic institute. In order to do this, he caused the Rule
to be revised by two Dominicans and moved the brethren
into towns and cities, laying a strong emphasis on the common life. The Order then became divided between isolated houses where the hermit life still continued in force,
and town houses where the common life was the rule and
everyone was engaged in apostolic work. In order to form
priests and apostles, houses of study were of course necessary. Hence the Carmelites founded in university cities, such
as Cambridge (1249), Oxford (1253), Paris (1259) and
Bologna (1260). In addition, each province had its own
studium generale.

To what extent was St. Simon Stock the savior of the
Carmelite Order? Would the Order have survived without
this transformation? If it had remained a small coterie of
hermits, would its destinies have been less flourishing? It is
impossible to answer these questions, but the debate is by
no means finished. In the eyes of the saint's immediate successors, the change had been a fatal mistake which could
only be repaired by a complete return to solitude. But such a
return was no longer possible. There are not lacking writers
today who believe that the abandonment of the hermit life
was the end of the genuine Carmelite ideal. Others, repre-
senting a more common opinion, like Fr Bruno de Jesus

Marie, prefer the view that only in Europe did Carmel find its true stature and identity, in the union of contemplation and the apostolate. Whatever the true answer may be (if a true answer can be found at all) the difficulties encountered by the nascent Order were truly enormous.

As anyone familiar with thirteenth century history realizes, the mendicants were thought by conventional minds to be turning the Church of God upside down. Their advent was regarded by the "old fashioned" as a dangerous revolution. In such circumstances, the appearance of yet another new and unconventional group could only increase the confusion and unrest. The Carmelite friars were forced to find themselves a recognizable place in the Church of their time: they had to belong to some category before they could be comfortably dealt with by anxious canonists. There was no need of a new monastic Order—or they could have become another group of hermits like the Carthusians or Camaldolese. However, there seemed to be a better reason why they should turn toward the mendicants. Not only did these Orders correspond with the most vital needs of the Church in the thirteenth century, but also Carmel itself had as one of its integral notes, the need of an apostolic outlet for the overflow of contemplation.

But for the Carmelite friar, it was not, as for the Dominican, a matter of a special vocation to preach the Gospel,— that is to say, the apostolate was not the main end of the Carmelite vocation. On the other hand, since contemplation was the main end of the life, it followed that the sharing of the fruits of contemplation was a secondary end, inseparable from the first. This was a new approach to the apostolic life, a development that had not been suspected in the old monastic setup, except in individual cases like those of St. Gregory the Great and St. Bernard of Clairvaux who were so to speak the exception to the rule, and as such were very articulate in bewailing their fate. For them it *was against the nature of their vocation* to be called to the apostolate. A paradoxical exception permitted by the inscrutable designs of God. But for the new thirteenth century mentality, explicitly formulated by St. Thomas Aquinas, an apostolate of preaching became on the contrary the ordinary outcome of perfect contemplation.

Not all the Carmelites accepted this spontaneously and without reserves. On the contrary, it was quite natural that the conservative, eremitical group should regard it with the same eyes as a Benedictine, a Cistercian or a Carthusian of that time.

The primitive Rule of St. Albert had been approved by the Holy See in 1226. But now that the Carmelites were in the west, and were beginning to see that their place was among the mendicant Orders, the Rule had to be revised. St. Simon Stock here called upon the aid of two Dominicans, Hugh of St. Cher and William of Antera. These two adjusted the primitive Rule with certain subtle, accidental changes which nevertheless made it possible for the whole life and outlook of Carmel to be completely transformed. In a word, the changes in the Rule resulted in a reorientation of the Carmelite life in the direction of apostolic activity, without however altering the basic obligation for the friars to be, before all else, contemplatives.

In brief, the changes introduced by the Dominican revisers of the Rule, in cooperation with St. Simon Stock and the western Superiors of the Order, were these:

1) Where there had only been a vow of obedience, now the vows of chastity and poverty became explicit. This was nothing new in itself, only a canonical step to put the Car-

melites on the same juridical footing as the other mendicants.

2) It was now made clear that the friars could live "anywhere suitable" which meant that they could live in towns, in order to engage in the apostolate. This was a radical departure from the primitive eremitical concept, and it was considered by many in the Order to be unacceptable. But in fact the Popes began to demand that this change be made. John XXII moved ten Carmelite communities from solitude into cities in order that they might more effectively carry on the apostolate.

3) Whereas in the first version of the Rule each one kept to his cell, and not even the divine office was recited in common, there now came to be a greater emphasis on the common life and common exercises. Meals, for instance, were to be taken in common. At the same time, the rules for fasting and abstinence were slackened, and meat was permitted at certain times.

4) The rules of silence were also mitigated.

5) Finally, the poverty of the Order was given a strictly mendicant character. It was stipulated that the Friars could not own land but that they could have certain domestic animals, including mules to ride on. This implied travel.

These changes were incorporated into the Rule and be came part of the primitive Rule of St. Albert. And it was to this Rule, modified in 1247 by St. Simon Stock and the two Dominicans, that St. Theresa was to return in her reform. Hence, in practical fact, the primitive Carmelite ideal is embodied in the Rule as adapted for the apostolate in the west, and not in the original, purely eremitical Rule first drawn up by the Patriarch, even though that allowed, implicitly, certain excursions into the apostolate. The struggle over the

primitive Rule in 16th century Spain was, then, a struggle for the Rule as adapted in 1247 against another greatly
relaxed version of the Rule which was put into effect in
1413 and which the Calced Carmelites followed, in opposition to St. Theresa's reform.

Nevertheless, in the thirteenth century there was a pronounced reaction in favor of the earlier, more eremitical
ideal of the Order, led above all by Nicholas the Frenchman.
And in the sixteenth century, within the Discalced Reform,
there was also an extreme wing which sought solitude along
with austerity and centralization: and this was the faction
of Doria and the Friars of Pastrana, who eventually perse-
cuted St. John of the Cross, and hounded him to his death.
The curious thing is that St. John of the Cross, the defender
of the pure Carmelite ideal of mystical contemplation, was
himself not an extremist in favor of pure solitude, nor did he
advocate extreme austerity, but took the middle way, favor-
ing the combination of solitude, and contemplation with
preaching and the direction of souls.

Hence it is evident that in the history of the Carmelites
the pure and primitive spirit of the Order always remains
incarnate in a kind of "prophetic" union of solitude and
apostolate. When this balance is disturbed, when the shift is
made too far in one direction or the other, then the primitive
spirit is lost. That is to say that when too much emphasis is
placed on apostolic action, the primitive spirit is of course
weakened and eventually destroyed. But that does not mean
that the return to the original ideal is a mere matter of abandoning the apostolate and embracing a solitary life that is
primarily ascetical and austere. It seems likely that the apostolate, when kept in its right place, *remains the true guarantee*
of the original purity of the ideal. For a Carmelite, the apostolate in its own way encourages contemplation, just as con-

templation is the source of a genuine apostolate. To abandon the apostolate altogether in what we might call a kind of "left wing deviation" would result not in a purification of the contemplative spirit, but rather its stultification in the rigidity of an artificial, formalistic cult of solitude and asceticism for their own sakes. This at any rate appears to be the lesson of Carmelite history, both in the 13th century and, more particularly, in the 16th. The problem was very successfully solved by St. John of the Cross and by those who, following him, remained true to the genial and inspired intuitions of St. Theresa of Avila.

III . *The Fiery Arrow*

What has just been said is no more than an opinion, a tentative judgment, which however seems to be the commonly accepted view among Carmelite theologians. But once the judgment has been made, we must face the provoking witness of that "prophetic" successor of St. Simon Stock: I mean the author of *The Fiery Arrow*, Nicholas the Frenchman.

The *Fiery Arrow*, is, for very good reasons, little known. One of the most urgent, most passionate of all the documents in a long literary history of contemplative religion, it is so outspoken that it has rarely, if ever, been printed in its entirety. It has not even been made known, except in fragmentary fashion, in the Carmelite Order itself. Even today, the *Ignea Sagitta* has been published only in part. The French translation (published in 1944) soon went out of print and as far as I know is no longer available. It is still quite likely that the *Fiery Arrow* is completely unknown to many members of the Carmelite Order. But in discussing the primitive ideal of Carmel, such a document can hardly be left out of the account. It must be considered with care.

It would of course be interesting to speculate on the reasons for the long-standing neglect of an important document. But that is a delicate question, and should not after all be brought by anyone who is not professionally concerned with Carmelite history. The outside observer may content himself with remarking that this seems to be another manifestation of something almost universal in religious history. Once an institution has been set up and is successfully running, anything that calls into question its validity, its authenticity or the quality of its achievement is feared and resented: not necessarily out of base motives, but for solid, though perhaps expedient reasons. It is always felt that once a stable situation has been reached, and problems have been to some extent solved, it is better not to cause unrest, to reopen old wounds, and needlessly to excite the aspirations of the members with reminders of some other ideal. This is especially true wherever there is question of some opposition between community life and life in solitude.

In the case of the *Fiery Arrow*, the author speaks with a fervor, a conviction and even a certain asperity of accusation which would scarcely admit of compromising acceptance. Those who could not receive all his arguments with favor would almost necessarily reject everything. For our own part, however, looking at the work objectively and free from administrative concern, we feel it is permitted to admire the author and sympathize with his ideals. Even admitting that he has missed the target in placing too exclusive an emphasis on solitude, it is permitted to feel that he has nevertheless spoken with the authentic voice of the first Carmelites, and that his witness is not to be rejected without serious consideration. Indeed, if he is accepted, he may have very much to contribute to the modern and current teaching that the Carmelite vocation is both contemplative and apostolic. This is something that the *Fiery Arrow* also asserts with explicit clarity. Its only complaint is that in aligning itself with the mendicants, the Carmelite Order sacrificed its own true and unique originality as an order of apostolic hermits.

It is all important to understand clearly the historical situation in which the *Fiery Arrow* was written. The first groups had left Carmel and had been in the west for some thirty years when Nicholas, a hermit who had come direct from Carmel, was elected Prior General. The religious community he took over from St. Simon Stock was to him completely unrecognizable. The Rule had been rewritten by Dominicans, and the Friars were building convents in cities, acting in practice as if their Order had been founded "in order to preach." It is true that there is something about the *Fiery Arrow* which suggests the violent anti-mendicant pamphlets of the time, like those of William of Saint Amour, refuted by St. Thomas Aquinas. It is possible that Nicholas was instinctively ultra-conservative and that he was shocked by the whole mendicant movement. But this fact is not enough to explain his vehement indignation against the Carmelite apostles. He was not simply inveighing against the apostolic life. Far from it. What seemed to him to be a scandal and a decline equal to the tragedy mourned by Jeremias in the Lamentations was the fact that men called to be hermits, men without sufficient preparation, without study, without discipline and without regular safeguards, were playing at the full-time apostolic life without having a sufficient appreciation of its responsibilities and burdens. Anyone who is intimately acquainted with communities of contemplatives can well understand with what concern a superior might see them suddenly precipitated into the active ministry.

The Carmelite Order was really in a state of grave crisis. The transition from east to west and from contemplation to apostolate had been too rapid. The Carmelites had not yet sunk deep roots in their new homes. Numerous postulants were entering, but their motives for entering were confused since the Superiors themselves were still disoriented. It is said that large numbers of the older members were leaving to join the established monastic Orders, while the younger ones, preferring to be frankly active, were attracted to the Franciscans and Dominicans. There were of course newly founded houses of study for Carmelites in the university cities. But these were not yet well established, and the level of doctrinal formation was as yet probably not very high. Furthermore, as Carmelite historians tell us[6] that academic degrees brought with them exemptions and privileges and this meant that there was a rush for doctorates that was not entirely based on zeal for theological science and for the apostolate, but on more human reasons as well. This was made worse by the fact that doctorates could be acquired by indult from Rome dispensing from the necessary studies. Such men were *doctores bullati*. In these circumstances it was natural that a contemplative like Nicholas should react energetically. In the presence of this dangerous situation, Nicholas had only one answer. His solution was naturally the only one he would be likely to think of: return to the desert! Live in Europe as you lived in the east. Live as you lived on Carmel. In this way he hoped to clarify the situation and salvage the originality of a hermit life with a very restricted and occasional apostolate.

From many points of view he was right. Yet facts and the

[6] Fr. Benedict Zimmerman, article "Carmes" in the *Dictionnaire de Théologie Catholique*.

decision of the Church were to contradict him. The Council of Lyons, in 1274, definitely ranked the Carmelites among mendicant and preaching Orders. The judgment of history upon the *Fiery Arrow* seems to be that, if Nicholas had been followed, the Carmelite Order would perhaps have had an ephemeral existence and would have died out with the thirteenth century. It would perhaps never have fulfilled its providential mission to contemplate and to share the fruits of contemplation in that very special way characteristic of it: by the formation and direction of interior souls in other orders and in the world.

Yet here is another case where a man who may in some sense have been proved pragmatically wrong by history, still remains as a noble witness not to a lost cause but to an undying truth: and the truth which, in the practical order, Nicholas was unable to defend in his own way, remains ideally speaking fundamental to the Carmelite spirit. It would be a serious mistake to regard Nicholas as a pathological crank. If he has been passed over in silence, it is not because he was a violent and deluded figure, but perhaps rather because his witness is too pure and too uncompromising to be accepted without confusion by generations unused to primitive simplicity. There is no reason why we should not pay attention to him, and be inspired by him, as long as we recognize at the same time that he must not be called upon to justify irresponsible and immature gestures of reformism, which do not take account of historical fact.

His modern editor, Pere Francois de Sainte Marie, O.C.D., sums up his case fairly and well:

Nicholas is not a tyrannical defender of solitude, nor a conservative clinging literally to the observance in which he himself was formed, he is simply an authentic contemplative, endowed with a keen sense of the mystery and of the exigencies of contemplation.[7]

We wonder if perhaps even more could be said for him than this: that he was not only an authentic contemplative, convinced by experience, of the beauties and nobility of the contemplative life, but that he was, above all, one who fully realized the implications of the early Carmelite ideal in all its originality and uniqueness: the ideal of a "prophetic" eremitism, in which solitude was essential and all important, but in which from time to time, as the Holy Ghost inspired or as occasion might demand, there was need for a brief and apostolic witness, perhaps only to a few isolated souls. What Nicholas opposed was not the apostolate, but a mass apostolate, on a large scale, with the need for much study and continuous preaching in towns.

In other words, Nicholas was, paradoxically, a representative of the pure and prophetic spirit of the early Carmelites, even though he appeared to be "prophetically" wrong. If we were to evaluate him by the kind of standard used by Marxists, we would simply say that he had judged wrongly and that his judgment was discarded by history, which he had not "interpreted correctly." As Catholics, though we may respect pragmatic judgments in historical matters, we owe loyalty to certain truths that are eternally valid. What Nicholas had to say as prophet and as contemplative cannot be discarded by history. It has meaning for contemplatives in every age. But it has a special meaning for Carmelites. He is then "prophetic" after all in the sense that he clearly enunciated what was essential and "Elianic" in the Carmelite ideal: the primacy of solitude and contemplation, not "in spite of" or

[7] *Les Plus Vieux Textes*, p. 161.

"against" apostolic work, but even for the sake of an apostolate that would be all the more effective on account of its restricted, occasional and even quasi-charismatic character.

In summary, the *Fiery Arrow* written as an encyclical to the Carmelite Order when Nicholas was giving up his office in disgust, is partly an earnest exhortation to return to the pure spirit of the Rule of St. Albert, and partly a commentary on the essential prescriptions of that Rule. In the mind of Nicholas the Frenchman, the Carmelites who were living in towns and attempting to preach the Gospel on a large scale without sufficient authority or preparation, were unfaithful to their vocation, were dividing and destroying their Order, and were accomplishing nothing of any pastoral value, that might justify or excuse their defection. They were losing their own souls without helping the souls of others. The reason for this, he thought, was not merely the physical fact that they lived in towns rather than in the forests, but rather that they had abandoned their ideal of prayer, solitude and charity. Let us hear his own words:

> As long as the brethren were united, bound together by sincere charity, and refused to violate their promises; as long as they remained in their cells instead of running about the world, as long as they meditated on the Law of the Lord and were vigilant in prayer, not out of obligation alone but because they were inspired by the impulsion of spiritual joy, as long as they persevered in this gladness, they were true sons (of Carmel). But disunity and inconstancy have split wide open the cement of charity and the stones of the sanctuary have been scattered to the four corners of the world. (p. 167)

> Did not the Lord our Savior grant us the favor of leading us into solitude, and speaking familiarly to our hearts, He who does not manifest Himself to His friends in public, in the

noise of the streets, but in intimacy, by the grace of spiritual joy, in order to reveal to them His mysteries and His secrets? Be not then like mules! Do not imagine that the Lord speaks with fools who seek their own enjoyment or the pleasure of their senses in the vanity of this world, among the crowd of men given to vice, or in the chaos of sinful thoughts that separate a man from God: He wishes, on the contrary, that each one may guard his heart in honor and sanctity, pure of all sin and far from all danger of it. Without mentioning the disgust which such profound stupidity inspires, I ask myself with astonishment why you have chosen the consolation of the world. You cannot possess the joy of God and the joy of this world at the same time. They do not go together, they cannot be reconciled. (p. 171)

It is easy to recognize in this passage the basic principles familiar to every reader of St. John of the Cross, particularly those with which he opens his *Ascent of Mount Carmel*. Nicholas the Frenchman was unable, unfortunately, to quote from the Carmelite Doctor of the Church who came only three centuries after him. Instead, he quoted another who had lived and preached a century before, St. Bernard of Clairvaux: "Divine joy is a delicate thing which is not given to one who seeks any other."

The important thing about this passage is the directness and clarity with which Nicholas attacks, not the apostolic life but simply the sensuality and inconstancy of contemplatives who have grown tired of solitude or have never learned to love it. Anyone can see that this is a vastly different matter. An apostolate that is merely an evasion of a more urgent and more personal responsibility is valueless before God and man. It is nothing but self-delusion, and cannot claim to be based on genuine charity. It can no longer be said with certainty to what extent Nicholas was fair in his judgment of his contemporaries, particularly of that restless younger generation which had not enjoyed the advantages he himself had enjoyed in the east. Doubtless there were shiftless and undisciplined men among them. But history has shown that the majority must have been worth more than the impatient old solitary believed. They must, after all, have developed into true apostles.

The first part of the *Fiery Arrow* is based on the experience, the contemplative instinct, by which Nicholas himself judged between the things of God and the things of the world. It was a bold declaration that if one lived alone and in silence with God, he received a gift of discernment, a kind of supernatural "taste" with which he could instinctively and spontaneously distinguish the true joys of the divine life from the false, nauseating counterfeit. But if one were unfaithful to solitude and to prayer, he would surely be deluded with false ideas of zeal and, in pretending to seek the salvation of others and the interests of the Church, he would in fact ruin his own soul in the pursuit of unreality.

The second part of the *Sagitta* appeals to the objective standard of the Rule and Nicholas sets about the work of commenting on that document, in order to bring out clearly what are the essential obligations of the Carmelite life.

First of all, he says, there are the three vows common to all religious: poverty, chastity and obedience. But each religious family has a special modality of its own: special means by which its members are to sanctify themselves and consecrate to God the aptitudes which He has given them. Nicholas points to the division between active and contemplative Orders, and here he is at least implicitly in agreement with St. Thomas in admitting the superiority of those Orders that engage in the apostolic life.[8] It must never be imagined that the author of the *Fiery Arrow* is concerned with a partisan defense of the contemplative Orders as such. Speaking in the practical language of one experienced in contemplation, he advocates the contemplative life and calls it superior only for those who have a contemplative vocation: and if it is superior for them this is perhaps because they do not have the necessary aptitudes for a life of apostolic action.

God has foreseen that those who would embrace the labors of Martha in the cities should be men with aptitude for intellectual work, for research in Holy Scripture, and men whose spiritual life is so firmly established that they can dispense to the multitudes the nourishment of the divine word. But the simpler sort, those with whom He communes in mystery, these the Lord keeps in solitude with the prophet who says: "Lo I have gone far off, flying away; and I abode in the wilderness. I waited for Him that saved me from pusillanimity of spirit and a storm." (Ps. 54:8-9)

Speaking from his own experience on Mount Carmel and in the west and basing his remarks on the actual persons he had known in the Order, Nicholas seemed to think that the Carmelites of his time were not cut out for the apostolic life except in a very simple and restricted form. But the principles on which he bases this judgment obviously allow for a totally different viewpoint, once the members of the Order are adequately prepared for an active mission. However, he does not envisage any other than the actual situation which confronted him. He writes only for men whom he knew to have been called to the hermit life and who had lost their

8 II IIae Q 188 a 6.c.

way, embracing an active mission for which they were unprepared.

For such men as these, the will of God, manifested by their vocation, was a truly solitary life. Nicholas knows no more satisfactory way of meeting this obligation, that the actual practice he had known and lived on Mount Carmel. The Carmelites, according to him, were obliged by their very vocation to live in isolated cells, in a deserted or rural area.

The Holy Spirit, knowing what is best for each of us, could hardly have inspired without good reason the Rule which says each one of us should have a separate cell. This does not mean neighboring cells, but cells separated from one another, in order that the heavenly spouse and His bride, the contemplative soul, might converse together in the peace of an intimate colloquy . . . Consequently, if we wish to live according to our profession, we must have separated cells, and stay in them, or at least near them, meditating day and night on the Law of the Lord, praying and watching, unless we have other legitimate occupations . . . But you, city dwellers, you have turned the separate cells into a house where you live in common: how can you prepare yourselves for those holy occupations which should be yours? At what hours do you meditate on the Law of the Lord in reflection and prayer? Are not your nights troubled by the remembrance of your vanity, since you pass your day in gossiping, running around, listening, speaking and acting? Your memory is filled with forbidden and impure thoughts to such an extent that your mind is incapable of meditating on anything else . . . If anyone who has made profession of our life finds himself out of his cell, he must ask himself in conscience if he is justified by a legitimate occupation; if he has no reasonable motive, he must get back to his cell. If he disobeys his conscience and does not return to it, he must realize that he is violating his promises. (177, 178)

In reading these bitter reproaches, we can understand why
Nicholas has been considered an extremist by his own Order. It is difficult, if not impossible, to interpret such a text
correctly unless one is able to see through the eyes of the
writer himself. All that is said here is to be understood exclusively from the point of view of one who in actual, concrete fact, was called by God to be a hermit and was fully
aware of it. For such a one, life in the cities would be an
obvious prevarication. But those who came after, who had
made a successful adaptation to the mendicant life, knew
well enough that they could carry on their active, preaching
mission without necessarily being in a state of habitual sin.
On the contrary, though that life had its dangers, it also had
its graces and compensations, and they were no doubt sincerely convinced that the *Fiery Arrow* could no longer be
applied to their case. But then, this could only be because
they had ceased to be what Nicholas believed they ought to
have been, and had become mendicants pure and simple.
Nicholas is not writing for mendicants, but for hermits.
Hence, he insists that for solitaries, life in towns is an infidelity to the Holy Spirit.

Among the reasons for this, he cites first of all ascetic
ones: exterior and interior silence, purity of heart and body,
recollection. But these are not simply ends in themselves.
The positive joys of solitary contemplation are for Nicholas
the most important reason why the hermit should remain in
solitude. These joys are inaccessible in the noise and tur-
moil of the active life. There is probably no more beautiful
chapter in the whole work than that in which he depicts the
hermit's life of praise in union with all creation:

The beauty of the elements and of the firmament of stars and
planets harmoniously ordered, attracts us and leads us on to

higher wonders. The birds, in some way putting on the nature of angels, gladden us by intoning their sweet songs. The mountains, according to the prophecy of Isaias, surround us with great sweetness and the hills flow with that milk and honey which are never tasted by those who, in their madness, have chosen the world. These mountains, our conventual brethren who surround us, unite themselves with the psalms which we sing to the glory of the Creator as a lute accompanying words. While we praise the Lord, the roots grow, the grass becomes green, the branches and trees rejoice in their own fashion and applaud our praises. Wonderful flowers, delicately scented, gladden our solitude with their laughter. The silent light of the stars tells us the hours set apart for God's service. Wild growing things cover us with shade and offer us their pleasant fruits. All our sisters the creatures who, in solitude, charm our eyes or our ears, give us rest and comfort. In silence they give forth their beauty like a song, encouraging our soul to praise the wonderful Creator. Isaias speaks to us in figure of this joy of solitude and of the desert: "The land that was desolate and impassable shall be glad and the wilderness shall rejoice, and shall flourish like the lily. It shall bud forth and blossom and rejoice in prayer and praise." (Isa. 35:1-2) So also in the Psalm: "The beautiful places of the wilderness shall grow fat: and the hills shall be girded about with joy." (Ps. 64:13) (182, 183)

There is no need to crown this beautiful passage with an obvious platitude by calling it Franciscan, as if St. Francis had a monoply on the contemplation of the Creator in His creation. This view of creation is so traditionally and essentially Christian that it is found in all the saints who have been at all articulate on the subject, and perhaps not least surprisingly in some of the most austere. It is certainly found in St. John of the Cross—in fact all through the *Fiery Arrow* we hear echoes of the saint of the *Dark Night* who is also the contemplative of the *Spiritual Canticle* and of the *Living Flame*. The principles are the same, the conclusions are identical. In order to seek true joy, the joy of God in all things, renounce joy in all things. That is, do not trouble and distract your soul with a concern that yearns for this or that limited joy, seeking happiness now here and now there, restlessly passing from one to the other, Renounce the vain quest, give your whole heart of God, and He Himself in return will give you joy in all things.

In order to arrive at having pleasure in everything, desire to have pleasure in nothing . . .

Through the eye that is purged from the joys of sight, there comes to the soul a spiritual joy, directed to God in all things that are seen, whether Divine or profane. Through the ear that is purged from the joy of hearing, there comes to the soul joy most spiritual an hundredfold directed to God in all that it hears, be it Divine or profane. Even so is it with the other senses when they are purged. For even as in the state of innocence all that our first parents saw and heard and ate in Paradise furnished them with greater sweetness of contemplation, so that the sensual part of their nature might be duly subjected to, and ordered by, reason; even so the man whose sense is purged from all things of sense and made subject to the spirit, receives, in his very first motion, the delight of delectable knowledge and contemplation of God.[9]

We can sum up our discussion of the *Fiery Arrow* with the following conclusions. It has certain superficial resemblances to the anti-mendicant tracts of the 13th century, but in reality it is an entirely different kind of thing. To reject it along with William of Saint Amour would be to misun-

[9] Ascent of Mount Carmel: i, xiii, vol. 1 p. 63 and iii, xxvi, id. p. 288.

derstand completely its deep and undying message. It is not an attack on the apostolic life, or on the mendicant Orders. Far rather it is a defense of an original, unique and quite unusual combination of contemplation and apostolate. It is a defense of a religious family that would necessarily always be isolated and small, and of an apostolate that would never be fruitful on a large external scale. The insistence of Nicholas on the Rule of St. Albert is less juridical than the spiritual, and he is not concerned with defending contemplation or action as specific ends and works to be achieved. On the contrary, what he insists on is the concrete, we might say existential value of the life itself that he had known on Mount Carmel. What he feared—and not without reason,— was that this unique life would be altogether lost to the Church and would vanish from the world.

That the Carmelites might go through a kind of "dialectical" development and reach a new solution, beyond and above the apparent opposition that troubled Nicholas the Frenchman, seems not to have occurred to the author of the *Fiery Arrow*. But in any case, for the dialectic to be valid, the new solution would have to include within itself all the values inherent in both the thesis and the antithesis that had been transcended. The Carmelites would have to be in the truest sense both hermits, and apostles. They would have to be something more than simple solitaries, more than ordinary preachers. They would have to be men of God who were "prophets" living and acting, by their poverty and nakedness of spirit, according to the austere laws of the desert, directly and continually dependent on God the Holy Spirit.

IV . *Reform and apostolate*

The whole subsequent history of Carmel is in fact the history of this endeavor. Whether the solution was ever fully achieved in the Middle Ages can perhaps be a matter for dispute. At any rate, the Order survived, prospered, declined, revived in many ways and in many places. There was the 15th century reform of Bl. John Soreth which brought into existence those Carmelite nuns who were to be reformed again by St. Theresa of Avila. In 1567, Father John Baptist Rubeo, General of the Carmelites, coming to apply in Spain the decrees of the Council of Trent for the reform of religious, laid down this principle as the basis for the renewal of life in what had now been for three hundred years a mendicant and apostolic Order:

> The chief and primitive ideal of the inhabitants of Mount Carmel—an ideal which every Carmelite must imitate and pursue—is this: day and night they must consecrate all the efforts of which they are capable to uniting their soul and their spirit to God the Father by meditation, contemplation and uninterrupted love. And this is to be done not only in a habitual fashion but also actually.[10]

St. Theresa herself had no other purpose in her reform than a return to the solitude and contemplation of the primitive Carmelite ideal. She says so explicitly:

> All of us who wear this sacred habit of Carmel are called to prayer and contemplation because that was the first principle

[10] Quoted by Bruno de Jesus-Marie, in "Traversées Historiques," *Etudes Carmelitaines*, Avril 1935, p. 18.

of our Order and because we are descended from the line of those holy Fathers of ours from Mount Carmel who sought this treasure, this precious pearl of which we speak, in such great solitude and with such contempt for the world.[11]

Yet at the same time, the reformer of Carmel clearly conceived that the prayers of the Discalced Nuns had an apostolic object: they were to pray especially for the salvation of souls and for the work of the priests engaged in the work of the Counter-Reformation. Such apostolic prayer was, indeed, "the principal reason for which the Lord has brought us together in this house." [12]

Hence, in one word, it is clear that the Discalced Carmelite Reform was a return to the primitive spirit of solitude, but at the same time a renewal of the apostolic spirit. But it can be said that this renewal was, in fact, given an original character of its own by the circumstances of the time.

It would be tedious and out of place here to enter into all the intricacies of the history of the Discalced Carmelite Reform in this matter. Let it be sufficient to indicate that once the reform broke off from the "Calced" and became autonomous in Spain, it was divided from within into two strongly opposed factions, especially after the death of St. Theresa who "protected Fr. Jerome Gratian against Doria and against himself." [13] On the one hand there was Fr. Doria, the hermit of Pastrana, the ferocious partisan of strict observance, solitude and austerity before all else. The sagacity of St. Theresa had held him in check as long as she was alive. As soon as she was dead, Doria would make short work of Fr. Jerome Gratian whom he considered a "radical," and who seemed to be undermining the reform with his zeal for

[11] Interior Castle, v, i. Vol. ii (Peers trans.) p. 247.
[12] Way of Perfection, iii, vol. ii, p. 10.
[13] cf. Fr. Bruno de Jesus Marie, art, cit. p. 25.

apostolic work and even for foreign missions. Once again it was the old opposition that had excited such anguish in the writer of the *Fiery Arrow*. In between the two stood St. John of the Cross, who transcended them both, who included in himself all that was good in either of them: who was an austere lover of solitude, but more prudent than Doria because he knew that solitude itself could become a fetish, an object of immoderate attachment. He knew that the love of austerity could become a mere "penance of beasts." He fully understood and carried out St. Theresa's apostolic ideals without being swept away by the volatile enthusiasms of a Gratian. He it was who embodied in himself the true prophetic spirit of Carmel, and it is remarkable that of the three, he was the one who was externally the least fiery, the least impressive, the most obscure. Of the three he was the most silent, the most retiring, the truest solitary, the greatest contemplative. But also, at the same time, he was of the three the greatest apostle, the one who had the surest and deepest effect on other people. These were not souls whom he had hunted out with the busy zeal of an aggressive convert maker: they were people who had been brought to him by God, without his knowing how they came to him. And they were transformed, as a result, without either he or they knowing what had happened.

The most remarkable thing about St. John of the Cross and Saint Theresa of Avila is that in their lives as well as in their words they represent the perfect flowering of the Carmelite ideal as it was conceived by Nicholas the Frenchman and glorified in the *Fiery Arrow*. The mystical works of St. John of the Cross are simply the flowering of seeds that germinate on every page of the 13th century encyclical of the hermit of Carmel. The "desert" doctrine of the Carmelite mystics is again the realization of all that is implied in the aspirations of Nicholas the Frenchman. Yet it cannot be said that the life of the first Discalced Carmelites was in every physical detail the life demanded by the earliest version of the Rule of St. Albert and defended with such ardor by Nicholas in the *Fiery Arrow*. It might at first sight seem that Doria and his party were tending, by their austerity and violent defense of primitive eremitism, toward a greater conformity with the ideals of Nicholas. But this is not the case. It is in Theresa and John of the Cross that we find the true successors to the one who fired that original arrow. Whether or not they were acquainted with the document is not, of itself, particularly important.

But it must be admitted that the apostolic ideal of a St. Theresa was much more far reaching than that of Nicholas the Frenchman. True, but her situation was different. The Carmelites had for centuries been established as a mendicant Order and they had a definite function to fulfil in the Church. They could fulfil that function and still return closer to the primitive ideal. This could be done in two ways: by a recovery of the original spirit of solitude and prayer, and by a reduction of the apostolate to a more occasional and more specialized level. And so, though the Discalced Carmelites did not reproduce in every detail the life of the first hermits on the Holy Mountain, they did revive the primitive spirit of the Order in a very authentic form particularly adapted to the post-Tridentine counter-reformation.

In spite of the apparent "victory" that rewarded the centralizing politics of Doria and his party, in spite of the fact that Gratian was broken and John of the Cross died, the policies of Doria did not prevail. On the contrary, it was the apostolic and missionary ideal, which had been the ideal of Theresa of Avila, came out on top in the end. Indeed,

Carmelite Friars began to cross the seas to Africa and Asia, and Mount Carmel itself was to be reconquered and resettled by them.

In 1582, even before the death of St. Theresa, Gratian had sent a party of Carmelites to make a foundation in Ethiopia which was almost as bad as sending them to the moon. When the party was shipwrecked and drowned, the Doria faction hailed the event with ferocious satisfaction as a manifest sign of divine displeasure with the apostolic party. A first party of friars that was sent out to the Congo was captured by British pirates and marooned. Renewed satisfaction on the part of the hermits! A second group which succeeded in getting to the Congo was left to die there by Doria who abandoned them after he got in power. Nevertheless the missionary ideal persisted. Eliseus of the Martyrs, who was to be provincial of the Carmelites in Mexico, well knew the apostolic zeal of St. John of the Cross, who believed that "it was not the will of God that the Order of His Mother should be limited and restricted to the boundaries of Spain, but that it should extend and spread out to every part of the Church provided that the institution of the Order could be kept there." [14]

These last words are very important, and whatever may have been St. John's sense of the apostolate, he, of all the Carmelite saints, certainly came closest to the author of the *Fiery Arrow* in his sense of the primacy of contemplation. We need only to quote here the celebrated passage from the *Spiritual Canticle* in which he says that the Carmelite who has been drawn into union with God by prayer should not be disturbed with active works, unless of course God Himself commands and inspires them. This is the obvious

[14] Quoted in art. cit. p. 26.

development of the doctrine expressed in the *Fiery Arrow*. It is worth remembering.

> When it reaches that estate (of unitive love) it befits it not to be occupied in other outward acts and exercises which might keep it back, however little, from that abiding in love with God, although they may greatly conduce to the service of God; for a very little of this pure love is more precious in the sight of God and the soul, and of greater profit to the Church, even though the soul appear to be doing nothing, than are all the works together. . . . Therefore if the soul have aught of this degree of solitary love, great wrong would be done to it and to the Church if, even but for a brief space, one should endeavor to busy it in active or outward affairs, of however great moment . . . Let those then that are great actives, that think to girdle the world with their outward works and their preachings, take not that here they would bring far more profit to the Church and be far more pleasing to God (apart from the good example which they would give of themselves) if they spent even half this time in abiding with God in prayer, even had they not reached such a height as this.[15]

This is a weighty statement, and one which disturbs us in our anxiety to be always producing some visible result to justify our existence in the Church. Clearly it cannot be adduced as an excuse to evade the normal duties of religious life. But it certainly shows that St. John of the Cross, for all his apostolic zeal, would never have countenanced the foundation of a Carmelite community under circumstances that would involve the Friars in extremely burdensome and continual active works, to the detriment of their main object which is solitude and contemplation. This did not prevent

---

[15] Spiritual Canticle, xxix, 2. Vol. ii (Peers trans.) p. 346.

him from desiring missionary foundations in Africa or America. When Doria was engineering his disgrace, St. John thought of retiring to the Carmelite foundation in Mexico, but died before this could be achieved. And Theresa of Jesus had wept at the convent grille when she heard, from a Franciscan missionary, of the millions of souls being lost in the Americas. Though the Doria party firmly refused to spread the Theresian reform outside of Spain, the gordian knot was cut by Pope Clement VIII who established the Discalced in Italy in a separate province, and instructed them to make foundations "at Rome and in all parts of the world." [16]

Carmelites established themselves in Persia (1607), Mesopotamia, Syria, India, Central and South America, Africa, the East Indies, and in 1631 a Spaniard of the Province of Genoa, Prosper of the Holy Spirit, returned to live as a hermit in a cave on Mount Carmel. The Friars had come back to the Holy Mountain of Elias and of the Blessed Virgin! This symbolic gesture was conceived in one of the desert hermitages of the Discalced Friars, and this important movement deserves consideration in the concluding words of our study.

v . Carmelite deserts

It has been said that the institution of the "deserts" was the closest approach to the primitive Carmelite ideal made by any reform of the Order since the middle ages. The author of the idea was Thomas of Jesus, and it is significant that he was first of all a faithful follower of St. Theresa and of St. John of the Cross, and secondly that he was of the apostolic group, rather than of the Doria party. When Thomas of Jesus first proposed to Doria the foundation of a "desert"

[16] Fr. Bruno de Jesus Marie, art. cit. p. 27.

—that is to say of a remote and isolated community where a small number would live as true hermits in separate cells, Doria refused permission on the ground that it would disrupt the Order and draw "all the best men" away from the cities into solitude. This paradoxical admission shows us at once how complex was the character of the organizer and hermit who took command of the Discalced Carmelites after the death of St. Theresa! Thomas of Jesus obediently renounced his plan. But it happened that one day in 1591 when he was professor and vice rector in the Carmelite house of studies at Alcala, he was re-reading his notes on the plan for a desert foundation and, being called suddenly away, left them lying open on his table. The rector chanced to see them, and becoming enthusiastic about the project, brought up the subject of its possibilities. Interest was aroused. The plan was once again presented discretely to Doria who, this time, accepted it. The definitory decreed the establishment of a desert foundation. A benefactor offered land, and the first Carmelite desert of Bolarque, in an isolated rocky valley of Castille, came into existence. Four Friars hastened to the spot and the first small buildings were erected in the summer of 1592.

What was the nature and purpose of a Carmelite "desert"? Physically it resembled a Camaldolese *eremo*: a village of separate cells, with a chapel, a gatehouse, an enclosure wall. There were also more isolated hermitages in the woods, to which the brethren might retire at certain periods of the year for more complete solitude. The population of a "desert" consisted of some twenty to twenty-four friars and a maximum of six lay brothers. Of the friars, four were permanent hermits, assigned to the desert at their own request for the rest of their days. Of these, one was the Prior, chosen for his contemplative wisdom, love of solitude, and aptitude to direct and moderate the lives of his companions. The majority of the hermits were temporary residents, assigned to the desert (usually at their own request) for periods of several months or for an entire year. In some provinces it was required that men spend a certain time in the desert before ordination to the priesthood or before being sent to a foreign mission.

Generally speaking, the desert was regarded as a special function of that contemplative solitude and necessary in an apostolic Order, though it would not be quite correct to say that the friars went to the desert *to prepare themselves for* apostolic work. That would be a misleading conception. Contemplative solitude has no ulterior purpose, and when it seems to have one, it becomes degenerate, and ceases to be what it pretends to be. The function of the Carmelite desert was not to be merely a place of retirement to which one would have access *before* apostolic labors in order to prepare oneself spiritually or *after* apostolic labor in order to recover and rest. No such pragmatism could ever be fully compatible with the true Carmelite ideal. On the contrary, it would be truer to say that the desert was a place to which the friars went to be most truly what they were called, Carmelites, faithful sons of the Virgin of Carmel and spiritual descendants of Elias. The purpose of the deserts was to give them access to that pure and perfect climate of solitude without which they would never fully be themselves. Even where the deserts do not exist (and in most provinces of the Carmelites they do not exist today), wherever the authentic spirit of Carmel prevails, Friars who have never seen a desert nevertheless have in their heart the hunger for solitude and prayer which only such a place as this could provide.

Even where deserts do not exist, the spirit of solitude and

contemplation is ever present in the Order. It is inescapable because of the fervor and the primitive purity of the Discalced Carmelite nuns, who, like the Carthusians, have had the distinction of never needing another reform.

In the seventeenth century there were deserts everywhere in the Order, even in Mexico. They were particularly numerous in Spain, Italy and France. Many ordinary Carmelite monasteries, though in towns, managed to maintain hermitages in their large gardens. An interesting history of these desert houses, unfortunately incomplete, was written by a historian of the Order, Father Benedict Mary of the Holy Cross.[17] He described twenty-two deserts of the Order of which all but one had ceased to exist in his time. But since then, especially since the second world war, the general return to contemplation which has manifested itself in various other forms, also produced this revival of a Carmelite desert in France. The Order took over an abandoned Camaldolese hermitage at Roquebrune, in the mountains of southern France. This became a desert for the French and Belgian Provinces of the Discalced Carmelite Friars. Two other deserts also exist in Spain and quite naturally there is talk of deserts in other provinces of the Order. There is no reason why such a desert should not soon be founded in the United States, and such a foundation would certainly correspond to the deepest desires of several American Carmelite friars known to the author.

Since this is the case, it is perhaps not useless to bring back to mind the strangely moving pages of the *Fiery Arrow*, and to reflect on the reasons why the document was so long passed over and forgotten.

It is true that the author of the *Fiery Arrow* was in some sense a failure, an idealist who rebelled against the trend of

[16] Les saints deserts des carmes dechaussés, Paris, 1927.

the times without being able to change anything. Let us be careful not to reject his testimony out of a kind of secret, semi-pelagian pragmatism which flourishes more vigorously than we realize among us today. There are signs that a revival of solitary life in its various forms is of great importance for the Church today. One of these forms is the Carmelite Desert, and here no special complications stand in the way of the project being easily realized. The Carmelites themselves have an easy and obvious way of putting to practical use such suggestions of their primitive tradition as can be applied to the needs of our day.

What about the rest of us? Have we something more than this to learn from the primitive tradition of Carmel? I think so. It may very well be that Nicholas the Frenchman was very far ahead of his time. It certainly seems that the very original form of contemplative life which he tried vainly to preserve in its simplicity in the 13th century, is one of the things we need, and ought to seek to establish in our own day. I refer to the conception of a small eremitical community practicing solitude, prayer, manual labor and the traditional exercises of the solitary life, but at the same time permitting and envisaging an informal apostolate, consisting of restricted, somewhat "special" contacts with people outside. This, after all, was something like the life planned by Charles de Foucauld for his hermits in the Sahara. His dream was never realized in his lifetime. It has been realized, in a modified form, by the Little Brothers of Jesus. But the Little Brothers, like the Carmelites of St. Simon Stock, are mostly in cities and towns. Their vocation is to work among men. There still remains a need for a purely eremitical community, isolated and quiet, to which perhaps a few people might have access by invitation or otherwise. The outside contacts would have to be small and selective.

There would be no question of a habitual apostolate. But there would be room for a contemplative and spiritual dialogue with laypeople or members of other Orders. The fruit would be the extension of the spiritual and intellectual lives: of contemplation in a broad and healthy sense, integrated in every form of human existence. Ideally speaking, such a community could engage in a very fruitful dialogue with non-Catholic intellectuals, with Oriental thinkers, with artists and philosophers, scientists and politicians—but on a very simple, radical and primitive level, though in full cognizance of the problems of our time. This is just one example that occurs, of a possible application to our day of the primitive ideal of a solitary, contemplative and apostolic group, with a primitive and "prophetic" character—a voice crying in the wilderness to prepare the ways of the Lord.

ABSURDITY IN SACRED DECORATION

Somewhere in his *Mont Saint Michel and Chartres*, Henry
Adams makes the remark that a medieval artist would sooner
have gone about with a landscape painted on the back of
his coat, than put one in a stained glass window. Of course,
the nineteenth century turned church windows into magic-
lantern slides of our Lord's life. The men of an earlier age
had a very keen sense of symbolism—a sense which we have
almost completely lost. In exchange, we have acquired a
rather more trite and compulsive need: the appetite for use
less decoration and for illustration, in the expressive German slang expression, the appetite for *Kitsch*.

1 . *Symbolism or illustration?*

This directly affects our true sense of liturgy and, consequently, our inner life of prayer. For while liturgical sym-

bol is a vital and effective force in the life of prayer—it plays an active part in our worship—mere decoration is inert, confusing, and a kind of dead-weight on prayer. It distracts not in the superficial sense of substituting one concept for another, but in a deeper way: by drawing us from the realm of intuition and of mystery into the more superficial level of sentimental fantasy.

Symbolism fortifies and concentrates the spirit of prayer, but illustration tends rather to weaken and to dissipate our attention. Symbolism acts as a very efficacious spiritual medium. It opens the way to an intuitive understanding of mystery—it places us in the presence of the invisible. Illustration tends rather to become an obstacle, to divert and to amuse rather than to elevate and direct. It tends to *take the place of* the invisible and to obscure it.

And note that in most cases symbolism is more concrete, more visible and tangible, more incarnate than mere decoration. Symbolic objects are effective by their own actuality, their concrete presence and function. Illustrations are rather vague reminders or suggestions, stimulants for the senses, meant to encourage a pious mood or to induce a sentimental sense of comfort. They have no constructive function, they merely entertain and soothe.

But when a person seeks the living God, and not mere psychological comfort, useless decoration does not entertain, it annoys. Needless to say, when the decoration itself is in bad taste, the results are even worse. No amount of subjective sincerity can completely offset the corrupting effect of vulgarity and materialism in prayer.

To approve of symbolism as we have just done, and to deprecate pictorial decoration, is not to say that every detail of liturgical ornament must be on a plane of high symbolic seriousness, and even have some "intellectual content" or precise meaning. There must always be room for free artistic play and for the exuberant use of line and color when it is really called for. A chasuble does not *have to be* covered with crosses, or fishes, or monograms of the holy Name. Simple decorative lines and designs without any specific reference to any symbol, are perfectly acceptable and entirely in the spirit of the liturgy. They are much more effective than labored and unimaginative conventions which repeat over and over again an outworn symbolic theme. But what is objectionable above all is the *illustrative* convention which harps on pictorial decoration without rhyme or reason, and with no concern for propriety or good sense.

There is a fundamental absurdity in using a liturgical vestment as a frame for a picture, or, more particularly, a portrait. Certainly there is a place for painting, for the ikon, in sacred worship: but that place is not on the back of the priest, or on the pall, the burse, the chalice veil, etc. The fact that a custom in this sense has grown up does not make it any more logical. Customs can sometimes be very illogical and silly.

II . *Selected absurdities*

Here is an extreme example of the absurdity of this spirit of illustration. This morning I said Mass, through no fault of my own, in a white chasuble which had, on the back, a picture of a lighted candle up against a design of a Gothic rose window. Now already on the altar two large candles were burning with bright flames perfectly and unobtrusively fulfilling their symbolic function. What possible sense could be made by a picture of a candle on the celebrant's back? We have no rose window in our chapel. But certainly the fact that we have none does not mean that we need one, still less that the need can be partially fulfilled by a picture of one—and, of all places, on the chasuble! An added note of absurdity came from the fact that the candle was realistically presented with a notch melted out of one side!

It is quite evident that the inane mentality of the Christmas card designer has now reached out into vestment making. What are we to suffer next? A bevy of merry choristers? Santa Claus? or even a Plum Pudding?

Another absurdity: you open the tabernacle, and there is the ciborium, covered with a veil. And on the veil, what? A picture of a chalice and a host. What need is there of a picture of a host on a ciborium full of real hosts? This question may at first seem surprising to some. But it will only surprise those who have a peculiarly modern mentality alienated from the sense of symbolism and completely dedicated to "illustration." I shall give what I think is the explanation for this mentality later on.

The priest stands at the altar, after the consecration. The sacred Body and Blood of the Lord are there before him. And on the pall—a highly colored, sugary painting of the divine Infant. I say "sugary" because the purpose seems to be to make Him look like candy, something "you could eat." On the burse, an equally overpowering, dramatic, even sentimental portrait of the Lord crowned with thorns.

An aid to faith? For one who has a deep sense of the meaning of bread and wine, of the reasons why the Lord purposely selected these elements for the Sacrament of His love, the accretion of pious pictures only confuses and disturbs faith.

To bring forth these useless stimuli is in reality like adding water to wine. You may think you are making the wine "go further" but actually you are weakening the wine to such an extent that the Mother of the Lord can say, as she said at Cana, that we have none left.

There is very definitely a place for artistic form and design on vestments and sacred objects, but we must conform to the noble logic of liturgical tradition. This logic is symbolic and objective and it requires that the sacred objects themselves should have full power to exercise their function as signs.

They are not mere vehicles for other signs, they are signs themselves, and therefore their signification depends first of all on the integrity of their own form. Any decorative additions should simply reinforce this symbolic character and not distract from it. They should be simple, hieratically significant, and perhaps even to a great extent abstract, depending on circumstances

On the face of the altar, sometimes one sees an elaborately carved and even painted representation of the Last Supper—inspired of course by Da Vinci. Is this necessary to remind the faithful that the Mass is the Lord's Supper?

Maybe so, if the altar has lost its true character and no longer looks even remotely like a table: if one forgets that Christ Himself is present and active in the priest as well as in the Blessed Sacrament and that the altar is at once the supper table and the Lord Himself. It may seem logical and even necessary to put a picture of Christ on the front of the altar, since without this perhaps the faithful will never think that the altar represents Christ. The trouble is that even with a picture they probably will not think of it either.

Someone might object that since the rubrics at present prescribe that there should be a crucifix on or above the altar during the eucharistic Sacrifice, the spirit of the liturgy *does* call for illustration: for a graphic representation of the sufferings of the Savior. That is not the idea at all. In the first place, this rubric itself presents a problem that has been discussed with some heat. I do not intend to discuss it here. The fact remains that there is little real sense in having a life-size, realistic representation of the Lord on the cross when the altar already symbolizes the divine Savior as priest and as victim.

In any events, the crucifix is not so much a picture of the passion as an eschatalogical sign of Christ's victory over sin and death. It is a sacred symbol with a sacramental quality of its own, not merely an illustration which arouses certain appropriate emotions and "affections" in the beholder. Certainly it may do this but such is not the primary function of the crucifix: the psychological effect is something derivative.

The crucifix is not a picture of something that once happened, it is a sacred presence, a sign of the Lord, a sign of victory and of power. And the efficacy of this great religious sign, the sign which makes us Christians before all else, is not necessarily increased by its specifically *representational* character.

It is certainly essential to the Christian spirit that the crucifix should be a *true sign* of Christ's suffering and triumph. And this truth depends on fidelity to Christian tradition. The sacred crucifix is a visual statement of the fundamental dogma of our faith, and hence the figure of Lord must at once be recognized as the Christ of faith, not as a subjective caricature. But this does not mean that realistic *graphic representation* is essential to the sacred sign.

On the contrary, while a definitely objective quality of truth is demanded, subjective emotionalism tends to lessen the true force of the symbol of the cross, and to create a diversion in favor of dramatic appeal which is not universal. It may strongly affect certain types and temperaments, but it will also, by that very fact, distract or even repel others of diverse character. It is precisely this emotional tone of subjectivity which paves the way for caricature.

Let us not forget that the vivid religious expressionism which strikes, and sometimes shocks us in modern sacred art, is simply a further derivation and purification of the subjectivism and drama of the past three centuries. How different are the objectivity and serene symbolic calm of the Byzantine and Italian Primitive styles!

One may object that in the most perfect chalices of the eighth, ninth and tenth centuries there are carved figures of personages like the Lord and His apostles. Yes, certainly. But these are not mere representations. Besides, a chalice has from time immemorial been a traditional place for visual symbolism, whether painted or carved. In adopting this tradition which flourished everywhere in the western world, the Church was simply doing what she did in everything else: taking ordinary and familiar things and consecrating them to the worship of God.

Needless to say, the carved figures on a sacred chalice should preferably have an austerely simple, hieratic character. They should not be efforts to represent psychological states or emotions. In any case, the chalice *need not* have such figures on it and indeed is usually much better without them.

III . *The heart of the matter*

In a word, the use of *symbol* and *design* in liturgical vestments and sacred objects is absolutely demanded by Catholic tradition. But the use of mere illustrative decoration is a modern accretion which disturbs the true liturgical effect of the sacred objects and tends to divert them, at least potentially, from their true spiritual purpose.

Actually, there is a kind of crypto-manicheanism that brings about this false attitude. We think that for a mere drinking cup to have a sacred and "spiritual" quality, we must add to it a "representation of something spiritual"—a stimulus for religious emotion or for psychological experience. In fact, however, a chalice, a vestment, a candle, or an altar cloth becomes a spiritual and sacred thing when its actual, physical entity is consecrated to the service of God.

Indeed, its ordinary form, by which it is adapted simply to its natural purpose, is already implicitly spiritual. It requires no camouflage in order to find its way into divine worship. It does not have to pretend to be something "more" than it actually is. To be "spiritual" a sacred object does not need to have its material being exorcised in some manner by the superaddition of something "mental" or "psychological," having an explicitly and obviously religious reference.

What we need to understand is that the candles on the altar fulfill their spiritual function by being candles, by burning, by giving light. That candlelight is itself more spiritual than electric light insofar as it is simpler, more primitive, more apt to be associated, in our minds, with silence, recollection and peace.

A vestment fulfills its function by being a garment. It does not have to become, at the same time, a holy picture, before it can be regarded as spiritual. Its shape, its texture, its color, all contribute far more to its "spiritual quality" than any adventitious pictorial accretions our fancy may see fit to tack on to it.

What is the source of this obsession with "illustration" and mere pictorial decoration in sacred art? I think in part it comes from an unconscious assimilation of the commercial mentality. It comes from the fact that our minds have been corrupted by the spirit of advertising. We think in terms of trade-marks, not of symbols.

In advertising, as we know, symbolism has reached its crudest and most degraded condition. Symbols have all but disappeared from commercial art, at least in America (Europe is still comparatively enlightened in this respect). Here, we simply present the material commodity in its crudest, rawest and most violently appetizing form. The idea is to give a picture of the goods that makes the consumer want them—and want them so badly that he cannot resist. The food in the picture looks "so luscious" that he has to go to the phone and order it immediately. It is a question of salesmanship.

Perhaps our concept of the love of God has been affected by this merchandising outlook. Certainly it seems to me that the "illustrations" I have talked about are simply representations of the "spiritual good" that is to be found in our liturgy, if it is sufficiently desired.

There is no question that desire is an essential element in prayer but perhaps it would be better to call this desire by a purer and more theological name, which is *hope*. But our liturgical designers, including perhaps chiefly those most innocent and fervent of them, the sisters, have ingenuously adopted the advertising technique: but of course with all the necessary decorum. They have decided to "show us" that good which we have come to Church to seek. The divine Child is so sweet that we can delay no longer, we must hasten to Communion and enjoy the sensible consolations He brings.

It is no longer a question of a symbolic presence, of a sacred sign, which is itself a concrete and very powerful source of grace. This we no longer understand. We think that would be too crude. The liturgical image has to be a picture of something else than itself. It must point to something "spiritual" in the sense of "psychological." "Interior" has now come to mean "subjective." And, let us face it, it means feeling.

Hence the function of liturgical "illustration" and "decoration" is to advertise certain possibilities of emotional satisfaction which we can make our own if we go to work and stir up the appropriate affections in the depths of our own soul. These illustrations are simply advertisements, seeking to arouse in us the desire for a good religious feeling—or indeed to impart that feeling directly.

I do not deny that there are some people for whom this may work. But I question the fact that it is the full and true traditional function of sacred art.

On the contrary, I think it represents a degradation and an impoverishment of Christian symbolism. I think it makes art a destructive and dissipating force, which leads the way in the long run to an equally unhealthy revulsion in the form of puritanical iconoclasm. Indeed, I would imagine that puritanism itself (that classically businesslike religion), having first removed valid art and then permitted the substitution of more corrupt and popular forms, has paved the way for the degradation of sacred art by sentimentality.

But at all events, the priest at the altar should be seen as Christ clothed in the chasuble of His priestly glory, not as a sandwich man advertising the emotional satisfactions that are to be derived from sacramental devotion

ST. BERNARD, MONK AND APOSTLE

A saint is a sign of God. His life bears witness to God's fidelity to promises made to man from the beginning. He tells us who God is by fulfilling God's promises in himself and by being *full of God*. For that is what God has promised us: that we shall know Him by the gift of His own Spirit living in our hearts.[1]

The saint is therefore a "sacrament" of God's mercy in the world, the pledge of heaven, the visible expression of God's presence in the Church and of God's power working in time to sanctify the world through the mystical body of His Christ. The very presence of the saint in the world affirms that Christ *lives*: that He is risen from the dead, that our faith is therefore not vain. The saint moreover reminds us that in yet a little while Christ will come again and take

---

[1] Ezech. 36:24-28; Gen. 17:7 f.; Exod. 6:7; II Cor. 6:16.

us to Himself,[2] so that we may be where He is, live by His life, and never be separated from Him. The life of the saint is concrete evidence of the marriage of the godhead and human nature. That marriage, first celebrated when the Blessed Virgin said "yes" to the message of the great Arch-angel Grabriel, reaches out to prolong and extend itself through all mankind in those who, by the Spirit of God, are transformed and perfected from glory to glory in the image of His Son.[3]

The saint is a living sign of Christ, a replica of Christ; in a sense, the saint *is* Christ.[4] The saints are the joy of the world. They fulfill the prophecies of freshness, renewal, re-birth, and abundance which spring up everywhere in Isaias. They prolong the great work of re-creation which took place when the fallen world rose from the tomb with Christ. Filled with the triumphant joy of Christ, living out perfectly the promises and grace of their baptism, the saints show forth most fully the supreme fecundity of those saving waters which pour forth from the font to turn the wilderness of a barren earth into a new paradise.[5] Living on a plane of full and supernatural wisdom, they are men of the Spirit, in whom the Holy Spirit Himself bears witness to God's love for the world. He sings in their hearts Christ's hymn of vic-tory over sin, the victory of life over death and of light over darkness. For love, and love alone, is the "new song" which is sung in heaven to the glory of Jesus our Redeemer. The prayers of the saints on earth are offered to God the Father like incense, by the blessed spirits standing before His throne. Sealed with the Holy Spirit of promise, the saint is

[2] John 14:2 f.
[3] II Cor. 3:18; cf. Gen. 1:26; I Cor. 15:49.
[4] II Cor. 13:3.
[5] Isa. 35:1 f.

an irrefutable witness of the mystery of God with us, in His Son Jesus Christ.

If this is true of all the saints, it is particularly true of St. Bernard of Clairvaux, whom we must never dishonor by a partial or fragmentary appreciation. Yet it is often difficult to see the vocation of the greatest saints in all its wholeness and all its simplicity. The greater and more popular the saints are, the better chance they have of being misinterpreted both by those who like them and by those who do not. And it must be admitted that not all the saints appeal to all Catholics. Even today there are many who would pay St. Bernard little more than a grudging and perfunctory honor. The preacher of an unsuccessful crusade may perhaps seem unattractive to a century as tired of war as it is suspicious of "crusades." The uncompromising defender of faith against the forerunners of rationalism may seem like an obscurantist in our age of science. The reformer of monasteries and of the clergy, the ardent Cistercian penitent who so ruined his flesh as to be hardly able to retain a morsel of food in his stomach and who only continued to live for fifty years by a kind of miracle—such a one may frighten us a little, preoccupied as we are with our own health and comfort. There will be many, even Catholics, in our own days, whose sympathies lie less with Bernard of Clairvaux than with Peter Abelard, whom the wild abbot is represented as having hounded to a dishonorable tomb.

Called as he was to exercise a dominant influence in the political and religious life of his time, St. Bernard could hardly avoid being a man of his times. Nor could he help being a many-sided saint. He himself complained ruefully of his vocation to be the chimera of his age.

Born in 1090, the son of a Burgundian nobleman, the

gifted and ardently religious Bernard turned away from the cultivated world of twelfth century France to enter the new monastery of Citeaux in 1112. Citeaux represented one of many reactions against the conventional monastic life of the time. It was a "reform" of the Benedictine rule, a return to the purity of the primitive Benedictine idea. Citeaux stressed poverty, manual labor, austerity, simplicity, separation from the world. In due time the writings of Bernard himself were to add to all this an emphatic call to contemplative union with God. Two years after his profession, Bernard went to found Clairvaux, and began the extraordinary expansion of the Cistercian Order, which by the time of his death numbered 343 monasteries in all parts of Europe. His influence soon extended to other religious orders and began to penetrate all levels of society. Before 1130, when he was called from his cloister to play a decisive part in settling the schism of Anacletus II, Bernard was already renowned as a miracle worker and a man of God, and could gain a respectful hearing from cardinals, kings, and popes, as well as from any bishop or baron in the land. He travelled from one end of Europe to the other, preached against heresy, quelled social revolution, launched the second Crusade, and rose from what was practically his deathbed to make peace between warring cities. His sanctity had been acclaimed even before his death in 1153 and he was canonized in 1174.

It is by no means a sufficient appraisal of St. Bernard to attribute to him merely the dissemination of a monastic ideal, or the contemplative life, the reform of the clergy, the healing of schisms, the reconciliation of heretics with the Church, or the preaching of a crusade. We cannot be content to praise him for all his works together. Nor is it enough to find an appropriate place for St. Bernard in the history of spirituality. We cannot dismiss him with the fantastic understatement which makes him, as it were, a discoverer of the "humanity of Christ." Still less was he merely a propagator of a new devotion of the Holy Mother of God. All these things are true of St. Bernard in a fragmentary way, but not all of them together can give us the true St. Bernard.

The foundation of many monasteries, the elaboration of a profound theology of divine love and contemplation, a charismatic apostolate that embraced his whole world, and roused Christendom to a new realization of the divine mercy manifested in Jesus, through Mary, were all, in St. Bernard, the accidental expressions of a vocation substantially the same as that of St. Paul. He was a witness of God. He gave testimony of the resurrection of Christ. Bernard was sent by God "to complete the preaching of His word amongst you." This was the secret that had been hidden from the ages and generations of the past; now He has revealed it to the saints, wishing *to make known the manifold splendor of this secret* . . . Christ among you, your hope of glory." [6] How else could he "complete" the preaching of the word than by manifesting in his whole life the mystery of the Cross? Like all the saints, Bernard was consumed with the desire to "exhibit every human being perfect in Christ Jesus." [7] Driven by the charity of Christ and impelled by the inward pressure of His Holy Spirit, St. Bernard could say with St. Paul that: "It is for this that I labor, for this that I strive so anxiously; and with effect, *so effectually does His power manifest itself in me.*" [8]

Every great saint is also a great apostle. The exigencies of the divine power make it impossible for them to be any-

[6] Col. 1:27.
[7] *Ibid.*, v. 28.
[8] *Ibid.*, v. 29.

thing else. Even when they remain hidden in the cloister, the vocation of saints remains, in its essence, apostolic,[9] for it is nothing else but the radiation of Christ, by the grace of the Holy Spirit. The saints are beacons in the darkness of a world of sin. They proclaim that the Word has come unto His own and His own receive Him not—but as many as receive Him can be born of God and become sons of God.

Yet we cannot account for St. Bernard by pointing to his apostolate any more than we can do so by extolling his contemplation. It is not even sufficient to discern the perfect union of action and contemplation in this apostolic soul wedded to the Word of God in the flame of His Spirit, and raised up in ecstasy to the bosom of the Father.[10]

Bernard of Clairvaux, crucified with Christ, lived in Christ and Christ lived in him. Bernard not only preached the gospel which he lived, but was, both by his preaching and his life, a living fulfillment of the gospel. That which was perfected in him was done as a sign and a promise for all those who were able to receive his message. For Bernard, like all the saints, was a weak thing of the world caught up by the Spirit of God and transformed in Christ. He became to the world

[9] Pius XII reminds cloistered nuns of this truth in *Sponsa Christi* (AAS, XLIII [1951], 14): "Let them realize that their vocation is fully and in its entirety apostolic, always and everywhere reaching forth to all things which in any way whatever have a regard either to the honor of their Spouse or the salvation of souls." This is exactly the spirit of St. Bernard (Cf. *Serm. 41 in Cant.* nn. 5-6).

[10] "Do you see that it is they whom the Son first humbled by word and example, upon whom in turn the Holy Spirit has poured forth charity, that the Father at last has received in glory? . . . They therefore whom the Son calls by humility to the first heaven, these the Spirit gathers by charity in the second, and the Father lifts to the third by contemplation. . . . It is purity by which we are raised to invisible things, that snatches us up to the third." *De gradibus humilitatis,* nn. 20, 23, 19; *PL,* 182, 953, 955, 952.

the folly of God—the power of God that destroys the wisdom of the wise. Bernard, it is true, had been born of a family that could be accounted great in his Burgundy. But he made himself small and contemptible in the eyes of the world by embracing the humility of Citeaux. He did not realize what God had in store for him and his subsequent career seemed to him, at times, to be the contradiction of his original vocation: but God had drawn him out of the world that he might be all the more perfect an instrument of the power and wisdom of God in the world. In Bernard, then, "God had chosen what the world holds base and contemptible nay, had chosen what is nothing so as to bring to nothing that which is now in being; no human creature was to have any ground for boasting, in the presence of God." [11]

Bernard was amazed at the paradox of his nothingness and of his greatness in Christ. He came to know that his nothingness was in fact his greatness, because Christ, and not Bernard, was great in Bernard. The Bernard who was loved and acclaimed by men saw, with astonishment and satisfaction, that he did not exist. "Neither is it I who am loved, when I am so loved: but I know not what it is that is loved instead of me, something which I am not; . . . without doubt, whatever is thought to be, and is not, is nothing!" [12]   What is man, then asks the Saint, if God be not known to him? Yet the extraordinary thing about this nothingness whom men admired as "Bernard" was that he was a nothing who had discovered God, an empty mirror in which God had cast some reflection of His own divine glory. The knowledge of God—the experience of God in that loving knowledge which is the wisdom of the saints—is the thing that makes the nothingness of man finally begin to *be*

[11] I Cor. 1:28.
[12] *Epist.* xviii, n. 1; *PL*, 182, 121

"The knowledge of God is the reason man is anything." [13]

"Likeness," "vision," and "charity" are, practically speaking, all one for Bernard of Clairvaux.[14] The charity of the saint, which is his sanctity, is nothing else but God's sanctity mirrored in the saint. God's love for Himself, mirrored in a fallen and redeemed creature, becomes God's mercy for man. And so the love of the saint for God is at the same time God's love for Himself, God's love for the saint, and God's love for all mankind.

Like every other saint, then, Bernard is a man who, plunging to the depths of his human nothingness comes back to us resplendent with the divine mercy. There is nothing left for us to see and praise in him but God.

God transforms souls in Himself in order to satisfy the infinite exigencies of His mercy. The soul that is fullest of God's mercy gives God the fullest glory. To see anything else in the saints is to see the accidental. Of course, we must admit the necessity of seeing the accidents of sanctity as well as its substance. But let us first of all insist on the substance, in order that the accidents may not be taken for what they are not. The mystery of Christ is known to us in the lives of the persons for whom to live is Christ and to die is gain. We cannot find Him in them except by studying the details of their history; but it is He above all that we must see in their history.

Bernard of Clairvaux was plainly conscious of the fact that his own life was to serve as evidence of the outpouring of God's mercy upon the world. Perplexed as he sometimes

---

[13] *Ibid.*, n. 2; *PL*, 182, 121.

[14] Such conformity weds the soul to the Word; . . . it (the soul) shows itself like to Him in the will, loving as it is loved." *Serm.* 83 *in Cant.*, n. 3; *PL*, 183, 1182.

was at the apostolic mission which drew him forth from the
cloister into the world, he clearly understood the nature of
that mission. He well knew that the zeal of the apostle, sent
to preach the word of God, does not end with intellectual
instruction, the handing-down of truths to be believed. It is
essentially charismatic and prophetical. It is like the flame of
sanctity that burned the lips of Isaias in his vision of God[15]
flaming forth in a fire of love and truth, radiant with prophetic vision coruscating with miracles and other charisms,
imparting the substance of its own life to other men and
making them share in something of the apostle's own vision
of eternity.[16]

This outpouring of divine grace through the apostle
sent by God is a manifestation of the inexhaustible fecundity of love and mercy within God Himself—a fecundity
which cannot contain itself but must pour itself out into the
hearts of men in order to inebriate them with the wisdom of
sanctity.[17]

---

[15] Isa., chap. 6.

[16] This is beautifully expressed in the ninth responsory of the night
office of St. Bernard's feast (Cistercian Breviary, August 20th): "O olive
tree, bearing fruit in the house of God! O oil of gladness, fomenting
with good deeds, shining with wonders! Make us sharers of that light
and sweetness which Thou dost enjoy! Thou hast entered into the
powers of the Lord and now art more powerful to accomplish by
prayer. Make us, etc." St. Bernard himself describes the apostolic vocation as follows: "Such love loves ardently; it befits the friend of the
Spouse; with it the faithful and wise servant whom the Lord has ap-
pointed over his family must be on fire. It fills up, it is boiling hot, it
bubbles over. Now at last it pours out, rushing forth and breaking out
and saying: 'Who is weak and I am not weak? Who is scandalized and
I am not on fire?' Let it preach, let it bear fruit, let it renew signs and
let it change wonders. There is no place for vanity to mingle where
charity has laid hold of all." Serm. 18 in Cant., n. 6; PL, 183, 862.

[17] "The Fount of life in itself full . . . has multiplied His mercy and,
pouring out in His manifold mercies, has visited the world and inebriated it." Serm. 18 in Cant., n. 4; PL, 183, 861.

St. Bernard saw that the joy of Pentecost must continue throughout all time until the consummation God's plans for the world, when the redeemed would at last be ushered, body and soul, into the marriage feast of the Lamb. The wine of the Holy Spirit would always be with us as a fore-taste and reminder of what is to come. The Spirit Himself is the "new wine" which flows in the streets of the heavenly Jerusalem. He is poured out upon us in exchange for the Bread of Angels, Jesus, who has been taken from earth to heaven at the Ascension.[18] Yet Christ continues by His Holy Spirit, to live in the world and to work among us. The Spirit indeed effects that "necessary presence of Christ" [19] by which the Church continues His work of redemption applying the fruits of His Cross to men.

Dizzy with the new wine of this doctrine, St. Bernard knew that he was called to make others share in the divine delights. Blazing with a holy impatience, his humility armed itself against the pride of the worldly wise, and strove to rouse them from their banquet of ashes, the apples of So-dom, upon which they feasted in their blind curiosity.[20] He would call men from the husks of swine to the school of Christ where they would not merely *learn about* God but would come to know God Himself in the ineffable love of Christ. Bernard would not merely instruct them, but as a minister of Christ he would give them the Holy Ghost. Then they would experience in all truth the fact that the

18 *Serm. 3, Pentecost,* n. 2: *PL, 183, 330.*
19 *Serm. 7, Advent.,* n. *PL, 183, 55.*
20 "We read that there have been some whose supreme desire and only care were to investigate the manner and order of things done . . . con-tent with the most sparse and wretched food. They indeed call them-selves philosophers; by us they are called, and more rightly, vain and curious men." *Serm. 3 Pentecost,* n. 3; *PL, 183, 331.*

charity of Christ is poured forth in our hearts by the Holy
Spirit who is given to us. If He is given, then He is ours.
Why then should we not show our gratitude by recognizing this tremendous Gift and using it? "It is granted us for
use, for a wonder, for salvation, for help, for comfort, for
fervor." [21] Best of all is this last aspect of the outpouring of
the Spirit. Few there are who know His divine fervor, which
glories in tribulations, rejoices in insult and humiliation,
and who are inebriated with the sweet bitterness of the
Cross.[22]

In this fervor of spirit the soul thirsts for more than liberty, more than any reward or any inheritance. It thirsts for
God Himself.[23] And it is to souls athirst for God that St.
Bernard loves above all to address himself. He found them
most of all in his own Cistercian monasteries where he
would cast aside all formalities and speak to his spiritual
sons from the depths of his own heart, exclaiming: "Today
let us read in the book of experience!"[24] Such familiarity
was only possible when he was dealing with souls who could
verify, from their own intimate experience, something of
the ineffable doctrine which only those can understand who
have seen and heard and looked upon and handled with
their hands the word of life.[25]

Speaking with the authority of his own experience, St.
Bernard promised all men a quick and easy way in which to
run to God: the way of apostolic renunciation which is

21 *Ibid.*, n. 8; *PL*, 183, 331.
22 *Ibid.*; *PL*, 183, 334.
23 "She loves who seeks a kiss. She seeks not freedom, not reward, not
an inheritance, not at last even learning, but a kiss." *Serm. 7 in Cant.*,
n. 2; *PL*, 183, 807. For the meaning of *kiss* see *Serm. 8 in Cant.*, *PL*,
183, 810 ff.
24 The opening words of *Serm. 3 in Cant.*; *PL*, 183, 794.
25 Cf. I John 1:1.

found in the monastery. This is the straight road to the heavenly Jerusalem and those who travel on it run with ease because they have cast away every burden. This is the *vita fortissima* in which we find Christ by giving Him all we have and imitating the first Apostles.[26] Indeed, there were some at Clairvaux who had left "more than boats and fishing nets," to rejoice that they had found Jesus.[27]

The monastic vocation is not only "apostolic" by virtue of its renunciation, it is "angelic" by that chastity which makes the monk live like the blessed souls in paradise, and it is also "prophetic" by the faith and hope which keep the heart of the monk living in expectation of things to come— the *vita venturi saeculi*. But St. Bernard insists that the perfection of the monastic life, which is situated in these three things[28] derives above all from the *presence of Christ* in the monastic community and in the hearts of the monks. It is indeed this living presence, this life-giving activity of Christ in us that makes our renunciation and monastic virginity possible. Above all, our hope of heaven is in fact the actual and present possession of the Word who is Himself the light of heaven, the glory of the Father, and the One on whom the angels desire to look. The very desire of the monk for Christ is produced by the secret action of the Spirit of Christ already dwelling in his heart. "I take it as a most certain proof and as an indubitable argument that you have Him whom you thus seek, and that He who so powerfully draws you to Himself is already dwelling within you." [29]

It is in this sense, then, that the monastic life is contem-

---

[26] *Serm.* 22 *de diversis; PL*, 595 ff.
[27] *Serm.* 37 *de diversis*, n. 7; *PL*, 183, 642.
[28] *Serm.* 37 *de diversis*, nn. 5-8; *PL*, 183, 641.
[29] St. Bernard again says: "Not from man, I say, is that form of conversation. Or seek we other evidence of that Christ who dwells in you than that you seek Christ in this manner?" *Ibid.*, n. 4; *PL*, 183, 641.

plative: not merely that the monk is segregated from the world, not merely that he is cloistered, that he abstains from certain active works and dedicates his existence to "the exercises of the contemplative life"—the office, *lectio divina*, and penance. The monastic vocation is contemplative because it makes possible the fullness of the Christian vocation to divine union in so far as that union can be achieved on earth. It is a life in which we take time to realize the fact that the Spirit of God is poured out in our hearts in order that we may know the things that are given to us from God.[30] It is a life in which we learn by experience that God has given us His Son and that Christ lives by His Holy Spirit in the Church.

It is true that not all in the monastery are called to be contemplatives in the strict sense of the word: not all will receive the gifts of contemplative prayer or the leisure in which to enjoy it with Mary. But those who have received the vocation of spouse of the Word, in the sense of a call to mystical union, will advance with a confidence born of humility and beg God for that "kiss of His mouth" which is nothing else than the Holy Spirit, the love of the Father and the Son, in whom the Son reveals both Himself and the Father.[31] In this secret and mysterious embrace the soul penetrates, in the Spirit of God, into the abyss of the mystery of God which is the mystery of infinite goodness and mercy. The spirit, in whom the Father and the Son are known to us, is the Spirit of love. Our knowledge of God, in this union, is a knowledge which is also love. "That vision is charity." [32] It is the very love which the Father manifests

[30] I Cor. 2:12. Cf. St. Bernard, *Serm.* 37 *de diversis*, n. 5; PL, 183, 641.
[31] "Therefore with desire she seeks to be given the kiss, that is, that Spirit in which the Son is revealed to her and the Father also." *Serm.* 8 *in Cant.*, n. 2: PL, 183, 811.
[32] *Serm.* 82 *in Cant.*, n. 8; PL, 183, 1180.

in the Son, drawing Him forth from the depths of His own godhead, and which the Father and Son manifest to us in turn, making "one spirit" with themselves. This "embrace" of the divine Spirit is the awakening in us of the *experience* that we are sons of God and brides of the Word. "In the spirit of the Son, know thyself to be daughter of the Father, spouse yet sister of the Son." [33]

In revealing His goodness, God reveals His mercy and His condescension to men. The way to this ineffable loving knowledge of the "one true God and Jesus Christ whom He has sent" [34] is through faith in Christ crucified. But the mystery of the Cross is the mystery of divine humility and therefore it can never be penetrated by those who, in the presumption of their own spirit, have raised themselves up to a false contemplation which insolently pries into the majesty of God without loving His goodness. The only contemplation that knows Him is one which casts itself down in adoration and gratitude before the mystery of a mercy for which the great ones of the world have never felt any need.[35]

Because he had been privileged with this embrace of the Holy Spirit, St. Bernard saw clearer than anyone else in his time that all the plenitude of God's love for us is contained in the mystery of the Incarnation. All the love and goodness of God are made manifest in Jesus. But St. Bernard contemplates Jesus, by preference in the arms of Mary. And therefore he sees that after all the whole mystery of divine

---

[33] *Serm. 8 in Cant; PL*, 183, 814.

[34] John 17:3.

[35] "Hence it is evident that they did not know Him perfectly whom they loved not at all. For if they had known Him wholly, they would not have failed to recognize the goodness by which He wished to be born in the flesh and to die for their redemption." *Serm. 8 in Cant.*, n. 5; *PL*, 183, 812.

mercy is contained in our Blessed Lady who is the Mediatrix
of all grace. She is the way by which we can ascend to Him.[36]
More precisely: since the presence of the Word among us is
effected by the Spirit of Love and verified in us by the intensity of our desire for Him, the incarnation of the divine
Word is due entirely to the *desire* for Him which the Holy
Spirit enkindled in the Immaculate Heart of the Most
Blessed Virgin Mary. The hunger and thirst of Mary for the
incarnation of the Word are the cause of our own hunger
and thirst for Him.[37] Mary is the Mother of Jesus in His mystical as well as in His physical body—the Mother of Jesus in
our hearts as well as in His own flesh. That is to say that

[36] "Let us take care, likewise, dearly beloved, through her to rise to
Him who came down to us through her; through her to come into His
grace, who through her came into our wretchedness." *Serm. 2 Advent.;*
PL, 183, 43.
[37] This is the climax and conclusion of the homilies on the *Missus est.*
It is the theme of *Homily IV* (PL, 183, 78-86). In this sermon, number eight expresses the ardent desire of the whole world for the Incarnation, through Mary, in which St. Bernard becomes the spokesman for all
mankind and with ardent humility urges Our Lady to consent to the
message of the angel, since our salvation depends on her. Then finally
in the last section, Mary herself responds and emphasizes the fact that
her *fiat* is nothing merely negative, an abandonment to something she
cannot possibly understand, but a positive desire for something of which
she clearly apprehends the consequences both for the world and for herself. Her answer is the most perfect expression of the desire of a created
soul for God and is rewarded by the most perfect union with God possible to any created nature short of the hypostatic union itself (See col.
86). Writing in an admirable article on *Citeaux et Notre Dame*
("Maria" Du Manoir, II, 593), a "monk of Sept Fons" brings this out
clearly and remarks: "All true mysticism, being famished for God, hun-
gers for the flesh of the Word, the living and necessary bread which
gives life to the world and contains God. . . . Bernard had only to let
his own heart speak passionately, taken as it was by the Word made
flesh, to show us with what love and with what holy appetite the
Mother of Jesus desired and received Jesus."

Mary causes in us something of her own love and her own desire of God: a love and a desire which are the direct result of the living presence of God in our souls. He is present to us through the intercession of Our Lady. Clearly, then, Mary will hold a central position in St. Bernard's theology which is a theology of love because it is not only a doctrine but a hunger and thirst for the living God. Remember: we cannot thirst for God unless we have already tasted Him. We cannot hunger for Him unless He is already present in our hearts. The "taste" for His living presence is true wisdom. This taste was lost and corrupted by sin. It was restored to us by the *fiat* of Our Lady, and it is in this sense that we are "re-formed to wisdom" by the new Eve. We recover our divine likeness and our capacity for a connatural love of God, only through Mary.[38]

When all this has been said, we can conclude where we began: St. Bernard remains a sign of God because like all the saints he has been filled with the revelation of the living God. The lance of Longinus and the nails of the executioners on Calvary made windows through which Bernard looked into heaven, and through these windows by virtue of a light which strikes not the eye but the depths of the heart, St. Bernard plumbed the depths of the "great sacrament of God's love for us." [39] The voice of Bernard still calls us to share with him the "blessings of sweetness" which he tasted in that light. The power and authority and the innocence of his voice teach us to thirst as he did for the multi-

[38] "Behold wisdom filled anew the heart and body of a woman, that we who through a woman were deformed to foolishness might through a woman be reformed to wisdom." *Serm.* 85 *in Cant.*, n. 8; PL, 183, 1192.

[39] *Serm.* 71 *in Cant.*, n. 4; PL, 183, 1072; cf. I Tim. 3:16.

tude of God's mercies. If we attend to him, we will find, as he did, the treasure of God's love hidden in the cleft of the rock.[40] And we will enter with him, through that wide wound, into the heart which is the sanctuary of God.

[40] "God . . . has led us into His holy places through the opened clefts." *Ibid.*; PL, 183, 1073.

APPENDIX A

Postscript to "The Pasternak Affair"

I had begun to correspond with Pasternak before the appearance of *Dr. Zhivago* in 1958, and exchanged two letters with him before the Nobel Prize affair. After that I received messages from him either through a correspondent of his in England, or through mutual friends with whom he corresponded in German. (It was through these friends that Pasternak made known his satisfaction with the article on the "People with Watchchains.") I continued, however, to reach him directly with three or four letters and some books. I am not sure that all my communications got through to him, and I believe at least one letter of his did not reach me. The last letter he wrote, in February 1960, was an acknowledgment of a privately printed Christmas book, *A Nativity Kerygma*, which I had sent him in late November. *Kerygma* is a Greek word meaning "proclamation" or "solemn announcement." Hence the Greek sentence at the beginning of the letter: "I acknowledge your *Kerygma* as soon as possible."

The letter, deeply moving in its hastily composed, impro-

vised English, reflects the titanic inner struggle which the
poet was waging to keep his head above water—no longer
because of political pressure but because of the almost infinite
complications of his life itself, as a result of his celebrity. I
reproduce the letter here in witness of the generosity, courage and boundless warmth of Christian charity which constitute the most eminent greatness of this great man, and
which made him the friend of all.

Febr. 7, 1960

My highly dear Merton,

Το κερυγμα ὑμέτερον ἀναγνώσομαι ὡς τάχιστα. I thank you immensely for giving me such inexhaustible marvelous reading
for the next future. I shall regain myself from this long and
continuing period of letter writing, boring trouble, endless
thrusting rhyme translations, time robbing and useless, and of
the perpetual selfreproof because of the impossibility to advance the longed for, half begun, many times interrupted, almost inaccessible new manuscript [his historical drama of the
1860's in Russia].

I thank you still more for your having pardoned my long
silence, the faintheartedness and remissness that are underly-
ing in this sad state of mind, where being mortally overbusy
and suffering constantly from lack of leisure and time priva-
tion. I am perishing of the forced unproductiveness that is
worse than pure idleness.

But I shall rise, you will see it. I finally will snatch myself
and suddenly deserve and recover again your wonderful confidence and condescension.

Yours affectionatedly,

B. PASTERNAK

Don't write me, don't abash me with your boundless bounty.
The next turn to renew the correspondence will be mine.

Although much has been said and written about Pasternak's death, there remain perhaps many unpublished facts about his illness. Here is one. Although his health was not good, and had obviously suffered to some extent as a result of his tribulations, Pasternak's "sudden" death in May came as a surprise to everyone, even those closest to him. And yet as early as November 1959 Pasternak himself was aware that he was gravely ill and was expecting to die. However, he kept this secret from his family and from all those near him "in order to avoid the slavery of compassion." He struggled on, supported by the hope that he might be able to finish the work in which he was engaged.

This information, which was kept hidden from his family, was revealed by Pasternak to one of his many correspondents: and here we gain new insight into the extraordinary character of these epistolary friendships the poet had contracted with people all over the world. In this case, it was a woman who, with her husband, runs a gas station in a small German city. Deeply impressed by the warmth and intelligence of her letters, Pasternak responded with characteristic generosity, not only replying to her letters with frank and open friendship but even arranging for some friends to get her a golden bracelet, on his behalf, as a present.

Everywhere in the world, even the readers of *Zhivago* who had never actually written to Pasternak, felt that with his death they had lost a close personal friend. The pictures and reports of his funeral evoked in a startling, almost awe-inspiring fashion, the funeral of Zhivago himself, even down to the grief of one of the women mourners. It is the lament of Lara, not in fiction but in reality.

But when the unknown doctor was buried, there were now the thousands of silent, deeply grieving mourners who filed in quiet procession through the trees of the valley at Peredelkino where Pasternak loved to walk alone. This was a witness to the love and respect of the Russian people for their greatest modern poet.

The parish priest was not present when the mortal remains of Boris Pasternak were laid to rest in the churchyard. But the religious rites of the Orthodox Church had been performed quietly, the evening before, in the *dacha*. The simple prayers ended with these words, repeated three times, by the priest and the people: "*May the memory of Boris Leonidovitch, who is worthy of praise, remain with us forever.*"

APPENDIX B

A New Book About Mount Athos

Since the publication of the article beginning on page 68, an unusual new book about Mount Athos has made its appearance. Written in English by an American scholar of Greek extraction, Constantine Cavarnos, it has been published in English by a company in Athens.*

Studying in Athens on a Fulbright Research Scholarship, the author has paid several visits to the Holy Mountain. His interest is mainly in the works of art to be found in the various monasteries, but he is also evidently a devout Orthodox Christian and this book consequently has the advantage of being impregnated with the religious spirit which other, more detached, accounts so obviously lack. There is no question that a phenomenon like Athos is really incomprehensible to the mere tourist: it reveals itself only to the pilgrim. Mr. Cavarnos is a pilgrim, and his work is nothing more than the

* *Anchored in God: Life, Art and Thought on the Holy Mountain of Athos,* by Constantine Cavarnos, Astir Pub. Co., Al & E. Papademe-hiou, 10 Lycurgus St., Athens, 1959. Illus. 232 pp.

plain, unadorned notebook of a pilgrim. There is nothing elaborate about it; facts, conversations and impressions are jotted down without embellishment. Everything is accepted fully at its face value, and some pages may strike the sophisticated reader as naïve. But if so, this is the naïveté of Cassian and Germanus at Scete, which I find vastly preferable to the naïveté of the black-goggled camera-bedecked modern traveller who turns the six-eyed gaze of spectacles, lenses, viewfinders and natural eyes upon everything—and still sees nothing except himself.

Whatever may be the reader's reaction to the literary plainness of this volume, it is well worth reading for the information it contains and for the idea it gives of the monastic spirit that still lives among the Hagiorites.

It will also complete and in many cases correct the information given above in my own essay.

For example, the first motor vehicles have now made their appearance on Athos. The monastery of St. Paul has constructed a motor road from its forests down to the shore, and has bought a truck with which to bring timber down for shipment by sea. Mr. Cavarnos remarks: "The monks of other, more conservative monasteries look upon this innovation very critically as one which, if extensively imitated, will spoil the Byzantine character of the Holy Mountain and will lead to excessive tourism there, destroying the seclusion they now enjoy."

The Serbian monastery of Chilandari (which now has only about twenty-five monks, who are mostly Yugoslavians) has installed a telephone connecting the monastery and the dock, and (a dire portent) the monks now operate a tractor donated by Tito! Not only that, but Tito has apparently presented the monks of Chilandari with a generator so that they can have electric light.

Certainly one of the most disturbing problems on the mountain is the interest of Russians, Yugoslavians, and other citizens of communist-dominated countries. It seems that there have been not a few applications from Russians desiring to become monks at Saint Panteleimon but the Greek government, fearing communist infiltration, refuses to grant entry visas to these postulants.

The numbers have continued to dwindle and the figures given by Mr. Cavarnos are in every case lower than those I have given in my study. The smallest monastery, Stavronikita, is now down to eight monks, according to this book. The number may have dropped still more since the book appeared.

One of the questions frequently raised by the author, in his conversations with the monks, is the cause for this decline in numbers and the prospects for the future. The monks, surprisingly, do not seem very disturbed. They trust in God and believe they will "get along." Yet it would seem evident that Athos may have to make some prudent adjustments in the various forms of observance, in order that modern postulants may be able to persevere more successfully.